PHILIP'S

ST...AS
Co...ntry

Bedworth, Kenilworth, Rugby

First published 2007 by

Philip's, a division of
Octopus Publishing Group Ltd
2–4 Heron Quays
London E14 4JP

First edition 2007
First impression 2007

ISBN-10   0-540-09039-5
ISBN-13   978-0-540-09039-6
© Philip's 2007

Ordnance Survey

This product includes mapping data licensed from Ordnance Survey®, with the permission of the Controller of Her Majesty's Stationery Office.© Crown copyright 2007. All rights reserved.
Licence number 100011710

Photographic acknowledgements:
CV One Limited
Rugby Burough Council

Printed by Toppan, China

Contents

II   **Key to map symbols**

III   **Key to map pages**

IV   **Route planning**

VIII   **Sights of Coventry**

2   **Street maps** at 4½ inches to 1 mile

96   **Street maps of Coventry city centre** at 7 inches to 1 mile

98   **Index**

118   **List of numbered locations**

Key to map symbols

Roads

(12)	**Motorway** with junction number
A42	**Primary route** – dual, single carriageway
A42	**A road** – dual, single carriageway
B1289	**B road** – dual, single carriageway
	Through-route – dual, single carriageway
	Minor road – dual, single carriageway
	Rural track, private road or narrow road in urban area
	Path, bridleway, byway open to all traffic, road used as a public path
	Road under construction
	Pedestrianised area
	Gate or obstruction to traffic restrictions may not apply at all times or to all vehicles
P P&R	**Parking, Park and Ride**

Railways

 Railway

Miniature railway

 Metro station, private railway station

Emergency services

Ambulance station, coastguard station

Fire station, police station

H **+** **Hospital, Accident and Emergency entrance to hospital**

General features

+ **PO** **Place of worship, Post Office**

i **Information centre** (open all year)

Bus or coach station, shopping centre

Important buildings, schools, colleges, universities and hospitals

Woods, built-up area

Tumulus FORT **Non-Roman antiquity, Roman antiquity**

Leisure facilities

  Camping site, caravan site

Golf course, picnic site

Boundaries

• • • • • •	**Postcode boundaries**
— • —	**County and unitary authority boundaries**

Water features

 River Ouse **Tidal water, water name**

Non-tidal water – lake, river, canal or stream

< **ı** **Lock, weir**

Enlarged mapping only

Railway or bus station building

Place of interest

Parkland

Scales

Blue pages: 4½ inches to 1 mile 1:14 080

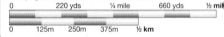

0	220 yds	¼ mile	660 yds	½ mile
0	125m	250m	375m	½ km

Red pages: 7 inches to 1 mile 1:9 051

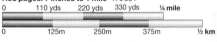

0	110 yds	220 yds	330 yds	¼ mile
0	125m	250m	375m	½ km

62

Adjoining page indicators The colour of the arrow and the band indicates the scale of the adjoining page (see above)

Abbreviations

Acad	Academy	Mkt	Market
Allot Gdns	Allotments	Meml	Memorial
Cemy	Cemetery	Mon	Monument
C Ctr	Civic Centre	Mus	Museum
CH	Club House	Obsy	Observatory
Coll	College	Pal	Royal Palace
Crem	Crematorium	PH	Public House
Ent	Enterprise	Recn Gd	Recreation Ground
Ex H	Exhibition Hall	Resr	Reservoir
Ind Est	Industrial Estate	Ret Pk	Retail Park
IRB Sta	Inshore Rescue Boat Station	Sch	School
		Sh Ctr	Shopping Centre
Inst	Institute	TH	Town Hall/House
Ct	Law Court	Trad Est	Trading Estate
L Ctr	Leisure Centre	Univ	University
LC	Level Crossing	Wks	Works
Liby	Library	YH	Youth Hostel

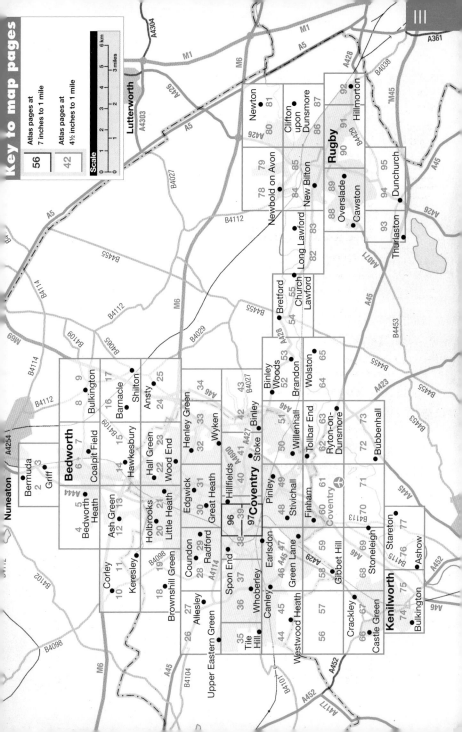

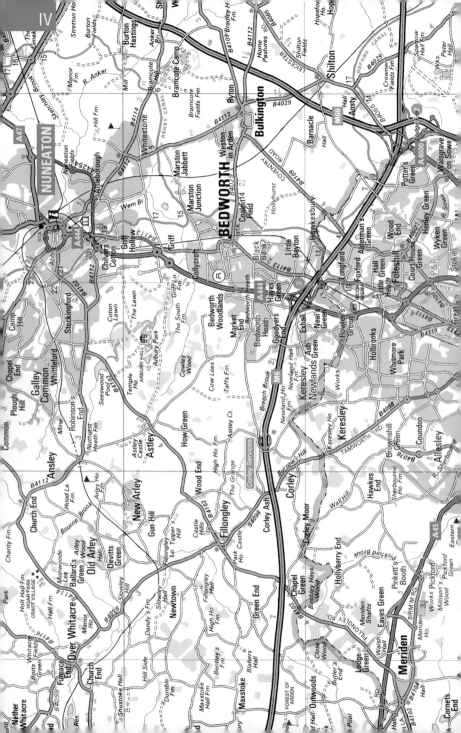

Route planning

Route planning

Scale

0   1   2   3   4 km

Sights of Coventry and Rugby

Museums and Galleries

Coventry Toy Museum *Much Park Street* Collection of toys and games from 1740. Housed in the 14th century Whitefriars Monastery gatehouse, where Queen Elizabeth I stayed on numerous occasions. 🖳www.visitcoventry.co.uk ☎024 7622 7560 97 C2

Coventry Transport Museum *Hales Street* The largest collection of British road transport of all types in the world. ☎024 7623 4270 🖳www.transport-museum.com 96 B3

The Herbert *Jordan Well* Art gallery and museum; visual arts, archaeology and natural history. The Priory Visitor Centre shows the discovery of Coventry's original Benedictine monastery dissolved by Henry VIII. 🖳www.theherbert.org ☎024 7683 2386 97 C2

Jaguar Daimler Heritage Trust *Browns Lane, Allesley* Development of the Jaguar over a century with more than 100 vehiicles on display, many just as they left the factory and fully operational. ☎024 7620 3322 🖳www.visitcoventry.co.uk 28 A4

Lanchester Gallery *Graham Sutherland Building, Gosford Street* Venue for emerging and established artists at the School of Art and Design. 🖳www.coventry.ac.uk ☎024 7688 7688 97 D2

The Lewis Gallery *Rugby School, Rugby* Opened in February 2006 and named after Sir Edward Lewis. Collection of Roman artefacts, social and industrial history of Rugby, and temporary exhibitions. ☎01788 556227 🖳www.rugbyschool.net 90 A4

Lunt Roman Fort Museum *Coventry Road, Bagington* Partial reconstruction of the fort established there in 64 AD. A glimpse of Roman military life. ☎024 7630 3567 🖳www.theherbert.org 60 C3

Mead Gallery *Warwick Arts Centre, University of Warwick* Contemporary gallery focusing on post-war British and American art, with sculptures and photography. 🖳www.warwickartscentre.co.uk ☎024 7652 4524 57 C4

▼ *The Close at Rugby School*

Midland Air Museum *Coventry Airport, Rowley Road, Baginton* The Sir Frank Whittle Jet Heritage Centre telling 'The Story of the Jet' and 'Wings over Coventry'. ☎024 7630 1033 🖳www.midlandairmuseum.co.uk 61 C3

Rugby Art Gallery & Museum *Little Elborow Street, Rugby* Displays of archaeology, fine art and social history. ☎01788 533201 90 A4 🖳www.rugbygalleryandmuseum.org.uk

Webb Ellis Rugby Football Museum *St Matthews Street, Rugby* History and memorabilia. Housed in the workshops where the first rugby ball was made. ☎01788 567777 🖳www.warwickshire.gov.uk 85 B1

Historic Sites

Cheylesmore Manor *New Union Street, opp Greyfriars Lane junction* Remains of the old gatehouse, which was once the hunting lodge of the Black Prince. 🖳www.coventry.gov.uk 97 B2

City Wall and Gates *Cook Street and Lady Herbert's Garden, Hales Street* Construction began in 1355 and reached 2 miles long and 18 feet high. Today only 2 gates of the original 12 have survived with a section of the old city wall in Lady Herbert's gardens, know as Cook Street and Swanswell Gate. 🖳www.coventry.gov.uk 96 B3

Christchurch Spire *New Union Street* The third of Coventry's spires. Henry VIII demolished the first church, and the second was lost to bombing in 1941. Exterior viewing only. 🖳www.visitcoventry.co.uk 97 B2

Fords Hospital *Greyfriars Lane* Built in 1509, consists of four half-timbered almshouses founded by William Ford for elderley men and women. 🖳www.visitcoventry.co.uk ☎024 7683 3141 97 B2

Kenilworth Castle *The Green, Kenilworth* The largest ruined castle in England. Tudor gardens, Norman keep and John of Gaunt's Great Hall. Audio tours and interactive exhibition. 🖳www.english-heritage.org.uk ☎01926 852078 66 B1

St Mary's Guildhall *Hay Lane* Medieval guildhall. Survived World War II bombing and contains a 500 year old tapestry. 🖳www.coventry.gov.uk 97 C2

Spon End *East of the city* Medieval suburb built outside the city wall. The present Spon Bridge was built in 17th century and close to this site are the remains of the ancient chapel of St Christopher and St John. 🖳www.sponend.org.uk 38 B3

William Webb Ellis Statue *Junction of Lawrence Sheriff Street and Dunchurch Road* Bronze statue at Rugby School, in memory of Ellis, who is credited with the invention of rugby. 🖳www.visitrugby.co.uk 90 A4

Places of Worship

Coventry Cathedral *Hill Top* Founded as a Benedictine community in 1043 (Priory of St Mary). Destroyed in 1940, HM The Queen laid the foundation stone in 1956 and today the ruins remain hallowed ground next to the present structure – St Michaels. 🖳www.coventrycathedral.org.uk ☎024 7652 1200 96 C3

Holy Trinity Church *Priory Row* Together with St Michaels and Christ Church spires these make the three spires of Coventry. 🖳www.holytrinitycoventry.org.uk ☎024 7622 0418 96 C3

St Andrew's Church *Church Street, Rugby* The West Tower dates to the 14th century and the present church was completed in 1920. Unique two sets of bells. ☎01788 565609 🖳www.standrewrugby.org.uk 85 B1

St John's Baptist Church *Fleet Street* Medieval church, carved from the parish of St Michael. It is said that no two walls are parallel and there are no perfect right angles in the church. ☎024 7655 2491 🖳www.stjohn-the-baptist.co.uk 96 B3

Other Sights

Arbury Hall *Nuneaton* The 'Gothic Gem' of the Midlands and home to the Newdegate family for over 400 years. Fine porcelain and portraits collection. ☎024 7638 2804 🖳www.visitcoventry.co.uk

Coventry City Farm *Clarence Street, Hillfields* Educational farm for the caring and training of animals. ☎024 7622 5323 🖳www.coventrycityfarm.org.uk 39 C4

Godiva Clock *Broadgate* The original statue of Peeping Tom was destroyed during World War II. Today an animated version watches over the Godiva Clock in Broadgate. 🖳www.visitcoventry.co.uk 97 B2

Lady Godiva Statue *Broadgate* Striking Grade II listed statue in the central square of Broadgate, commemorating the legend of Lady Godiva. 🖳www.visitcoventry.co.uk 97 B2

Millennium Place *Hales Street* Public space with numerous pieces of art: the Glass Bridge links Millenium Place to the Garden of International Friendship and the Whittle Arch celebrates Coventry-born Sir Frank Whittle, who invented the jet engine. 🖳www.coventry.gov.uk 96 C3

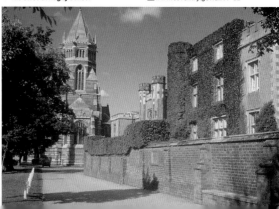

▲ *Whittle Arch & Glass Bridge, Millennium Place, Coventry*

Stoneleigh Abbey *Kenilworth* Founded in 1154 by Cistercian monks, it has some 690 acres of parkland. Many famous people have been entertained here, including Jane Austin and Charles I. ☎01926 858535 🖥www.stoneleighabbey.org 76 B3

Green Spaces

Brandon Marsh Nature Centre *Brandon Lane, Brandon* A 200 acre nature reserve – a Site of Special Scientific Interest. Tranquil area with lots of wildlife. Tea room and shop. 🖥www.warwickshire-wildlife-trust.org.uk ☎024 7630 8999 63 B4

Coombe Abbey Country Park *Brinklow Road, Binley* With 500 acres of gardens, woodland, lakeside walks, bird watching and fishing. 🖥www.coventry.gov.uk ☎024 7645 3720 43 C3

Garden of International Friendship *Hales Street* A modern garden near Lady Herbert's Garden and the ancient Coventry gates. ☎024 76 🖥www.visitcoventry.co.uk 96 C3

Greyfriar's Green *Greyfriar's Road* A restful garden on the site of the old Coventry Fair. Now a conservation area. 🖥www.visitcoventry.co.uk 97 B2

Miners' Welfare Park *Rye Piece, Bedworth* Awarded 'Best Public Park in the Country', this beautiful park has a cricket ground, roller skating, bowls, tennis, football pitch and aviary. 🖥www.visitcoventry.co.uk 6 C3

Peace Garden *Bayley Lane* Opened by HM the Queen Mother, it commemorates the blitz of 1940. A pillar in the centre shows the 26 cities with which Coventry is twinned. 🖥www.visitcoventry.co.uk 97 C2

Ryton Organic Gardens - HDRA *Ryton-on-Dunsmore* Ten acres of landscaped organic grounds, a safe haven for wildlife. Fully interactive visitor centre, restaurant and cafe. 🖥www.gardenorganic.org.uk ☎024 7630 3517 64 C2

Ryton Pools Country Park *Ryton Road, Bubbenhall* 100 acres of wildlife and ancient woodland, with a visitor centre and picnic area. 🖥www.warwickshire.gov.uk ☎01926 410410 72 C1

War Memorial Park *Kenilworth Road* 120 acres of park with golf course, tennis courts and tea room. 🖥www.visitcoventry.co.uk 47 C3

Activities

Bedworth Civic Hall *High Street, Bedworth* Multi-purpose entertainment centre with a gallery. Hosts concerts, pantomimes and ballet. 🖥www.civichallinbedworth.co.uk ☎024 7637 6705 6 B2

Bedworth Leisure Centre *Coventry Road, Bedworth* Swimming pool with flume, fitness studio, squash court, cafe and creche. The Brink is an outdoor floodlit multi sports area. 🖥www.nbleisuretrust.co.uk ☎024 7637 6714 6 B2

The Belgrade Theatre *Belgrade Square* An eclectic programme of drama, musicals, live comedy, music and community theatre. Re-opening September 2007. ☎024 7655 3055 🖥www.belgrade.co.uk 96 B3

City College Theatre (The Butts Theatre) *The Butts* Both amateur and professional productions of musicals and concerts. 🖥www.visitcoventry.co.uk ☎024 7679 1705/1709 38 B2

Clock Towers Shopping Centre *Market Mall, Rugby* Over 45 high street shops with restaurants and cafes, in the heart of Rugby. Multi-storey car park on site. ☎01788 572630 🖥www.clock-towers.co.uk 85 B1

Coventry Canal Art Trail Five and a half miles of art alongside the canal by over 30 artists. From Coventry Canal Basin to Hawkesbury Junction. ☎024 7678 5507 🖥www.coventry.gov.uk

Coventry City FC *Ricoh Arena, Phoenix Way, Foleshill* Founded in 1883, it recently moved to Ricoh Arena from Highfield Road. ☎0870 421 1987 🖥www.ccfc.co.uk 21 B3

Coventry Farmers Market *Spon Street* Over 20 stalls selling local produce. ☎024 7622 7264 🖥www.visitcoventry.co.uk 96 A3

Coventry Greyhound Track *Coventry Stadium, Rugby Road, Brandon* Racing track with panoramic views. ☎024 7654 2395 🖥www.coventrygreyhounds.com 53 A3

Coventry International Speedway & Karting *Coventry Stadium, Rugby Road* Home of the Coventry Bee's Speedway Team. 🖥www.coventrymotorspeedway.com ☎024 7654 2395 53 A3

Coventry Rugby FC *Butts Park Arena, The Butts* Established in 1874, many famous England players have been produced here. 🖥www.coventryrugby.co.uk ☎0871 750 9100 38 B2

Criterion Theatre *Berkeley Road, South Earlsdon* Comedy to classical productions, with visits from other theatre groups and folk concerts. 🖥www.criteriontheatre.co.uk ☎024 7667 5175 47 B4

National Agricultural Centre *Stoneleigh Park, Kenilworth* Equine centre, exhibition and conference centre, arts centre and 'food experience'. ☎024 7669 6969 🖥www.stoneleighpark.com 76 C4

Priory Theatre *Rosemary Hill, Kenilworth* Member of the Little Theatre Guild of Great Britain. 🖥www.priorytheatre.co.uk ☎01926 863334 67 A1

Rugby Theatre *Henry Street, Rugby* Amateur Theatre Society, also hosting films. ☎01788 541234 🖥www.rugbytheatre.co.uk 85 B1

Shysters Theatre Company *AUEW Building, Corporation Street* Unique performances by young people with learning disabilities. 🖥www.theshysters.co.uk ☎024 7623 9186 96 B3

Skydome *Planet Ice Arena, Croft Road* Home to Coventry Blaze ice hockey club. Hosts skating clubs. 🖥www.planet-ice.co.uk ☎024 7663 0693 97 A2

Talisman Theatre & Arts Centre *Barrow Road, Kenilworth* Also a member of the Little Theatre Guild with regular house productions. 🖥www.talismantheatre.co.uk ☎01926 856548 74 B4

Warwick Arts Centre *University of Warwick, Coventry* Largest arts centre in the Midlands. Music, drama, dance, comedy, literature, films and visual art performances. 🖥www.warwickartscentre.co.uk ☎024 7652 4524 57 C4

West Orchards Shopping Centre *Smithford Way* Range of high street shops with a large food court. 🖥www.westorchards.co.uk ☎024 7623 1133 96 B3

Wheatsheaf Theatre (aka Co-operative Theatre) *Watersmeet Road, Wyken* Recent Godiva Award winners, this small theatre is dressed in Cabaret style, with a variety of performances. ☎024 7645 6179 🖥www.wheatsheafplayers.com 31 C2

Information

Tourist Information
🛈 *Coventry: Priory Row*
☎024 7622 7264 96 B3
🛈 *Rugby: Rugby Art Gallery & Museum, Little Elborow Street* ☎01788 534970 85 B1
🛈 *Kenilworth: Smalley Place*
☎01926 748900 74 B4

Coventry City Council
Council House, Earl Street
☎024 7683 3333, parking ☎024 7622 7264
🖥www.coventry.gov.uk 97 C2

Rugby Borough Council
own Hall, Evreux Way
☎01788 533533, parking ☎01788 533729
🖥www.rugby.gov.uk 85 B1

NCP Car Parking
☎0870 606 7050 🖥www.ncp.co.uk

National Rail Enquiries
☎0845 748 4950 🖥www.nationalrail.co.uk

Local Bus and Rail
☎0870 608 2608 🖥www.traveline.org.uk

A   B   C

C

90

BERMUDA RD

HAZELL WAY

Ind
Est

BERMUDA
VILLAGE

BERMUDA RD

HAREFIELD LA

The
Lawns

Centenary Way

HAREFIELD LA

WATER LILY WAY

1

CARNATION WAY

2   3

MARIGOLD
WLK

PETUNIA
CL

Bermu

4

1 POPPY CL
2 DAHLIA WLK
3 ASTER WLK

Tea
House

Dennis
Farm

Arbury Park

CV10

3

HARRINGTON

Bermuda
Bsns Pk

WALSINGHAM DR

89

Works

GRIFF LA

ST D

2

Coventry
Wood

GRIFF LA

South Farm

Arbury Mill
Farm

Griff Lodge
Farm

1

Collycr

88

CV12

GLENWOOD GDNS

CONSTABLE
CL

DR

A444

REYNOLDS RD

GAINS...

TURNE...

COZENS

CL

W

STC...

SUTHE...

34   A   5   B   35   C   6

BEDWORTH LA

COTMAN
CL

CL

NINGTON DR

GIRTIN
CL

LOWRY CL

SAND...

LLAS CL

GHT...

SUTHE...

AMO...

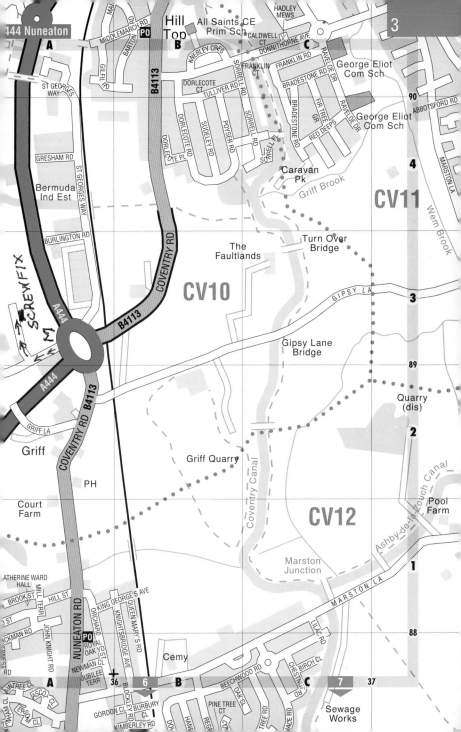

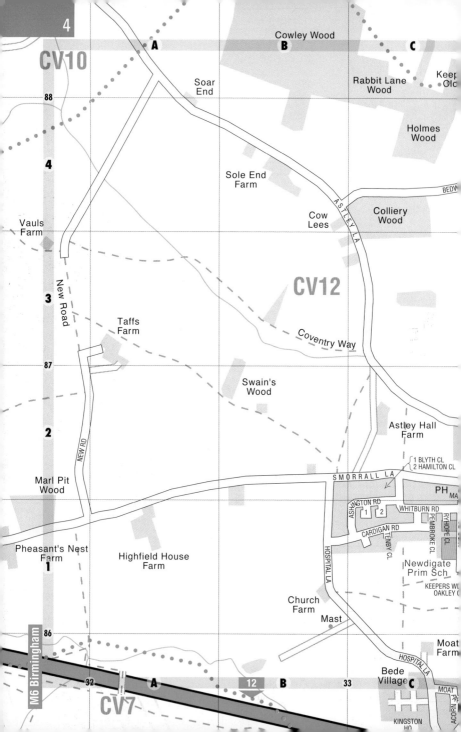

CV10

88

4

A

Soar
End

B Cowley Wood

C

Rabbit Lane
Wood

Keep
Old

Holmes
Wood

Sole End
Farm

Vauls
Farm

Cow
Lees

Colliery
Wood

BEDW

ASTLEY LA

CV12

New Road

3

Taffs
Farm

Coventry Way

87

Swain's
Wood

Astley Hall
Farm

2

NEW RD

1 BLYTH CL
2 HAMILTON CL

SMORRALL LA

PH
MA

Marl Pit
Wood

ASHINGTON RD

1 2

WHITBURN RD

CARDIGAN RD

PEMBROKE CL

TENBY CL

RYHOPE CL

Pheasant's Nest
Farm

1

Highfield House
Farm

Newdigate
Prim Sch

KEEPERS WI
OAKLEY C

HOSPITAL LA

Church
Farm

Mast

Moat
Farm

86

M6 Birmingham

HOSPITAL LA

Bede
Village

MOAT

ACORN

KINGSTON
HO

32

A

CV7

12 **B**

33

C

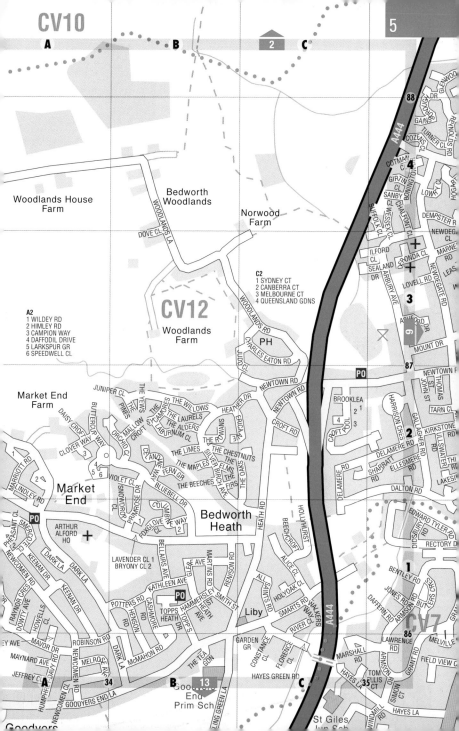

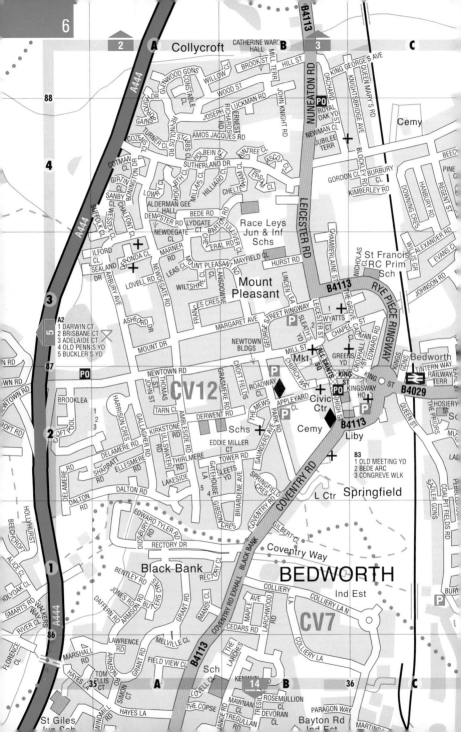

Marston
Junction
3

A

MARSTON LA

LILAC RD

B

Marston Hall
Farm

Marston
Jabbett

C

Eastland
Farm

88

CHESTNUT RD

BIRCH CL

FURNACE RD

TREE RD

Sewage
Works

Weston
Wood

4

ACACIA CRES

FURNACE
CL

CV12

Coventry Canal

Centenary Way

WESTON
STAB

3

ST

St Michael's
CE Prim Sch

1 BIRVELL CT
2 BRICK KILN WAY

8

87

SEVERN RD

CLYDE

Nicholas
Chamberlaine
Tec Coll

LKINGTON RD

BEDWORTH RD

B4029

BEDWORTH RD

EAST
AVE

WEST
AVE

NORTH AVE

COLUMBIA GDNS

Bulkington
Bridge

Camp
Farm

2

BEDWORTH RD

BYROW AVE

YORK AVE

POPLAR AVE

POPLAR
HO

SHAKESPEARE
AVE

GEORGE ELIOT AVE

Weston Lawns
Farm

Sewage
Works

TON RD

MILTON CL

**Coalpit
Field**

SHELLEY
CL

DSWORTH
RD

1

86

CV2

A 37 **B** **15** **C** 38

COVENTRY RD **B4109**

Hollyhurst
Farm

Hollyhurst

Sweet

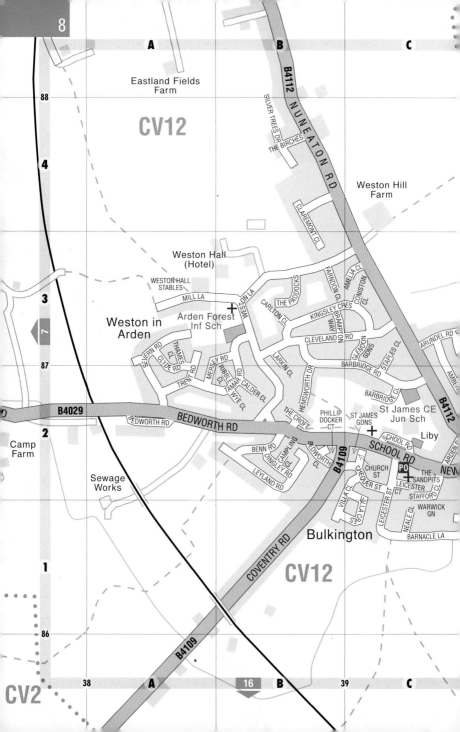

A　　　　　B　　　　　C

CV2

CV12

Eastland Fields
Farm

88

4

B4112 NUNEATON RD

SILVER TREES DR

THE BIRCHES

CLAREMONT CL

Weston Hill
Farm

Weston Hall
(Hotel)

WESTON HALL
STABLES

MILL LA

WESTON LA

THE PADDOCKS

FARNDON CL

AMELIA CL

COMISTON CL

Weston in
Arden

Arden Forest
Inf Sch

CARLTON CL

KINGSLEY CRES

BRAMPTON WAY

CLEVELAND RD

GLENDON GDNS

STAPLES CL

ARUNDEL RD

3

7

SEVERN RD

THAMES CL

CLYDE RD

TRENT RD

MERSEY RD

RIBBLE CL

TAMAR CL

CALDER CL

WYE CL

LARKIN CL

HEMSWORTH DR

BARBRIDGE RD

BARBRIDGE CL

St James CE
Jun Sch

B4112

AMB...

87

B4029

BEDWORTH RD

BEDWORTH RD

THE CROFT

PHILLIP
DOCKER
CT

ST JAMES
GDNS

SCHOOL RD

School Rd

Liby

2

Camp
Farm

BENN RD

CAMPLING CL

DINGLE CT

LEYLAND RD

BEDWORTH CL

B4109

CHURCH ST

CHEQUER ST

PO

LEICESTER CT

THE
SANDPITS

LEICESTER

STAFFOR...

NEW...

Sewage
Works

VILLA CL

LA CRES

LEICESTER ST

NEALE CL

WARWICK GN

BARNACLE LA

Bulkington

CV12

1

COVENTRY RD

86

B4109

38　　　　　A　　　　　16　　　　　B　　　　　39　　　　　C

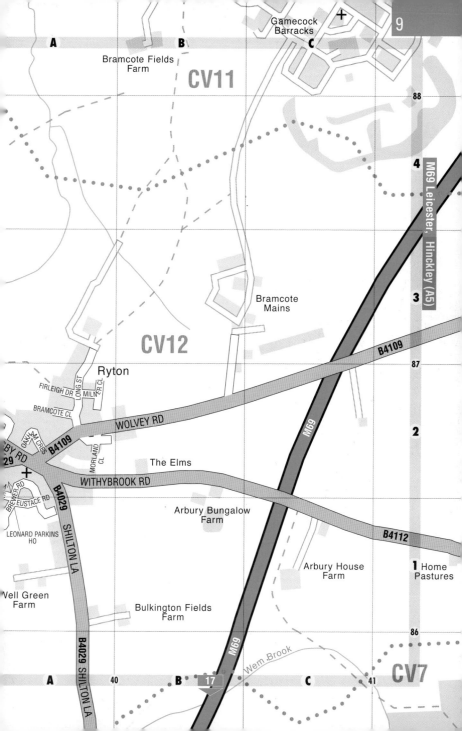

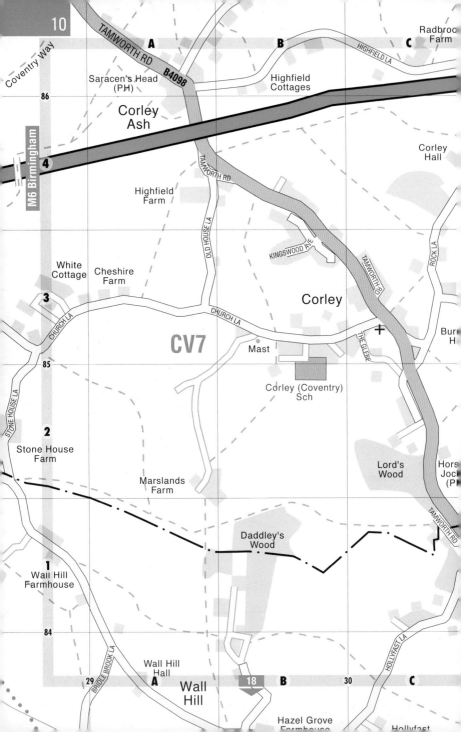

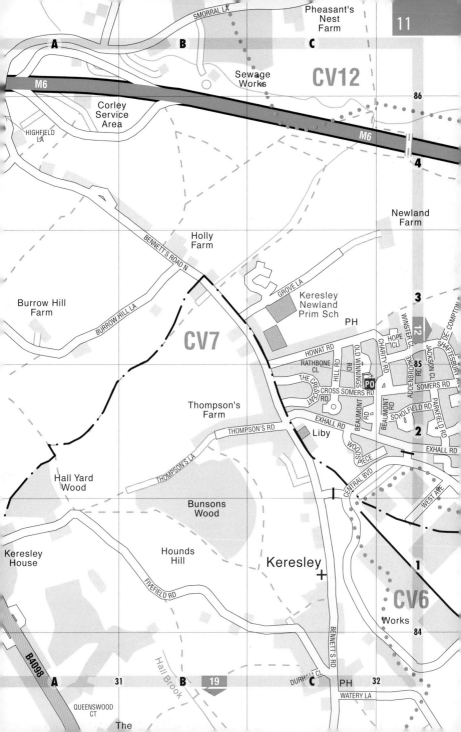

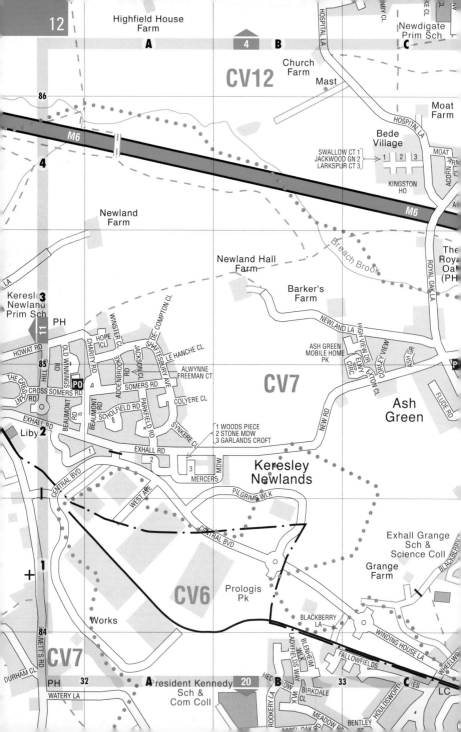

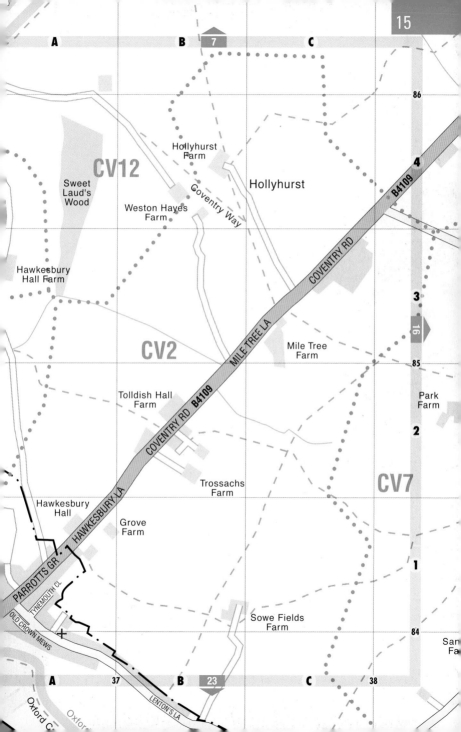

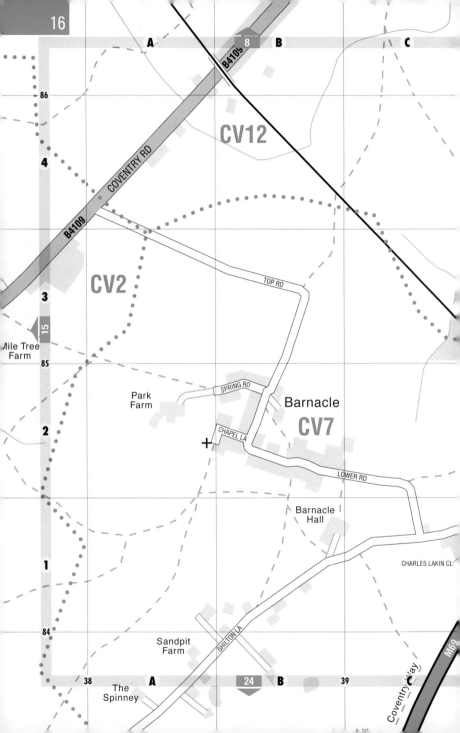

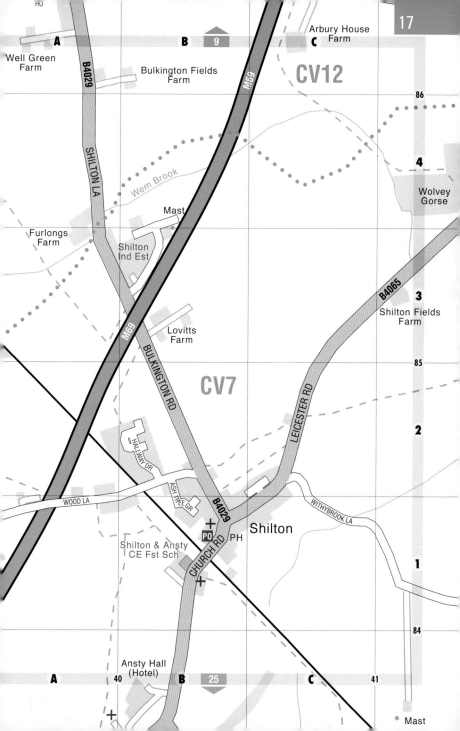

Well Green
Farm

Bulkington Fields
Farm

Arbury House
Farm

CV12

B4029

SHILTON LA

Wem Brook

Mast

Furlongs
Farm

Shilton
Ind Est

Wolvey
Gorse

B4065

Shilton Fields
Farm

Lovitts
Farm

M69

CV7

LEICESTER RD

HALLWAY DR

ASH TREE GR

WOOD LA

WITHYBROOK LA

PO

CHURCH RD

B4029

PH

Shilton

Shilton & Ansty
CE Fst Sch

Ansty Hall
(Hotel)

Mast

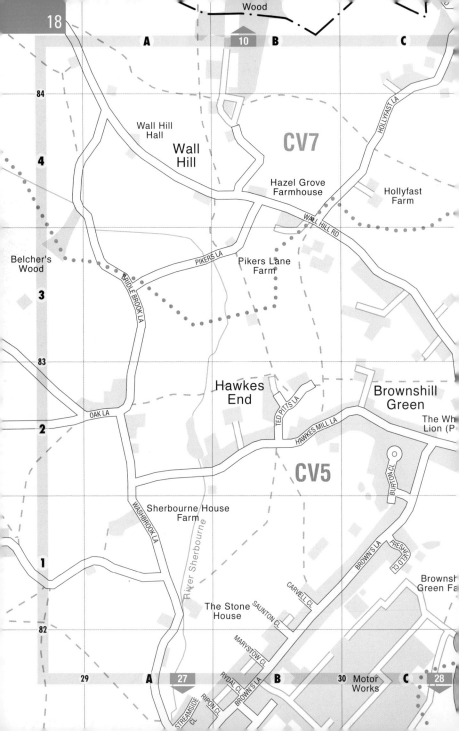

Wood

84

CV7

Wall Hill
Hall

Wall
Hill

4

Hazel Grove
Farmhouse

Hollyfast
Farm

HOLLYFAST LA

WALL HILL RD

Belcher's
Wood

PIKERS LA

Pikers Lane
Farm

BRIDLE BROOK LA

3

83

OAK LA

Hawkes
End

Brownshill
Green

2

TED PITTS LA

HAWKES MILL LA

The Wh
Lion (P

CV5

BURTON CL

Sherbourne House
Farm

WASHBROOK LA

BROWN'S LA

FRESHFIELD CL

Brownsh
Green Fa

River Sherbourne

1

CARVELL CL

The Stone
House

SAUNTON CL

82

MARYSTOW CL

RYDAL CL

BROWN'S LA

STREAMSIDE CL

RIPON CL

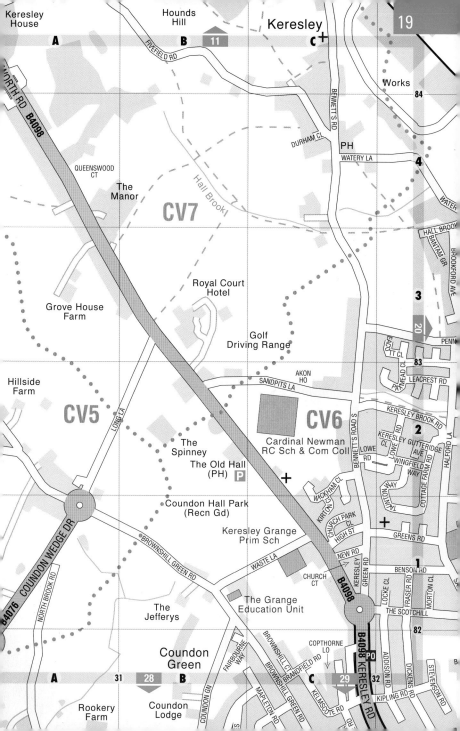

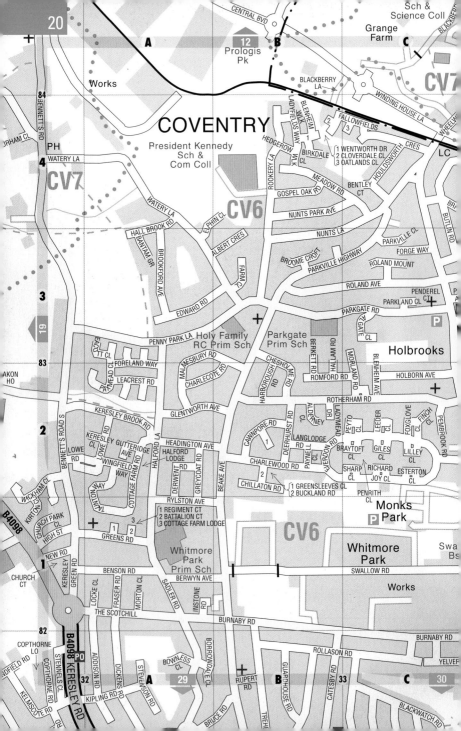

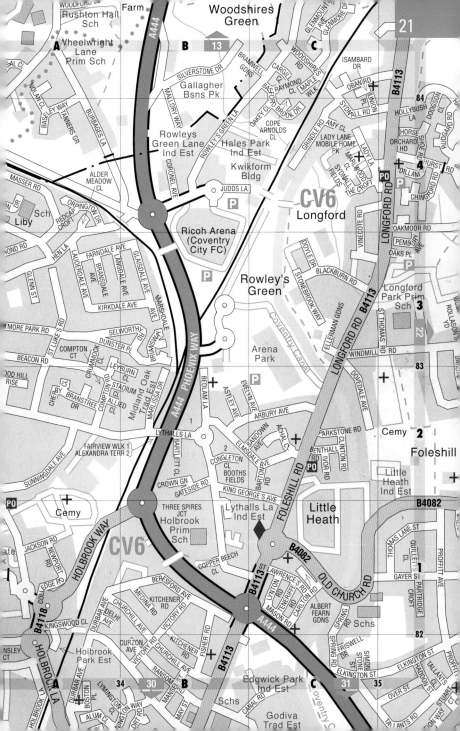

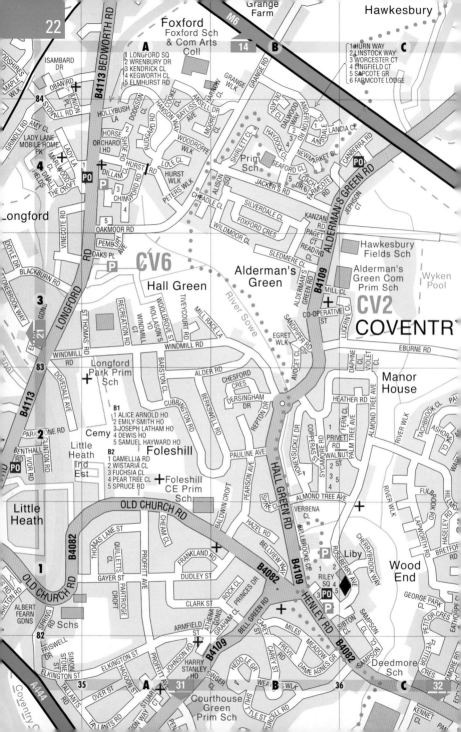

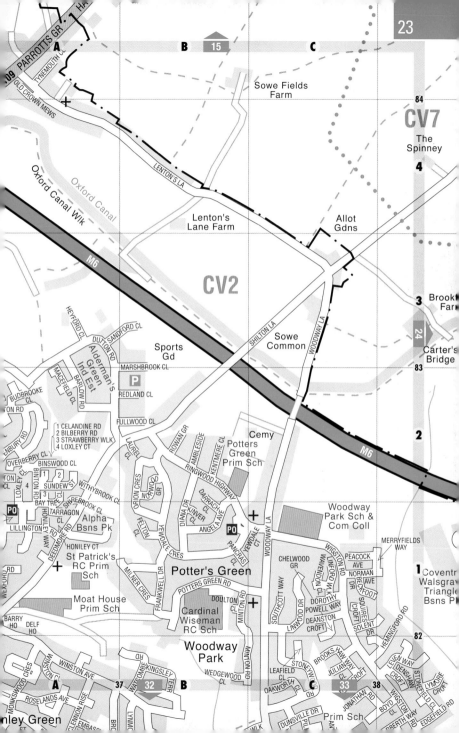

PARROTTS GR. HA-
.09
A
B
15
C

TYNEMOUTH LA

OLD CROWN MEWS

Sowe Fields
Farm

84

CV7

The
Spinney

4

LENTON'S LA

Oxford Canal

Oxford Canal Wlk

M6

Lenton's
Lane Farm

Allot
Gdns

CV2

3

Brook
Far

24

Carter's
Bridge

83

SHILTON LA

WOODWAY LA

Sowe
Common

HEYFORD CL

DUTTON RD

SANDFORD CL

Sports
Gd

MARSHBROOK CL

P

MACEFIELD CL

BARLOW RD

Alderman's
Green
Ind Est

2

BUDBROOKE
CL

-TON RD

REDLAND CL

FULLWOOD CL

M6

-NBURY RD

1 CELANDINE RD
2 BILBERRY RD
3 STRAWBERRY WLK
4 LOXLEY CT

OVERBERRY CL

BINSWOOD CL

LOXLEY
CL

-TON
CL

1   2

4   3

SUNDEW ST

WITHYBROOK CL

BINTON RD

Cemy

Potters
Green
Prim Sch

LAUREL CL

ROWAN GR

AMBLESIDE

KENTMERE CL

Woodway
Park Sch &
Com Coll

MERRYFIELDS
WAY

BAY TREE CL

SHREBROOK CL

TARRAGON

Alpha
Bsns Pk

RINGWOOD HIGHWAY

ORION CRES

ROTHESAY
CL

NW3
GR

DAGNACE

DIANA DR

KINVER
CL

ANGEL AVE

P
O

YEWDALE
CT

WOODWAY LA

1 Coventr
Walsgra
Triangle
Bsns P

P
O

HONILEY WAY

DEEDMORE RD

LILLINGTON

HONILEY CT

St Patrick's
RC Prim
Sch

FELTON CL

YEWDALE CRES

PANGRAS

CHELWOOD
GR

WIGSTON RD

LINCROFT

PEACOCK
AVE

NORMAN
AVE

BRICKFOOT
DR

SQUIRES
CROFT

SOLENT
DR

HENINGFORD RD

82

WEXFORD
RD

-WEXFORD

Moat House
Prim Sch

MILNER CRES

FRANKWELL DR

POTTERS GREEN RD

Potter's Green

DOULTON
CL

MINTON RD

SOUTHCOTT WAY

LINWOOD DR

DOROTHY
POWELL WAY

DEANSTON
CROFT

BARRY
HO

DELF
HO

Cardinal
Wiseman
RC Sch

Woodway
Park

WEDGEWOOD
CL

LEAFIELD
CL

STONEYWOOD

BROOKS HAW WAY

JULIAN CL

CROFT

LEVEN WAY

DEMSHAW
CROFT

STONEFIELD CL

WYMORE

EDGEFIELD RD

MONKSWOOD CRES

WINSTON AVE

WINSTON
ST

WATCOMBE RD

KINGSLEY TERR

A

37

32

B

ROSELANDS AVE

LENNON RISE

EMBASSY

LYNMO-

BRO-

OAKWORTH

DUNSVILLE DR

C

33

38

WIGSTON

BOYD
CL

JONATHAN
RD

BRERETH WAY

nley Green

Prim Sch

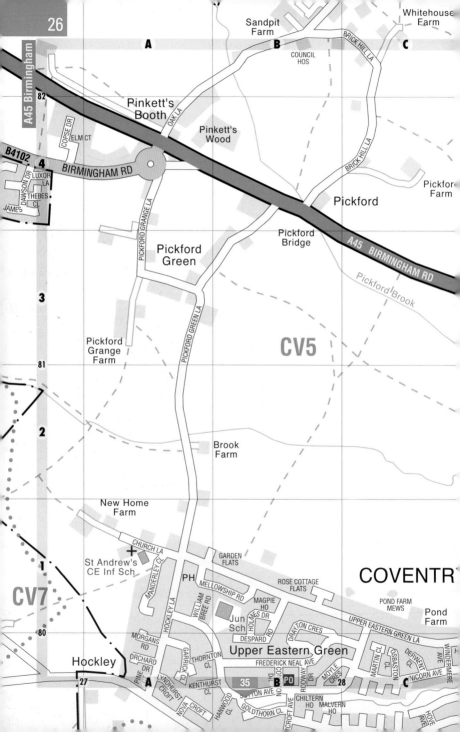

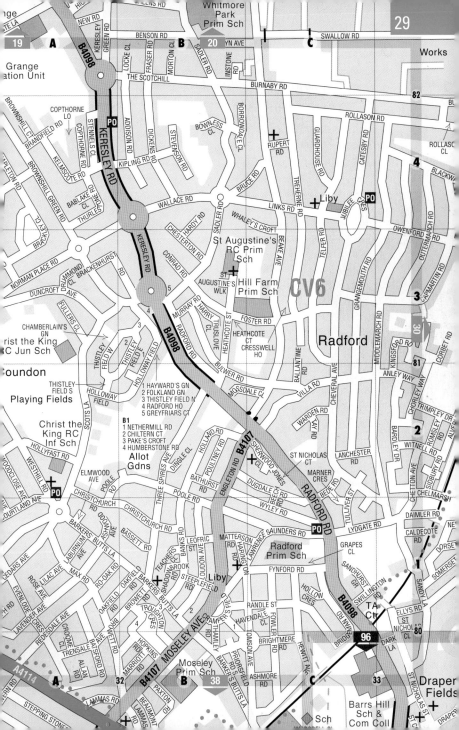

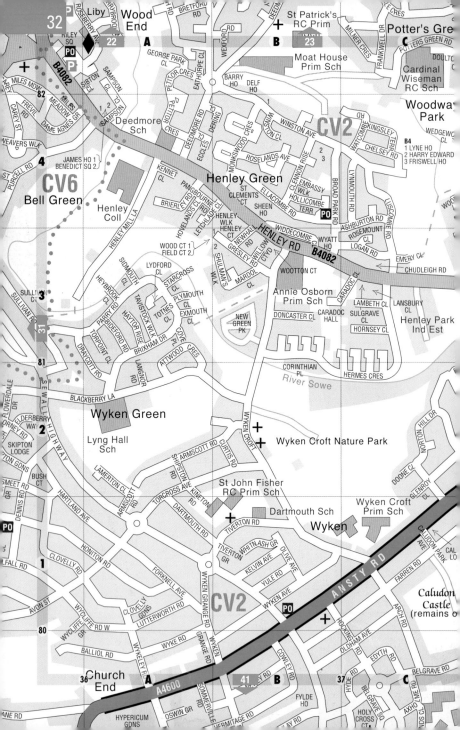

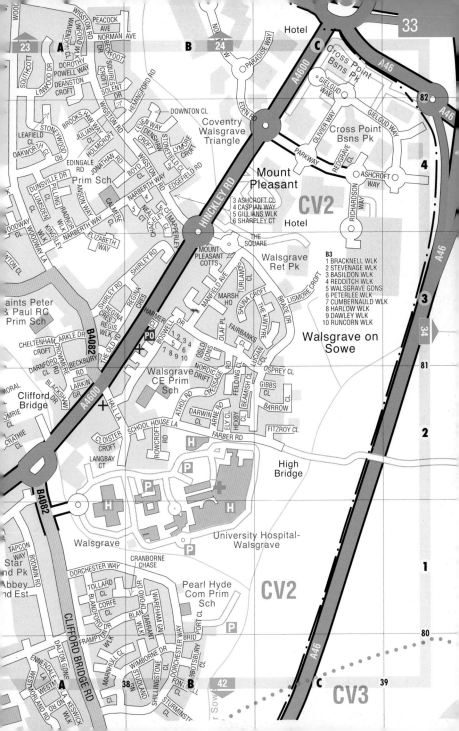

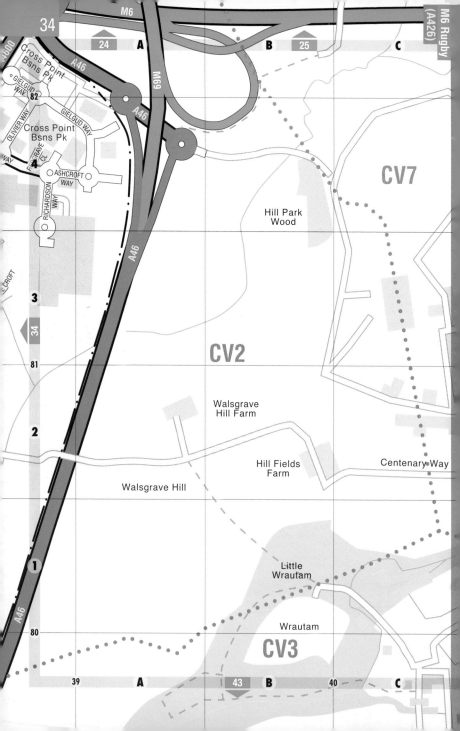

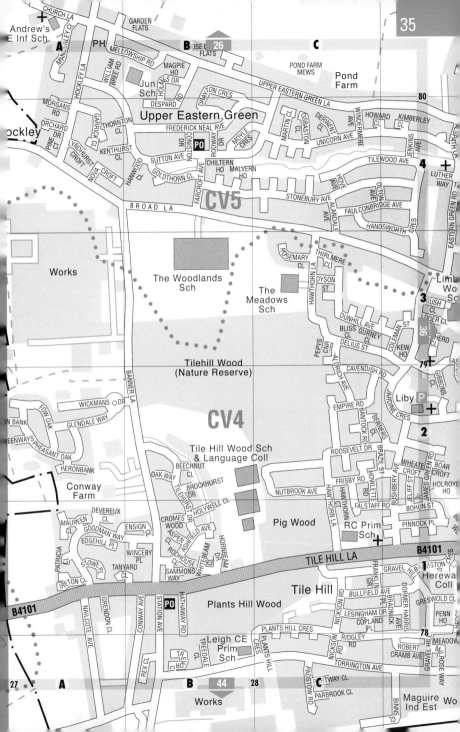

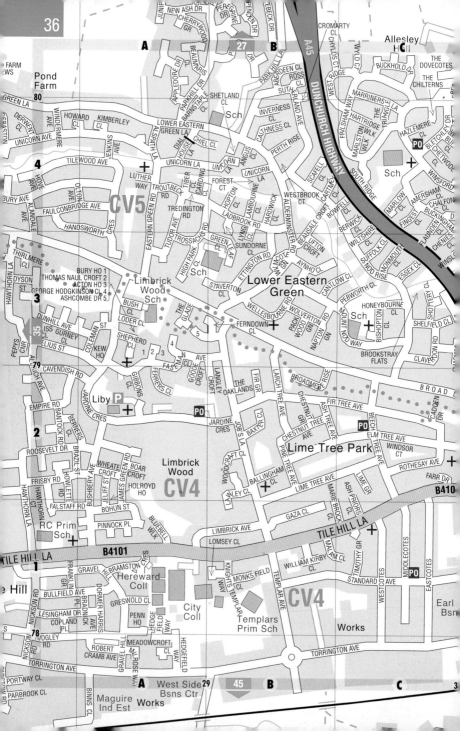

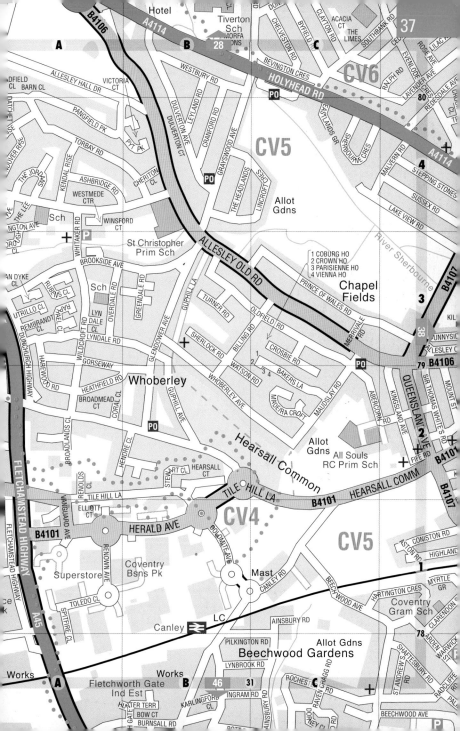

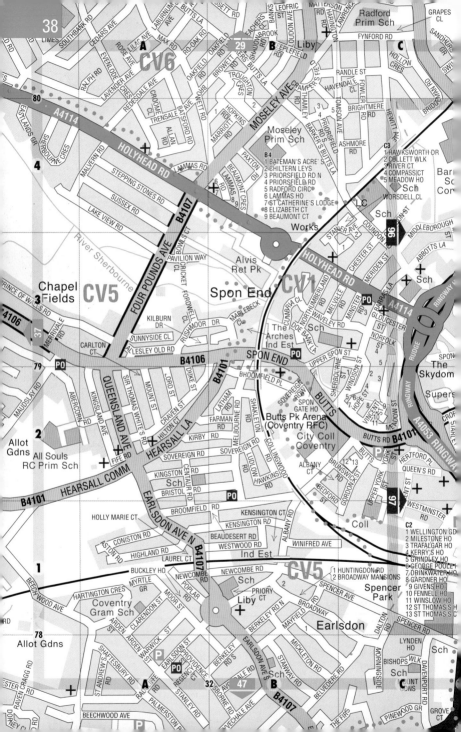

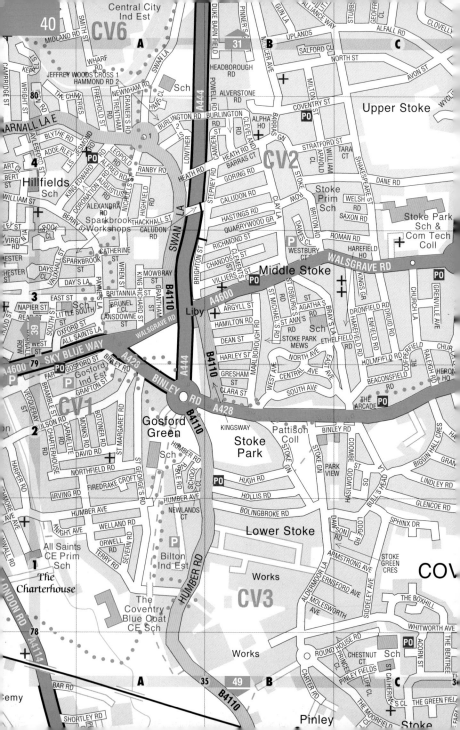

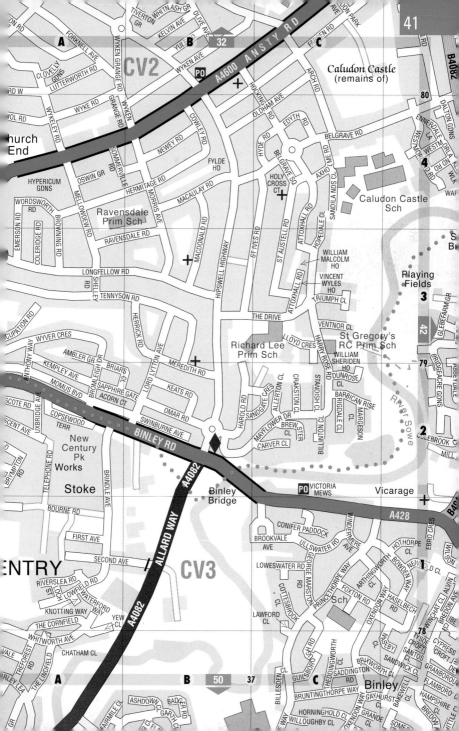

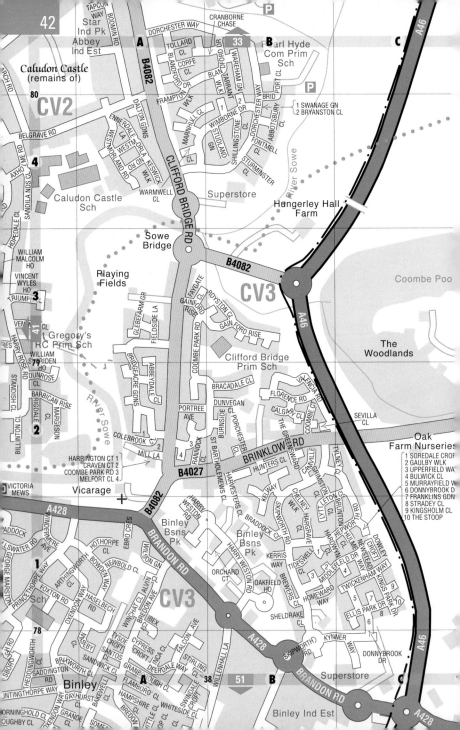

A

Little
Wrautam

B

34

C

Wrautam

Coombe Abbey
Farm

80

*Coombe
Abbey*
Hotel

4

Visitor
Ctr

P

Coombe Abbey
Country Park

COMBE FIELDS RD

3

CV3

B4027

COVENTRY RD

79

B4027

Centenary Way

2

Old
Pools

1

Old Lodge
Farm

The Grove

CV8

Little
Rough

78

One O'clock Ride

Twelve O'clock Ride

A Big Rough

B

52

40

New Close
Wood

C

Roseycombe
Cottages

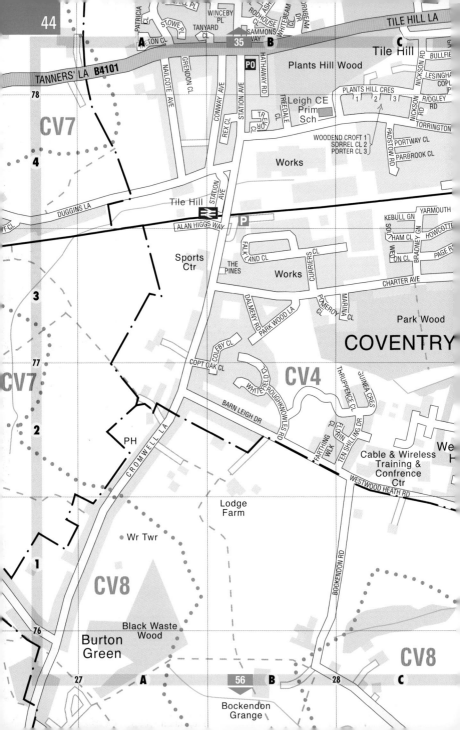

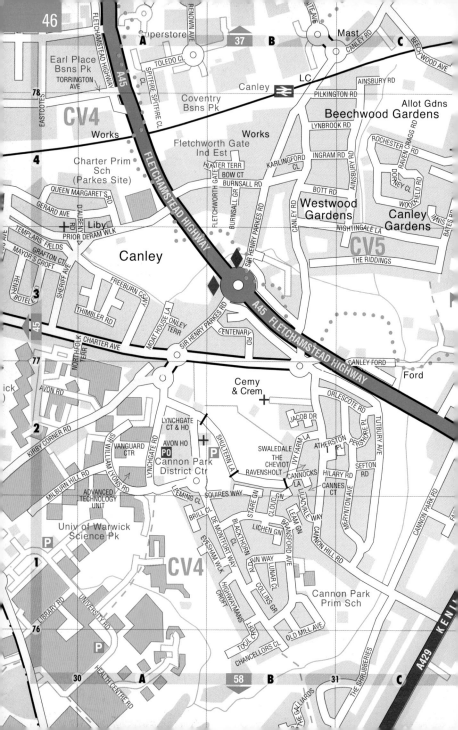

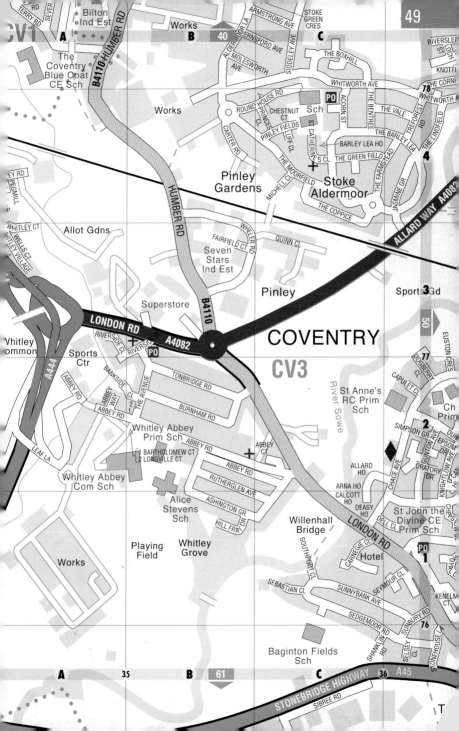

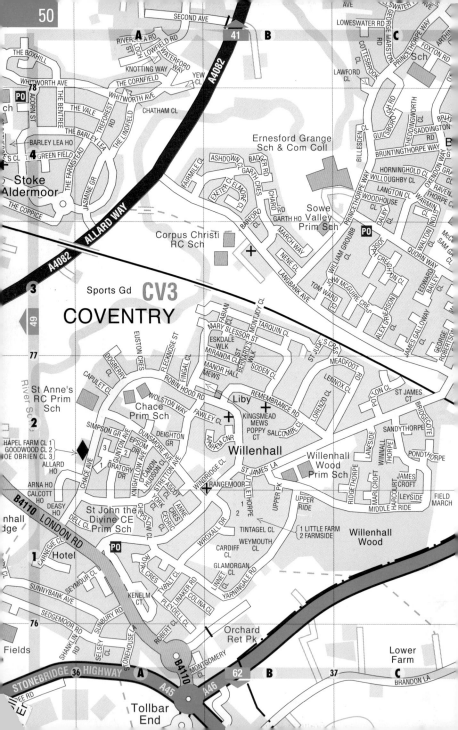

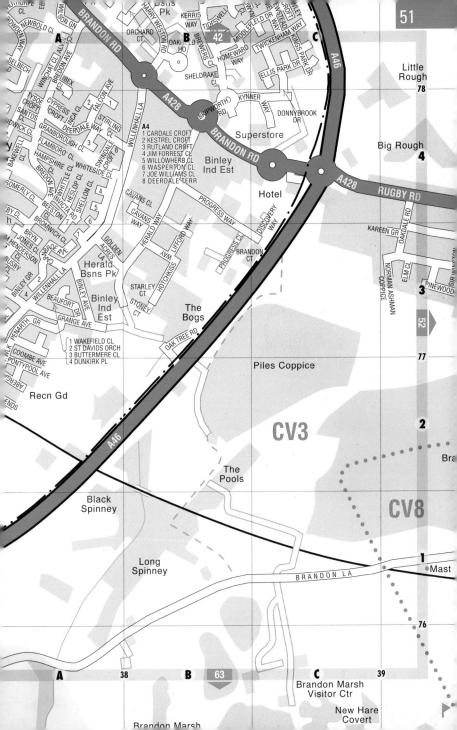

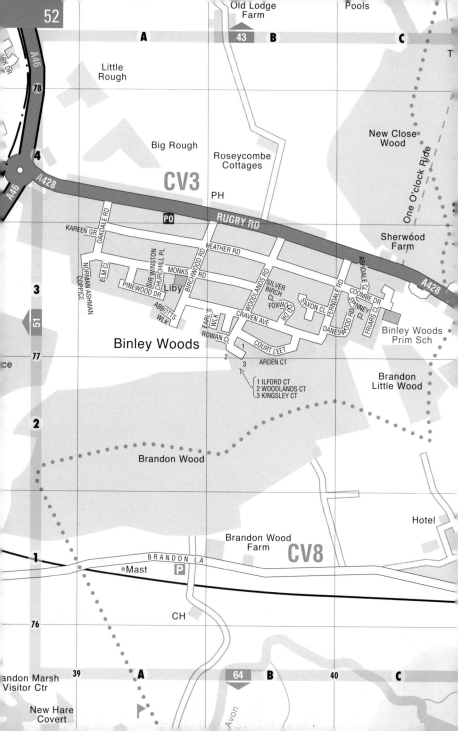

A 43 B C

Old Lodge Farm

Pools

T

Little Rough

Big Rough

Roseycombe Cottages

New Close Wood

CV3

PH

One O'Clock Ride

A46

78

A428

4

A46

51

KAREEN GR

OAKDALE RD

PO

RUGBY RD

Sherwood Farm

A428

NORMAN ASHMAN COPPICE

ELM CL

PINEWOOD DR

SIR WINSTON CHURCHILL PL

MONKS

Liby

BIRCHWOOD RD

HEATHER RD

WOODLANDS RD

SILVER BIRCH CL

FOXWOOD

SAXON CL

FERNDALE RD

COOMBE DR

WOOD RD

ASHDALE CL

SANNEY CL

FRIARS CL

Binley Woods Prim Sch

3

77

ABBOTTS WLK

EARL'S WLK

CRAVEN AVE

ROWAN CL

1

COURT LEET

DANES

Binley Woods

2

3

ARDEN CT

Brandon Little Wood

1 ILFORD CT
2 WOODLANDS CT
3 KINGSLEY CT

2

Brandon Wood

Brandon Wood Farm

CV8

Hotel

1

BRANDON LA

Mast

P

CH

76

Brandon Marsh Visitor Ctr

39

A

64

B

40

C

New Hare Covert

Avon

ce

52

51

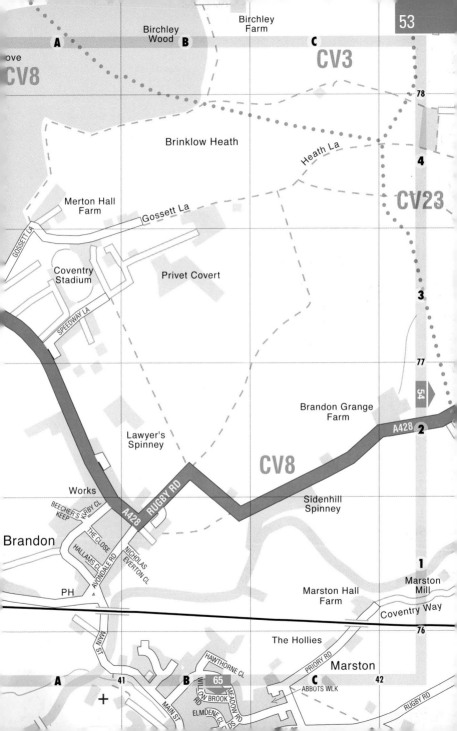

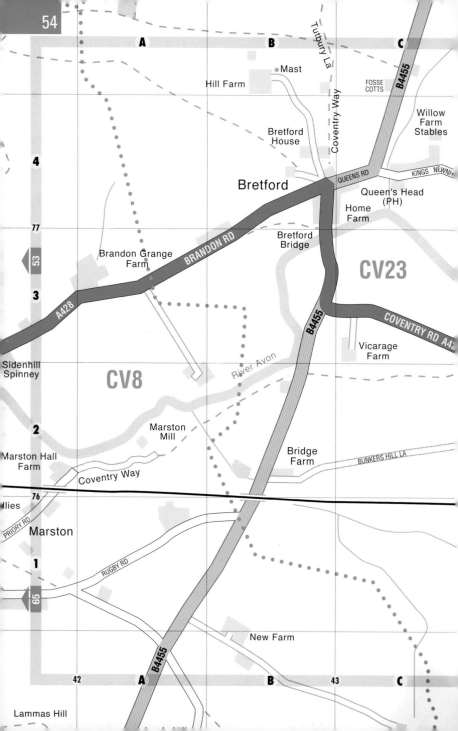

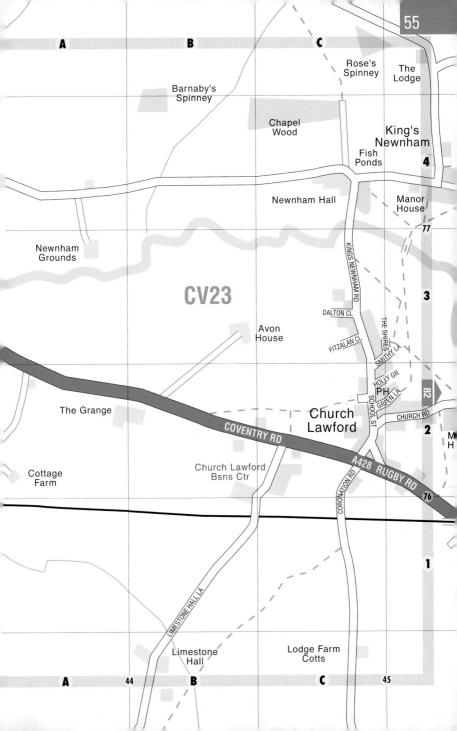

A
44
B
C

CV4

BOCKENDON RD

Black Waste
Wood

76

Burton
Green

4

Bockendon
Grange

Broadwells
Wood

South
Hurst
Farm

Burton Green
CE Prim Sch
Wr
3 Wr

75

Coventry Way

RED LA

CV8

2

Long
Meadow
Wood

Long Meadow
Barn Farm

HOLLIS LA

1

Dunns Pitts
Farm

A452 Balsall Common

74

27
A
66
B
28
C

Engadine
House

BIRMINGHAM RD

RED LA

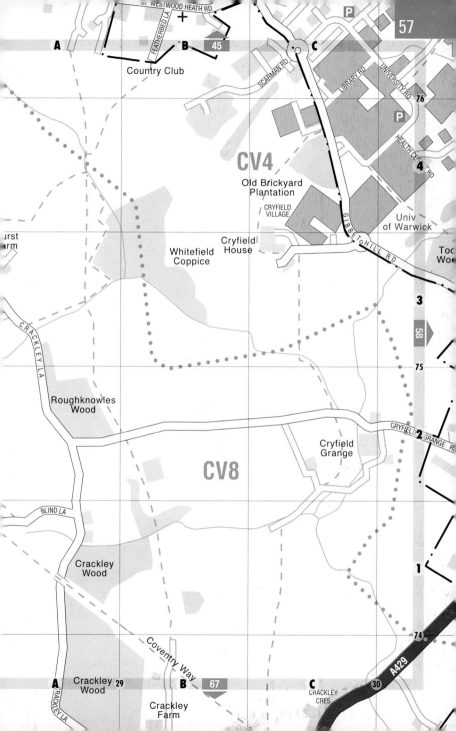

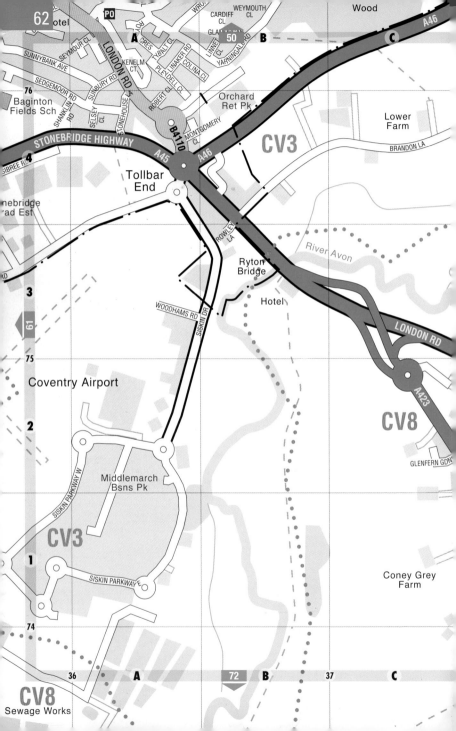

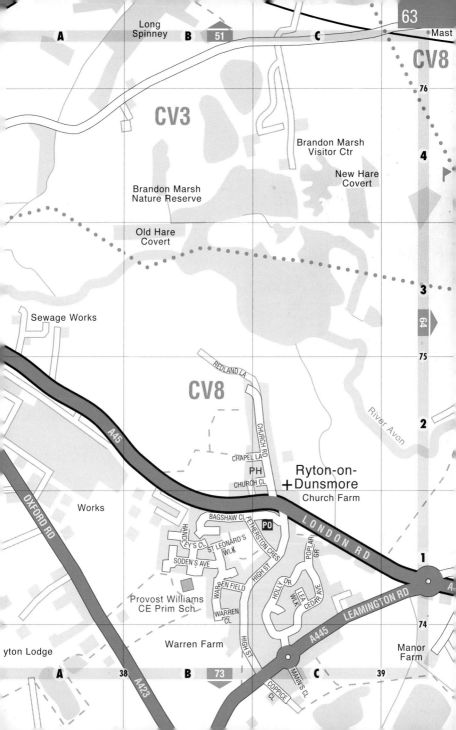

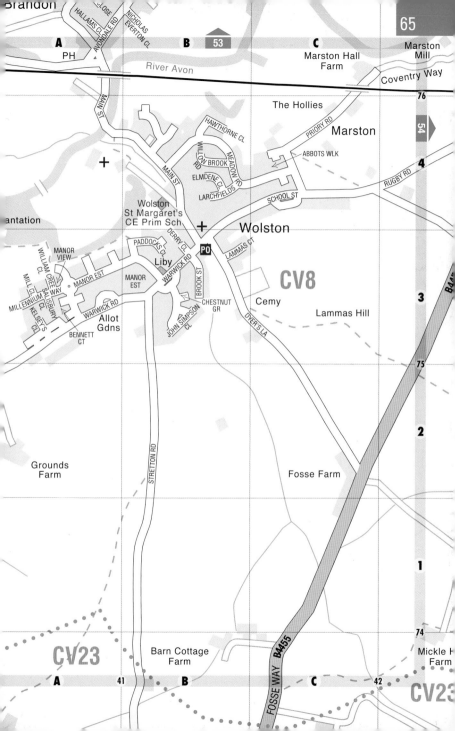

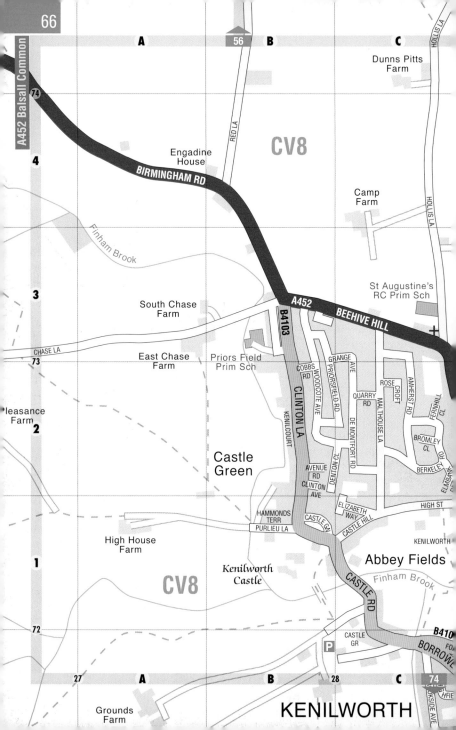

A452 Balsall Common

74

A

56

B

C

Dunns Pitts
Farm

4

RED LA

CV8

HOLLIS LA

Engadine
House

BIRMINGHAM RD

Camp
Farm

HOLLIS LA

Finham Brook

St Augustine's
RC Prim Sch

3

South Chase
Farm

A452

BEEHIVE HILL

B4103

CHASE LA

East Chase
Farm

Priors Field
Prim Sch

COBBS
RD

GRANGE
AVE

ROSE
CROFT

AMHERST RD

73

WOODCOTE AVE

PRIORSFIELD RD

FERNHILL CL

leasance
Farm

2

CLINTON LA

KENILCOURT

QUARRY
RD

MALTHOUSE LA

BROMLEY
CL

ELMBANK RD

DE MONTFORT RD

BERKELEY

DENTON CL

Castle
Green

AVENUE
RD

CLINTON
AVE

1

High House
Farm

ELIZABETH
WAY

HIGH ST

HAMMONDS
TERR

CASTLE GN

CASTLE HILL

KENILWORTH

PURLIEU LA

CV8

Kenilworth
Castle

Abbey Fields

Finham Brook

CASTLE RD

72

B410

FO

BORROWE

27

A

28

C

74

28

B

KENILWORTH

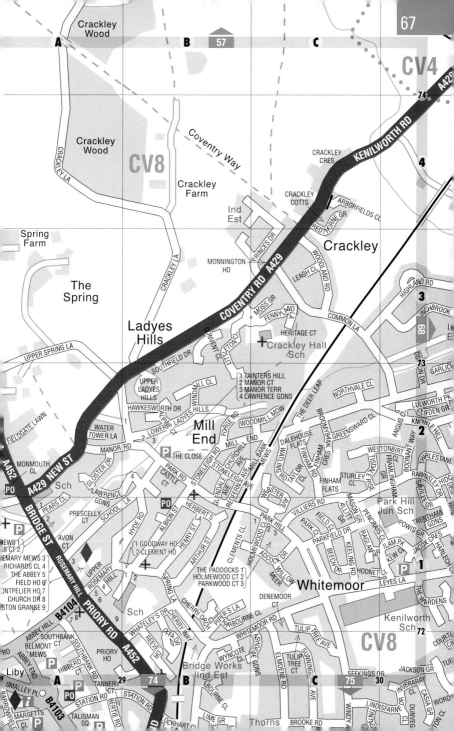

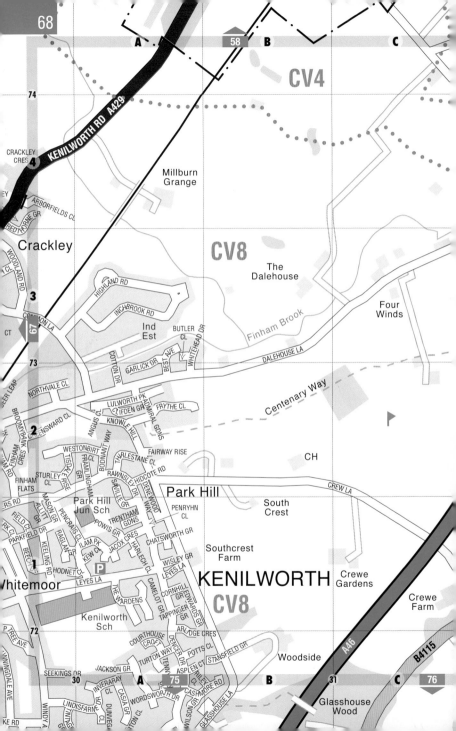

A 58 B C

CV4

74

KENILWORTH RD A429

CRACKLEY CRES

4

Millburn Grange

Crackley

CV8

The Dalehouse

ARBORFIELDS CL

FREDTHORNE GR

WOODLAND RD

CL

Four Winds

HIGHLAND RD

3

INCHBROOK RD

COMMON LA

69

CT

Finham Brook

Ind Est

BUTLER CL

WHITEHEAD DR

COTTON DR

73

GARLICK DR

BEST AVE

DALEHOUSE LA

Centenary Way

DEER LEAP

NORTHVALE CL

BROOMBANK RD

GREENSWARD CL

LULWORTH PK

IFDEN GR

ADMIRAL GDNS

FRYTHE CL

ANGUS CL

KNOWLE HILL

FINHAM CRES

2

WESTONBIRT

BODNANT WAY

TISDALE RISE

THIRLESTANE CL

FAIRWAY RISE

CH

FINHAM FLATS

STURLEY CL

FRAMLINGHAM GR

RAWNSLEY DR

HIDCOTE RD

DENEWOOD WAY

CREW LA

RS RD

WEDGNOCK

Park Hill Jun Sch

SAVILLE DR

Park Hill

South Crest

FIELD CL

MASON GR

ALLITT GR

PENCRAIG CL

POWIS GR

TRENTHAM GDNS

PENRYHN CL

PARKFIELD DR

RAGLAN GR

ILAM PK

JACOX CRES

CHATSWORTH GR

Southcrest Farm

BEECH CL

KEELING RD

KEW CL

HARLECH CL

WISLEY GR

1

HODNETT CL

P

LEYES LA

CAMELOT GR

LEYES LA

CORNHILL GR

KENILWORTH

Crewe Gardens

Whitemoor

THE WARDENS

EDWARDS GR

TAPPINGER GR

CV8

Crewe Farm

Kenilworth Sch

COURTHOUSE CROFT

DENCER DR

BRIDGE CRES

72

TURTON WAY

TENNYSON

POTTS CL

STANSFIELD GR

Woodside

A46

B4115

TREE AVE

SEEKINGS DR

JACKSON GR

ASPLEN CT

CASHMORE RD

30 A 75 B 31 C 76

INVERARAY CL

CASIA GR

WORDSWORTH DR

GLASSHOUSE LA

WILSON CL

Glasshouse Wood

TINNINGDALE AVE

LINDISFARNE

DUNVEGA

CASTON CL

WINDY A

KE RD

P Coventry Airport

STONELEIGH RD

BUBBENHALL RD

A

B

61

C

S/SKIN PARKWAY

CV3

Rock Farm

74

Sewage Works

4

CV8

Rock Spinne

River Avon

3

Vehicle Test Track

72

73

Bubbenhall Bridge

2

AVON TERR

PO

LOWER F

CHURCH RD

SPRING CT

PH

WAGGO

+

SPRING HILL

RIVERSIDE

DARFIELD CT

PIT HI

Manor Farm

Piece Barn

1

CV8

Old House Farm

A445

72

A

35

B

Broomhill Farm

C

36

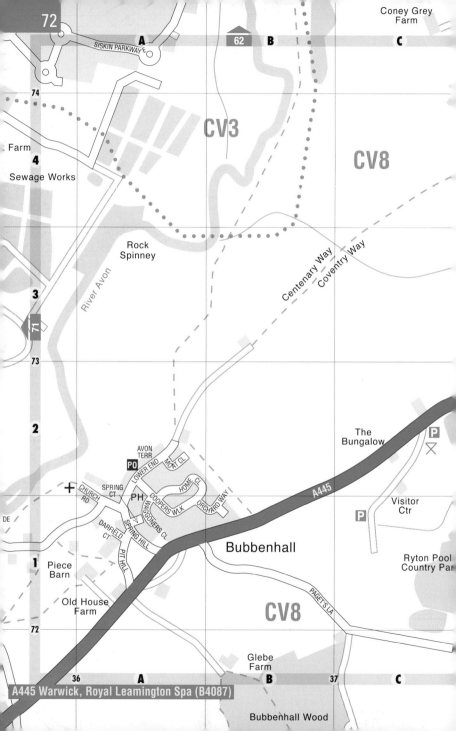

Coney Grey
Farm

A   62   B   C

SISKIN PARKWAY E

74

CV3

CV8

Farm

4

Sewage Works

Rock
Spinney

Centenary Way

Coventry Way

River Avon

3

71

73

2

The
Bungalow

P

AVON
TERR

PO

LOWER END

MCKT CL.

HOME CL.

ORCHARD WAY

A445

Visitor
Ctr

P

CHURCH RD

SPRING CT

PH

COOPERS WLK

WAGGONERS CL

Bubbenhall

Ryton Pool
Country Par

DE

DARFIELD CT

SPRING HILL

1

Piece
Barn

PIT HILL

PAGETS LA

CV8

Old House
Farm

72

Glebe
Farm

36   A   B   37   C

Bubbenhall Wood

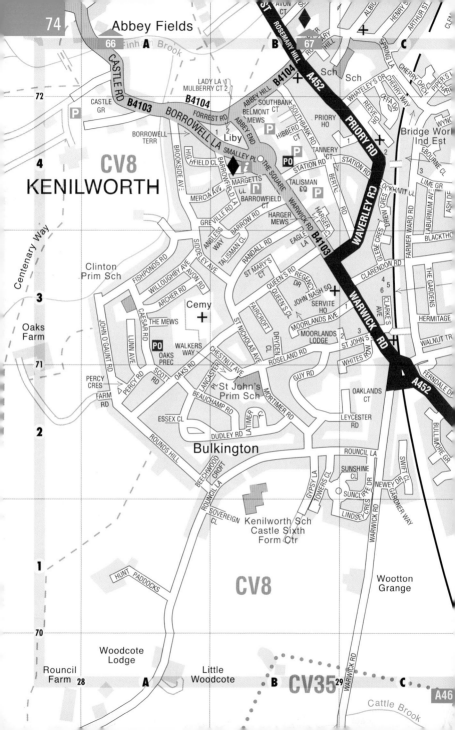

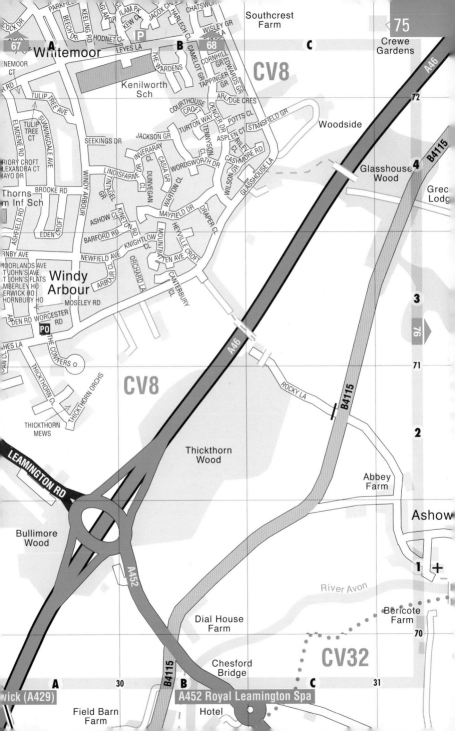

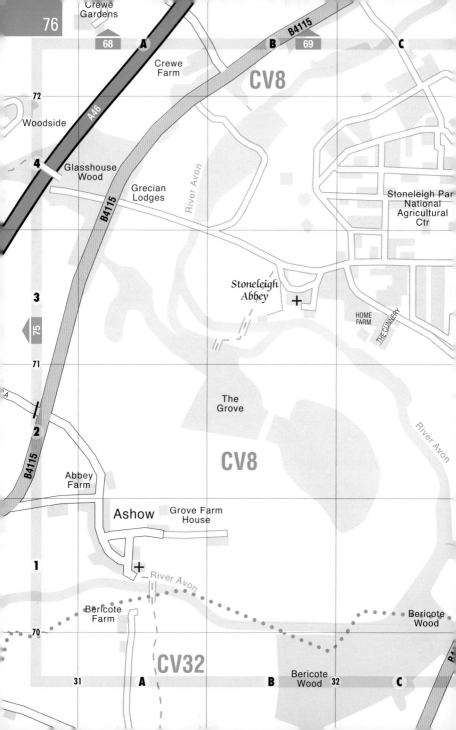

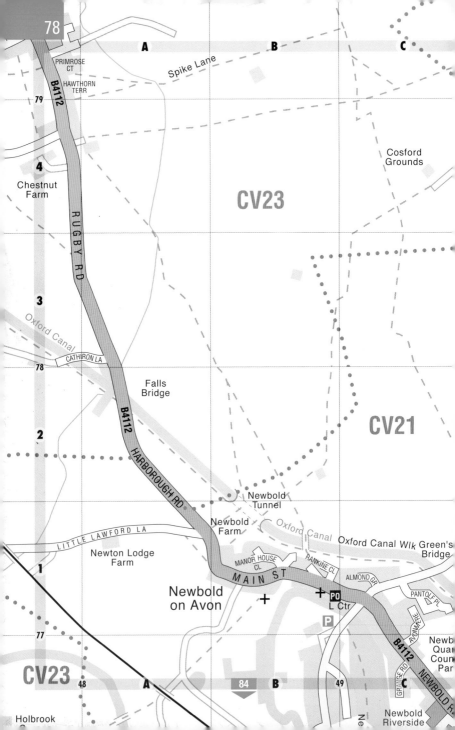

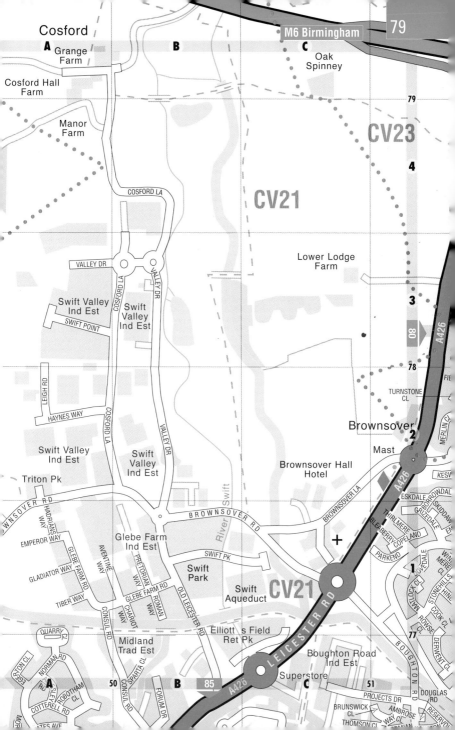

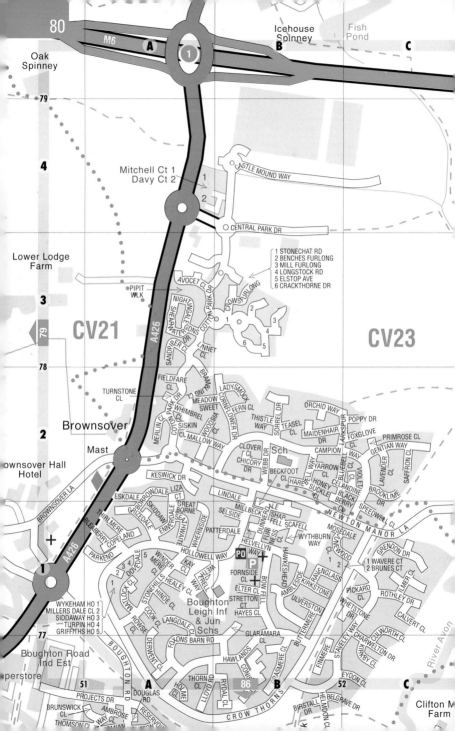

80

M6 Ⓐ ①

Ⓑ Icehouse Spinney

Fish Pond

Ⓒ

Oak Spinney

79

4

Mitchell Ct 1
Davy Ct 2

CASTLE MOUND WAY

CENTRAL PARK DR

1 STONECHAT RD
2 BENCHES FURLONG
3 MILL FURLONG
4 LONGSTOCK RD
5 ELSTOP AVE
6 CRACKTHORNE DR

Lower Lodge Farm

3

CV21

PIPIT WLK

AVOCET CL

NIGHTINGALE GDNS
SHEARWATER CL

COTTON PARK DR

CROW FURLONG

SANDPIPER CL

LINNET CL

78

79

TURNSTONE CL

FIELDFARE CL

WHIMBREL CL
BRAMBLING CL

LADYSMOCK
MEADOW SWEET

CORNFLOWER CL

FERN CL

ORCHID WAY

POPPY DR

Brownsover

2

MERLIN CL

COTON PARK DR

SISKIN CL

MALLOW WAY

WOODSIA CL

THISTLE WAY

SORREL DR

TEASEL CL

MAIDENHAIR DR

LARKSPUR CL

FOXGLOVE WAY

PRIMROSE CL

GENTIAN WAY

CV23

Mast

CLOVER CL

CHICORY DR

WEBB CL

Sch

BECKFOOT CL

CAMPION

HARE CL

FELL WAY

YARROW CL

HONEY SUCKLE CL

BLUEBELL CL

CELANDINE CL

BLACK BERRY CL

VIOLET CL

LAVENDER CL

SAFFRON CL

BROOKLIME DR

ownsover Hall Hotel

KESWICK DR

ESKDALE

BORROWDALE

BROWNSOVER LA

SKIDDAW CL

GATEDALE

LIZA CT

ENNERDALE

GREAT BORNE

WHERNSIDE

LINDALE

SELSIDE

MILLBECK CL

SHAP FELL

PATTERDALE

HELVELLYN

DUNNERDALE

FURNESS CL

SCAFELL

MOSEDALE

WYTHBURN WAY

NEWTON MANOR LA

SPEEDWELL DR

GRENDON DR

ULLSWOOD

THIRLMERE
BLEABERRY
COPELAND

DOVEDALE

WINDER MERE

HEALEY CL

KAY CL

HOLLOWELL WAY

BOW WAY

PO

FORNSIDE CL

HAWKSHEAD

ESKDALE

KIRKSTONE CL

RAVENGLASS

1 WAVERE CT
2 BRUNES CT

PICKARD CL

ILMER CL

ROTHLEY DR

PARKEND

MATLOCK CL

COCK CL

STONEHILL

HINDE CL

MERRIE

FELL WAY

WELHAM

Boughton Leigh Inf & Jun Schs

ELTER CL

STRETTON CT

HAYES CL

AMBLESIDE

BUTTERMERE

ULVERSTON

WHETSTONE CL

CALVERT DR

WYKEHAM HO 1
MILLERS DALE CL 2
SIDDAWAY HO 3
TURPIN HO 4
GRIFFITHS HO 5

ROWSE

COCK CL

LANGDALE CL

DERWENT CL

FOXONS BARN RD

GLARAMARA

HAWLANDS

GRASMERE CL

CONISTON

FINMERE

STAVELEY WAY

CWORTH CL

CHARWELTON DR

KIRBY CL

Boughton Road Ind Est
perstore

51

PROJECTS DR

BRUNSWICK CL

THOMSON CL

AMBROSE

Ⓐ

BOUGHTON RD

DOUGLAS RD

RESERVOIR

HOME CL

THORN CL

LLOYD CL

RYDAL CL

CROW THORNS

86

EYDON CL

Ⓑ

BIRSTALL DR

HEMDON CL

BELGRAVE DR

52

Ⓒ

River Avon

Clifton M
Farm

77

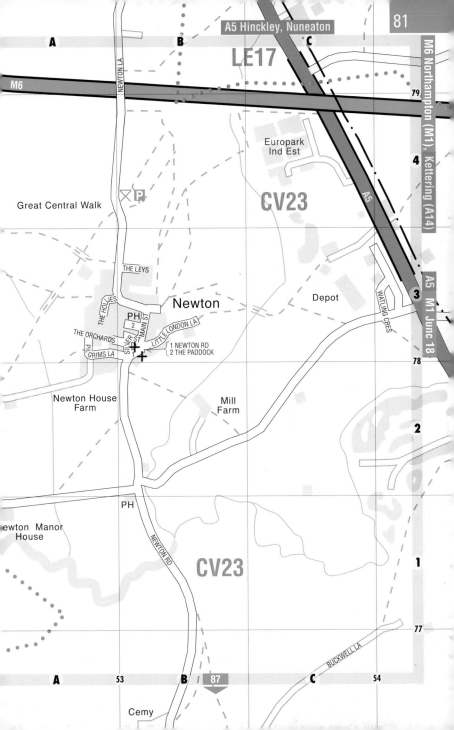

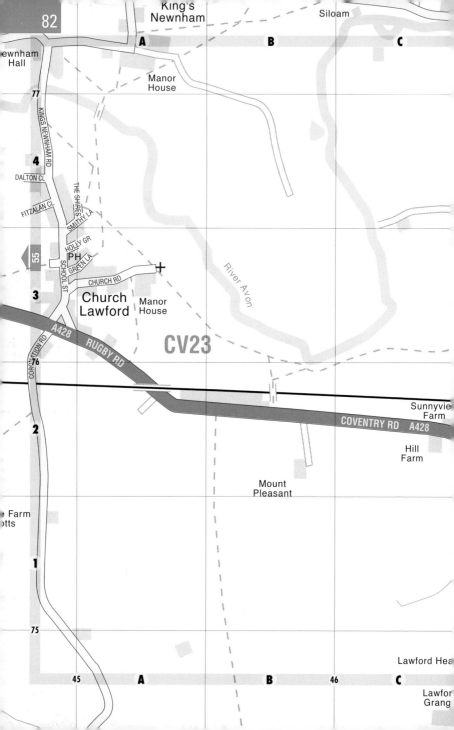

King's
Newnham

Siloam

A **B** **C**

ewnham
Hall

Manor
House

77

KINGS NEWNHAM RD

4

DALTON CL

FITZALAN CL

THE SHIRES

SMITHY LA

HOLLY GR

GREEN LA

55

PH

SCHOOL ST

3

CHURCH RD

Church
Lawford

Manor
House

River Avon

CV23

A428

RUGBY RD

CORPORATION RD

76

2

COVENTRY RD A428

Sunnyvie
Farm

Hill
Farm

Mount
Pleasant

e Farm
otts

1

75

Lawford Hea

45 **A** 46 **B** **C**

Lawfor
Grang

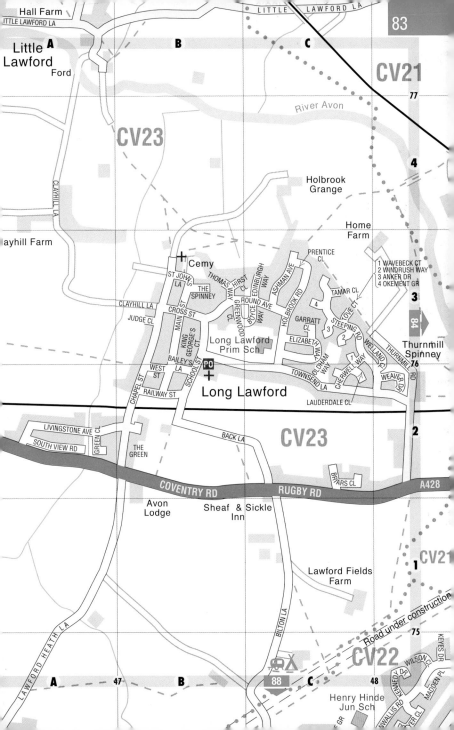

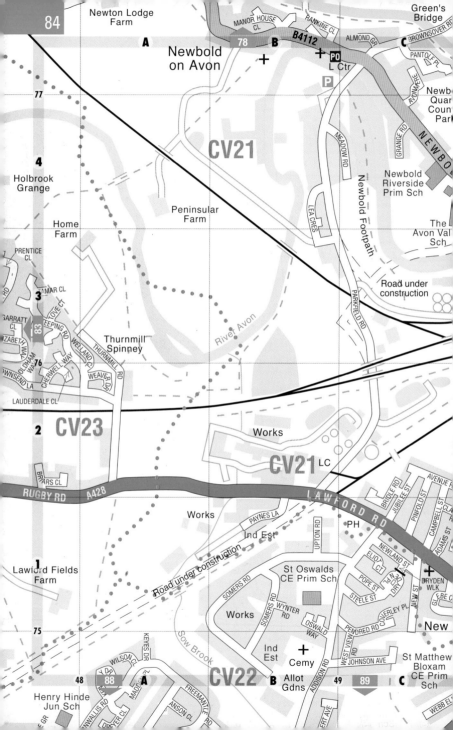

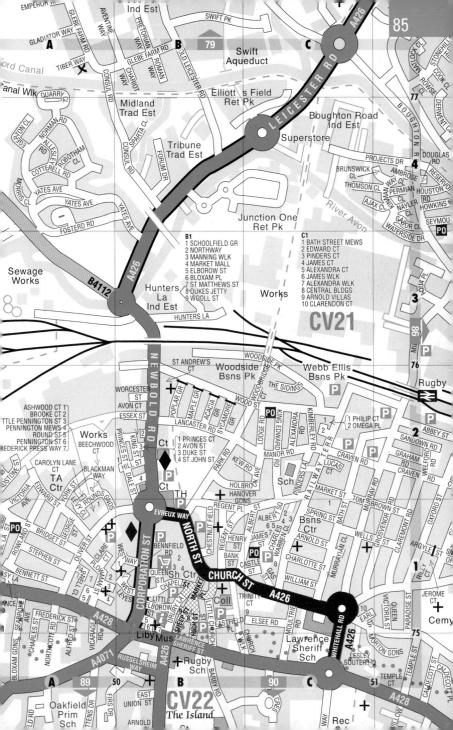

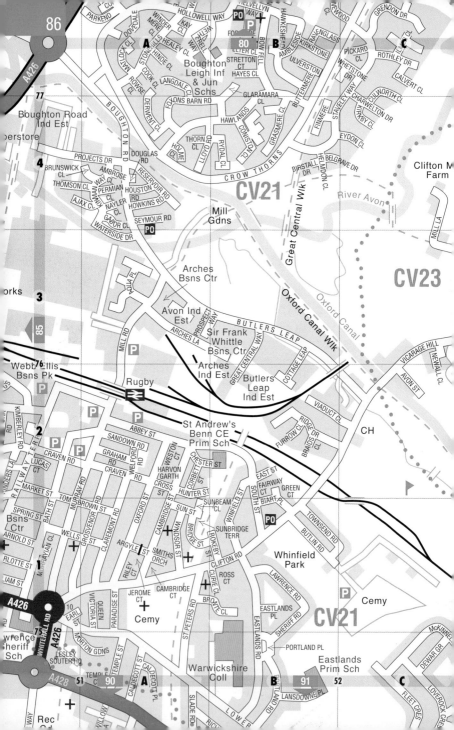

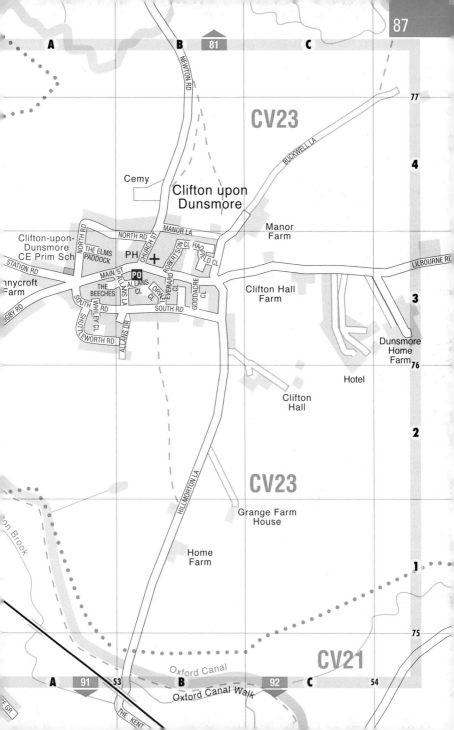

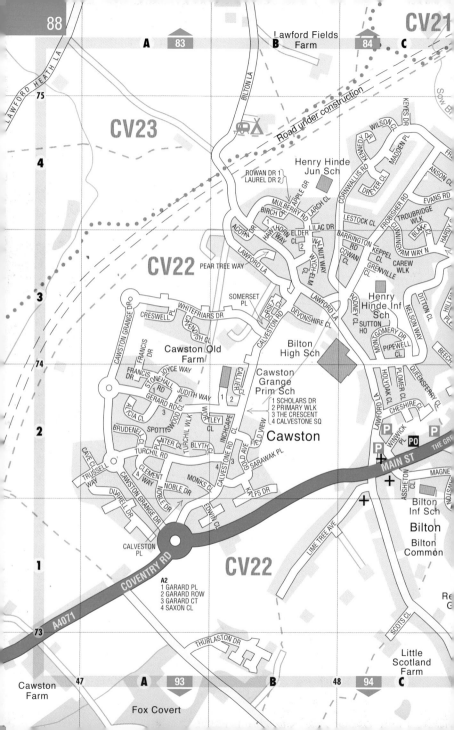

A 83

B Lawford Fields Farm

C 84

LAWFORD HEATH LA

75

BILTON LA

CV23

Road under construction

4

KEYES DR

WILSON

CORNWALLIS RD

KENNEDY

DREYER CL

MADDEN PL

ANSON CL

FROBISHER RD

EVANS RD

ROWAN DR 1
LAUREL DR 2

Henry Hinde Jun Sch

APPLE GR

MULBERRY RD

BIRCH CT

LARCH CL

LILAC DR

LESTOCK CL

TROUBRIDGE WLK

BLAKE CL

HARDY

CV22

ALCORN

HAWTHORN WAY

ELDER

WALNUT WAY

WYCH-ELM CL

BARRINGTON RD

COWAN CL

KEPPEL CL

CUNNINGHAM WAY N

CAREW WLK

PEAR TREE WAY

LAWFORD LA

SOMERSET PL

GRENVILLE CL

3

DEVONSHIRE CL

LAWFORD LA

RODNEY CL

Henry Hinde Inf Sch

DITTON CL

NELSON WAY

HILL

CAWSTON GRANGE DR

CRESWELL

WHITEFRIARS DR

CAVENDISH CL

FRANCIS DR

Cawston Old Farm

SOMERSET CL

CALVESTON CL

SUTTON HO

MONTGOMERY DR

PIPEWELL CL

BEECH

74

Bilton High Sch

HOLYOAK CL

PLOMER CL

QUEENSFERRY CL

FRANCIS DR

JOYCE WAY

STONEHALL RD

JUDITH WAY

CALLIER CL

Cawston Grange Prim Sch

1 SCHOLARS DR
2 PRIMARY WLK
3 THE CRESCENT
4 CALVESTONE SQ

CHESHIRE CL

2

GERARD RD

ACACIA CL

3

WOOD

WHATLEY CL

FIELD VIEW

BRUDENELL CL

SPOTTIS

PLANTER CL

TURCHIL WLK

INCHCAPE CL

CALVESTONE RD

GOLD AVE

Cawston

WINWICK

PO

P

CAVE CL

TURCHIL RD

BLYTH

SARAWAK PL

MAIN ST

THE GR

TRUSSELL WAY

CLEMENT WAY

NOBLE DR

MONKS CL

KALFS DR

MAGNE

ASSHETON CL

DURRELL DR

CAWSTON GRANGE DR

EDWIN CL

Bilton Inf Sch

CALVESTON PL

LIME TREE AVE

Bilton

1

COVENTRY RD

CV22

A2
1 GARARD PL
2 GARARD ROW
3 GARARD CT
4 SAXON CL

Bilton Common

Re G

A4071

SCOTS CL

73

THURLASTON DR

Little Scotland Farm

Cawston Farm

47

A 93

B

48

C 94

Fox Covert

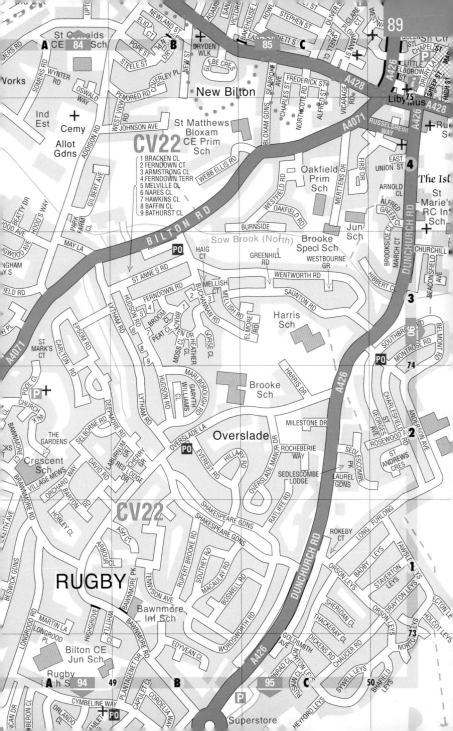

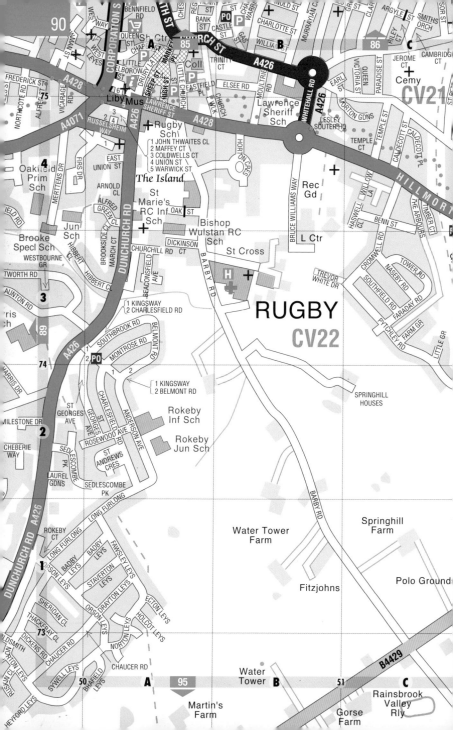

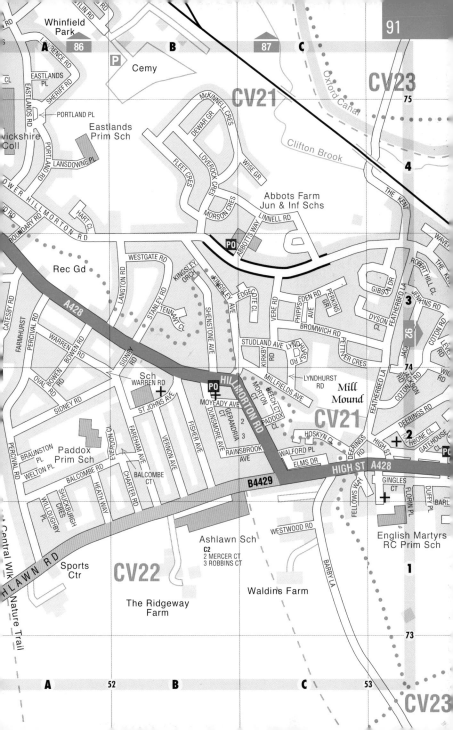

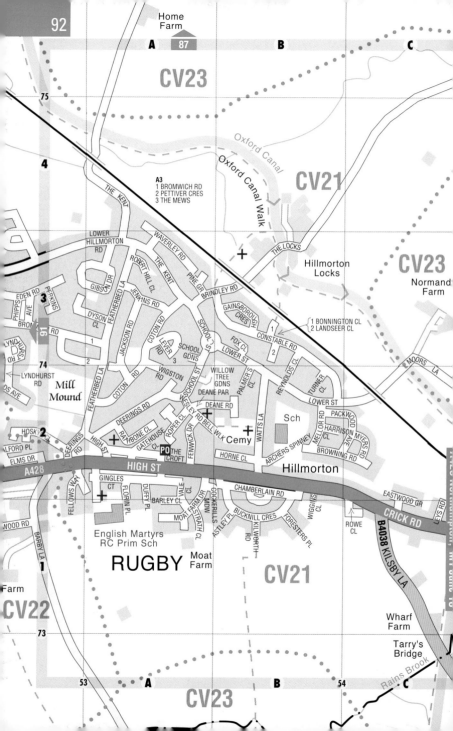

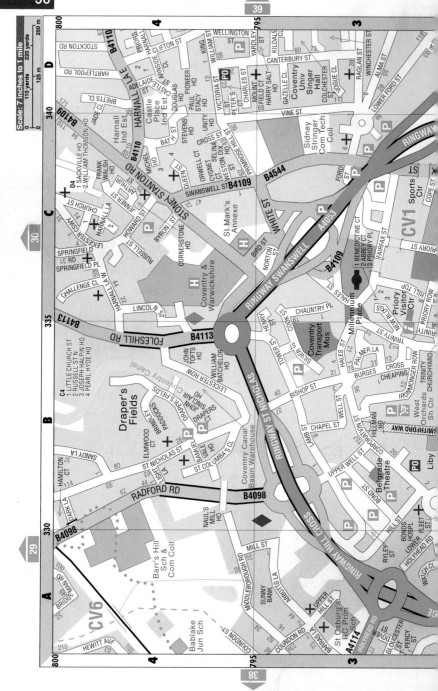

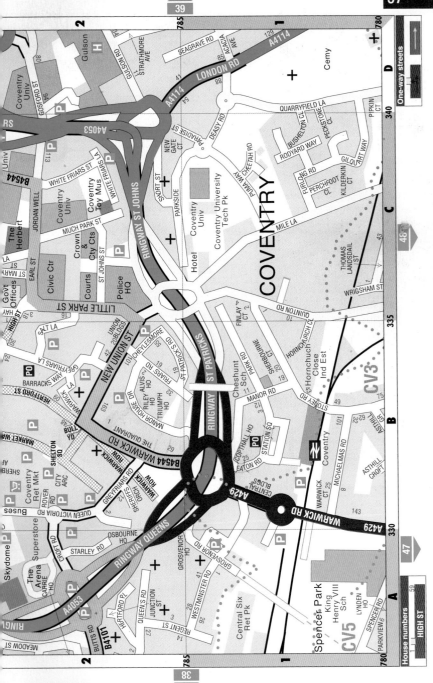

COVENTRY

One-way streets

House numbers
HIGH ST

CV5
CV3

Index

Street names are listed alphabetically and show the locality, the Postcode district, the page number and a reference to the square in which the name falls on the map page

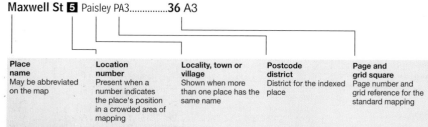

Maxwell St 5 Paisley PA3...............36 A3

Place name
May be abbreviated on the map

Location number
Present when a number indicates the place's position in a crowded area of mapping

Locality, town or village
Shown when more than one place has the same name

Postcode district
District for the indexed place

Page and grid square
Page number and grid reference for the standard mapping

Towns and villages are listed in CAPITAL LETTERS
Public and commercial buildings are highlighted in magenta. **Places of interest** are highlighted in blue with a star ★

Abbreviations used in the index

Acad	**Academy**	Ct	**Court**	Hts	**Heights**	Pl	**Place**
App	**Approach**	Ctr	**Centre**	Ind	**Industrial**	Prec	**Precinct**
Arc	**Arcade**	Ctry	**Country**	Inst	**Institute**	Prom	**Promenade**
Ave	**Avenue**	Cty	**County**	Int	**International**	Rd	**Road**
Bglw	**Bungalow**	Dr	**Drive**	Intc	**Interchange**	Recn	**Recreation**
Bldg	**Building**	Dro	**Drove**	Junc	**Junction**	Ret	**Retail**
Bsns, Bus	**Business**	Ed	**Education**	L	**Leisure**	Sh	**Shopping**
Bvd	**Boulevard**	Emb	**Embankment**	La	**Lane**	Sq	**Square**
Cath	**Cathedral**	Est	**Estate**	Liby	**Library**	St	**Street**
Cir	**Circus**	Ex	**Exhibition**	Mdw	**Meadow**	Sta	**Station**
Cl	**Close**	Gd	**Ground**	Meml	**Memorial**	Terr	**Terrace**
Cnr	**Corner**	Gdn	**Garden**	Mkt	**Market**	TH	**Town Hall**
Coll	**College**	Gn	**Green**	Mus	**Museum**	Univ	**University**
Com	**Community**	Gr	**Grove**	Orch	**Orchard**	Wk, Wlk	**Walk**
Comm	**Common**	H	**Hall**	Pal	**Palace**	Wr	**Water**
Cott	**Cottage**	Ho	**House**	Par	**Parade**	Yd	**Yard**
Cres	**Crescent**	Hospl	**Hospital**	Pas	**Passage**		
Cswy	**Causeway**	HQ	**Headquarters**	Pk	**Park**		

Index of towns, villages, streets, hospitals, industrial estates, railway stations, schools, shopping centres, universities and places of interest

Abb – Ald

A

Abberton Way CV4...... 58 C3
Abbey Ct
Coventry CV1 .... 96 C3
Coventry, Pinley CV3...... 49 C2
Abbeydale Cl CV3..... 42 A2
Abbey End CV8 ...... 74 B4
ABBEY FIELDS 66 C1
Abbey Hill CV8 ...... 67 A1
Abbey Ind Est CV2... 33 A1
Abbey Rd CV3 .... 49 B2
Abbey St CV21........ 86 A2
Abbey The CV8 ...... 67 A1
Abbey Way CV3....... 49 A2
Abbotsbury Cl CV2...... 42 B4
Abbots Farm
  Jun & Inf Schs CV21 ... 91 C3
Abbotsford
  Sch CV8............... 67 A2
Abbots Wlk CV8 ...... 65 C4

Abbotts La CV1........ 96 A3
Abbotts Way CV21 ..... 91 C4
Abbotts Wlk CV3 ...... 52 A3
Abercorn Rd CV5...... 37 C2
Aberdeen Cl CV5 ...... 27 B1
Abergavenny Wlk CV3 .. 51 A2
Acacia Ave CV1........ 39 C1
Acacia Ct CV6........ 28 C1
Acacia Gr CV21........ 85 B2
Achal Cl CV6........ 21 C2
Achilles Rd CV6........ 31 B3
Acorn Cl
  Bedworth CV12........ 12 C4
  Stoneleigh CV8 .... 69 C3
Acorn Ct CV5........ 41 A2
Acorn Dr CV22........ 88 B3
Acorn St CV3......... 49 C4
Acton Ho CV4 .... 36 A3
Adam Rd 1 CV6...... 31 A3
Adams St CV21........ 84 C1
Adare Dr CV3......... 48 A4
Adcock Dr CV8 .... 67 C1
Addenbrooke Rd CV7.. 12 A2
Adderley St CV1....... 39 C4

Addison Rd
  Coventry CV6 .... 29 B4
  Rugby CV22............ 89 A4
Adelaide Ct 3 CV12 ....6 A2
Adelaide St CV1 .... 96 D4
Adkinson Ave CV22 .... 94 A2
Admiral Gdns CV8 ..... 68 A2
Advanced Tech Unit
  CV4 .... 46 A2
Agincourt Rd CV3 ..... 48 C3
Ainsbury Rd CV5....... 46 C4
Ainsdale Cl CV6 .... 22 B4
Aintree Cl
  Bedworth CV12...........6 B4
  Coventry CV6 .... 30 C1
Ajax Cl CV21.......... 86 A4
Akon Ho CV6 .... 19 C2
Alandale Ave CV5...... 35 C4
Alandale Ct CV12...... 12 C4
Albany Ct CV1........ 38 B2
Albany Rd CV5 .... 38 B1
Albert Cres CV6 ...... 20 B3
Albert Fearn Gdns CV6.. 21 C1

Albert Sq CV21 .... 85 C1
Albert St
  Coventry CV1 .... 39 C4
  Rugby CV21............. 85 C1
Albion Ind Est CV6 ..... 30 B3
Albion St CV8 .... 67 B1
Aldbourne Rd CV1...... 30 A1
Aldbury Rise CV5....... 37 A4
**Alderman Callow Sch &
  Com Coll** CV4 .... 45 B2
Alderman Gee Hall CV12 ..6 A4
ALDERMAN'S GREEN .. 22 B3
Alderman's Green Com
  Prim Sch CV2 .... 22 C3
Alderman's Green Ind Est
  CV2 .... 23 A2
Alderman's Green Rd
  CV2 .... 22 B3
Alder Meadow Cl CV6... 21 A4
Alderminster Rd CV5 ... 36 B4
Aldermoor Farm Prim Sch
  CV3 .... 49 C4
Aldermoor La CV3...... 40 B1
Alderney Cl CV6 ...... 20 B2

Alder Rd CV6 . . . . 22 A2
Alders The CV12 . . . . 5 B2
Aldrich Ave CV4 . . . . 35 C2
Aldrin Way CV4 . . . . 46 B1
Alexander Rd CV12 . . . . 6 C3
Alexandra Ct
Kenilworth CV8 . . . . 74 C4
5 Rugby CV21 . . . . 85 C1
Alexandra Rd
Coventry CV1 . . . . 40 A4
Rugby CV21 . . . . 85 C2
Alexandra Terr CV6 . . . 21 B2
Alexandra Wlk **7** CV21 . 85 C1
Alex Grierson Cl CV3 . . 50 C3
Alfall Rd CV2 . . . . 31 C1
Alfred Green Cl CV22 . . . 90 A4
Alfred Rd CV1 . . . . 40 A4
Alfred St CV21 . . . . 85 A1
Alfriston Rd CV3 . . . . 60 A4
Algate Cl CV6 . . . . 20 C3
Alice Arnold Ho **1** CV2 . 22 B1
Alice Cl CV12 . . . . 5 C1
Alice Stevens Sch CV3 . . 49 B2
Alicia Cl CV22 . . . . 88 A2
Alison Sq CV6 . . . . 22 B4
Allan Rd CV6 . . . . 38 A4
Allans Cl CV23 . . . . 87 B3
Allans Dr CV23 . . . . 87 B3
Allans La CV23 . . . . 87 B3
Allard Ho CV3 . . . . 49 C2
Allard Way CV3 . . . . 50 A3
Allerton Cl CV2 . . . . 41 C2
ALLESLEY 27 C3
Allesley Croft CV5 . . . . . 27 B2
Allesley Ct CV5 . . . . 27 B2
Allesley Hall Dr CV5 . . . 28 A1
Allesley Hall Prim Sch
CV5 . . . . 36 C4
Allesley Old Rd CV5 . . . 37 B3
Allesley Prim Sch CV5 . . 27 B3
Allesley Rd CV21 . . . . . . 85 A4
Alliance Way CV2 . . . . . . 31 B1
Allied Cl CV6 . . . . 21 A2
Allitt Gr CV8 . . . . 67 C1
All Saints CE Inf Sch
CV12 . . . . 6 C2
All Saints CE Prim Sch
CV1 . . . . 39 C1
All Saints La CV1 . . . . . . 40 A3
All Saints Rd CV12 . . . . . . 5 C1
All Saints Sq CV12 . . . . . . 6 B3
All Souls RC Prim Sch
CV5 . . . . 37 C2
Alma St CV1 . . . . 96 D3
Almond Gr CV21 . . . . . . 78 C1
Almond Tree Ave CV2 . . 22 C2
Almshouses CV8 . . . . . . 70 A2
Alpha Bsns Pk CV2 . . . . 23 A1
Alpha Ho CV2 . . . . 40 B4
Alpine Ct CV8 . . . . 67 B2
Alpine Rise CV3 . . . . 47 B1
Alspath La CV5 . . . . 36 A4
Alton Cl CV2 . . . . 23 A2
Alum Cl CV6 . . . . 30 B4
Alverley Rd CV6 . . . . 30 C3
Alverstone Rd CV2 . . . . . 40 B4
Alvin Cl CV3 . . . . 42 A1
Alvis Ho CV1 . . . . 97 B2
Alvis Ret Pk CV5 . . . . . . 38 B3
Alwynne Freeman Ct
CV7 . . . . 12 A2
Alwyn Rd CV22 . . . . 94 A4
Amberley Ave CV12 . . . . . 8 C2
Amberley Ho CV8 . . . . . . 74 C3
Ambler Gr CV2 . . . . 41 A3
Ambleside
Coventry CV2 . . . . 23 B2
Rugby CV21 . . . . 80 B1

Ambleside Rd CV10 . . . . . . 6 A2
Ambrose Cl CV21 . . . . . . 86 A4
Amelia Cl CV12 . . . . 8 C3
Amersham Cl CV5 . . . . . 36 C4
Amherst Rd CV8 . . . . . . 66 C2
Amos Jacques Rd CV12 . . 6 A4
Amy Cl CV4 . . . . 21 C4
Anchorway Rd CV3 . . . . 59 C4
Anderson Ave CV22 . . . . 90 A2
Anderton Rd
Bedworth CV12 . . . . 4 C1
Coventry CV6 . . . . 22 B4
Andrews Cl CV8 . . . . 61 A2
Angela Ave CV2 . . . . 23 B1
Anglesey Cl CV5 . . . . . . 27 C3
Angless Way CV8 . . . . . . 74 B3
Angus Cl
Coventry CV5 . . . . 36 B4
Kenilworth CV8 . . . . . . 68 A2
Anker Dr CV23 . . . . 83 C3
Anley Way CV6 . . . . 30 A2
Anne Cres CV3 . . . . 50 A1
Annie Osborn Prim Sch
CV2 . . . . 32 B3
Ansell Dr CV6 . . . . 14 A1
Anson Cl CV22 . . . . 88 C4
Anson Way CV2 . . . . 33 A4
ANSTY 25 A4
Ansty Rd CV2 . . . . 32 C1
Anthony Way CV2 . . . . . 41 A2
Antrim Cl CV5 . . . . 27 C3
Applecross Cl CV4 . . . . . 45 A2
Appledore Dr CV5 . . . . . 27 A1
Apple Gr CV22 . . . . 88 B4
Appleyard Cl CV12 . . . . . . 6 B2
Aqua Pl CV21 . . . . 86 A3
Aragon Ho CV3 . . . . 48 A4
Arboretum The CV4 . . . . 58 B3
Arborfields Cl CV8 . . . . . 67 C4
Arbour Cl
Kenilworth CV8 . . . . 75 A3
Rugby CV22 . . . . 89 A1
Arbours The CV22 . . . . . 90 C4
Arbury Ave
Bedworth CV12 . . . . 6 A3
Coventry CV6 . . . . 21 C2
Arcade The CV3 . . . . 40 C2
Archer Rd CV8 . . . . 74 A3
Archers Spinney CV21 . . . 92 B2
Arches Bsns Ctr CV21 . . . 86 A3
Arches Ind Est CV21 . . . 86 A3
Arches Ind Est The CV3 . 38 B3
Arches La CV21 . . . . 86 A3
Arch Rd CV2 . . . . 32 C1
Arden Cl CV22 . . . . 94 C4
Arden Ct CV3 . . . . 52 B2
Arden Forest Inf Sch
CV12 . . . . 8 B3
Arden Rd
Bulkington CV12 . . . . . . 8 C2
Kenilworth CV8 . . . . 75 A3
Arden St CV5 . . . . 47 A4
Arena Pk CV6 . . . . 21 C3
Argyle St CV21 . . . . 86 A1
Argyll St CV2 . . . . 40 B3
Ariel Way CV22 . . . . 94 B4
Arkle Dr CV2 . . . . 33 A3
Arlidge Cres CV8 . . . . . . 68 A1
Armfield St CV6 . . . . 31 B4
Armorial Rd CV3 . . . . . . 47 C3
Armscott Rd CV2 . . . . . . 32 A2
Armson Rd CV7 . . . . 6 A1
Armstrong Ave CV3 . . . . 40 C1
Armstrong Cl CV22 . . . . 89 B3
Arna Ho CV3 . . . . 49 C2
Arne Rd CV2 . . . . 33 B2
Arnhem Cnr CV3 . . . . . . 50 B2
Arnold Ave CV3 . . . . 48 A1

Arnold Cl CV22 . . . . 90 A4
Arnold St CV21 . . . . 85 C1
Arnold Villas **9** CV21 . . 85 C1
Arnside Cl CV1 . . . . 96 D4
Arthingworth Cl CV3 . . . 41 C1
Arthur Alford Ho CV12 . . 5 A1
Arthur St
Coventry CV1 . . . . 96 C4
Kenilworth CV8 . . . . . . 67 B1
Arundel Rd
Bulkington CV12 . . . . . . 8 C3
Coventry CV3 . . . . 48 B2
Ascot Cl
Bedworth CV12 . . . . 6 B4
Coventry CV3 . . . . 50 A2
Ashbridge Rd CV5 . . . . . 37 A4
Ashburton Rd CV2 . . . . . 32 C4
Ashby Cl CV3 . . . . 51 A4
Ashcombe Dr CV4 . . . . . 36 A3
Ashcroft Cl CV2 . . . . 33 B4
Ashcroft Way CV2 . . . . . 33 C4
Ash Ct CV22 . . . . 89 B1
Ashdale Cl CV3 . . . . 52 C3
Ashdene Gdns CV8 . . . . 75 A4
Ashdown Cl CV3 . . . . . . 50 B4
Ash Dr CV8 . . . . 74 C4
Ashfield Ave CV4 . . . . . . 35 B1
Ashfield Rd CV8 . . . . 75 A4
Ashford Dr CV12 . . . . 6 A3
Ash Gr CV7 . . . . 12 C3
ASH GREEN 12 C2
Ash Green La CV7 . . . . . 13 A2
Ash Green Mobile Home
Pk CV7 . . . . 12 C3
Ash Green Sch CV7 . . . . 13 A2
Ashington Gr CV3 . . . . . 49 B1
Ashington Rd CV12 . . . . . 4 C1
Ashlawn Rd CV22 . . . . . 91 A1
Ashlawn Sch CV22 . . . . . 91 B1
Ashman Ave CV23 . . . . . 83 C3
Ashmore Rd CV6 . . . . . . 38 C4
Ashorne Cl CV2 . . . . 22 C2
ASHOW 76 A1
Ashow Cl CV8 . . . . 75 A4
Ash Priors Cl CV4 . . . . . 36 C1
Ash Tree Ave CV4 . . . . . 36 B2
Ash Tree Gr CV7 . . . . . . 17 B1
Ashurst Cl CV6 . . . . 14 B1
Ashwood Ave CV6 . . . . . 29 A1
Ashwood Ct CV21 . . . . . 85 A1
Aspen Cl CV4 . . . . 35 B1
Aspen Dr CV8 . . . . 14 C2
Asplen Ct CV8 . . . . 75 B4
Assheton Cl CV22 . . . . . 88 C2
Aster Wlk CV10 . . . . 2 C4
Asthill Croft CV3 . . . . . . 48 A4
Asthill Gr CV3 . . . . 48 A4
Astley Ave CV6 . . . . 21 B2
Astley La CV6 . . . . 4 C3
Astley Pl CV21 . . . . 92 B1
Aston Rd CV5 . . . . 38 A1
Athena Gdns CV6 . . . . . 22 A1
Atherston Pl CV4 . . . . . . 46 B2
Athol Rd CV2 . . . . 33 B2
Attoxhall Rd CV2 . . . . . . 41 C4
Attwood Cres CV2 . . . . . 32 A3
Augustus Rd CV1 . . . . . . 40 A4
Austin Dr CV6 . . . . 31 B3
Aventine Way CV21 . . . . 79 A1
Avenue Rd
Kenilworth CV8 . . . . . . 66 B2
Rugby CV21 . . . . 84 C2
Avenue The CV3 . . . . . . 49 B2
Avocet Cl
Coventry CV2 . . . . 22 B3
Rugby CV23 . . . . 80 A3
Avon Ct
Kenilworth CV8 . . . . . . 67 A1

Avon Ct continued
Rugby CV21 . . . . 85 B2
Avondale Rd
Brandon CV8 . . . . 53 A1
Coventry CV5 . . . . 47 B4
Avon Ho CV4 . . . . 46 A2
Avon Ind Est CV21 . . . . . 86 A3
Avonmere CV21 . . . . 78 C1
Avon Rd
Coventry CV4 . . . . 45 C2
Kenilworth CV8 . . . . . . 74 A3
Avon St
Clifton u D CV23 . . . . . . 86 C2
Coventry CV2 . . . . 31 C1
Rugby CV21 . . . . 85 B2
Avon Terr CV8 . . . . 72 A2
Avon Valley Sch The
CV21 . . . . 84 C4
Awson St CV6 . . . . 31 A2
Axholme Rd CV2 . . . . . . 41 C4
Aylesdene Ct CV5 . . . . . 47 A4
Aylesford St CV1 . . . . . . 39 C4
Aynho Cl CV5 . . . . 36 B3

B

Babbacombe Rd CV3 . . . 48 B1
Bablake Cl CV6 . . . . 29 A4
Bablake Jun Sch CV1 . . . 96 A4
Bablake Sch CV1 . . . . . . 38 C4
Back La CV23 . . . . 83 B2
Badby Leys CV22 . . . . . . 89 C1
Badger Rd CV3 . . . . 50 B4
Baffin Cl CV22 . . . . 89 B3
BAGINTON 61 A2
Baginton Fields Sch
CV3 . . . . 61 C4
Baginton Rd CV3 . . . . . . 48 A1
Bagshaw Cl CV8 . . . . . . 63 B1
Bailey's La CV23 . . . . . . 83 B2
Bakehouse La CV21 . . . . 85 A1
Bakers La CV5 . . . . 37 C2
Baker St CV6 . . . . 14 B2
Bakewell Cl CV3 . . . . 51 A4
Balcombe Ct CV22 . . . . . 91 B2
Balcombe Rd CV22 . . . . 91 B2
Baldwin Croft CV6 . . . . . 22 B1
Ballantine Rd CV6 . . . . . 29 C2
Ballingham Cl CV4 . . . . . 36 B2
Balliol Rd CV2 . . . . 41 A4
Balmoral Cl CV2 . . . . . . 32 C2
Bankside Cl CV3 . . . . . . 49 B2
Banks Rd CV6 . . . . 29 B1
Bank St CV21 . . . . 85 B1
Bank The CV8 . . . . 70 A2
Banner La CV4 . . . . 35 B2
Bantam Gr CV6 . . . . 20 A3
Bantock Rd CV4 . . . . 35 C2
Barbican Rise CV2 . . . . . 41 C2
Barbridge Cl CV12 . . . . . . 8 C3
Barbridge Rd CV12 . . . . . 8 C3
Barby Rd CV22 . . . . 90 B1
Bardley Dr CV6 . . . . 30 A2
Barford Cl CV3 . . . . 50 B4
Barford Rd CV8 . . . . 75 A3
Barkers' Butts La CV6 . . 29 B1
Barker's Butts La CV6 . . 38 B4
Barley Cl CV21 . . . . 92 A2
Barley Lea Ho CV3 . . . . . 49 C4
Barley Lea The CV3 . . . . 50 A4
Barlow Rd CV2 . . . . 23 A2
Barnack Ave CV3 . . . . . . 47 C1
BARNACLE 16 B2
Barnacle La CV12 . . . . 8 C1
Barn Cl CV5 . . . . 28 A1

Barnfield Ave CV5 ... **27** C2
Barn Leigh Dr CV4 .... **44** B2
Barnsley Ct CV6 .... **30** B4
Barnstaple Cl CV4 ..... **27** A1
Barnwell Cl CV22 ...... **94** A2
Baron's Croft CV3 .... **48** C3
Baron's Field Rd CV3 ... **48** C4
Barracks Way CV1 .... **97** B2
Barras Ct CV2 .... **40** B4
Barras Gn CV2 .... **40** B4
Barras La CV1 .... **38** C3
Bar Rd CV3 .... **48** C4
Barrington Rd CV22 .... **88** C3
Barrow Cl CV2 .... **33** C2
Barrowfield Ct CV8 .... **74** B4
Barrowfield La CV8 .... **74** B4
Barrow Rd CV8 .... **74** B4
Barr's Hill Sch & Com Coll
CV1 .... **96** A4
Barry Ho CV2 .... **23** A1
Barston Cl CV6 .... **22** A2
Bartholomew Ct CV3 .. **49** B2
Bartlett Cl CV6 .... **21** B2
Barton Rd
Bedworth CV12 .... **6** A4
Coventry CV6 .... **21** C2
Rugby CV22 .... **89** A2
Barton's Mdw CV2 ..... **31** C2
Baseley Way CV6 ..... **21** A4
Basford Brook Dr CV6 .. **21** C4
Basildon Wlk **3** CV2 ... **33** B3
Bassett Rd CV2 ...... **29** B1
Bateman's Acre S **1**
CV6 .... **38** B4
Bates Rd CV5 .... **46** C4
Bath St
Coventry CV1 .... **96** C4
Rugby CV21 .... **85** C1
Bath Street Mews **1**
CV21 .... **85** C1
Bathurst Cl CV22 ..... **89** B3
Bathurst Rd CV6 ..... **29** B2
Bathway Rd CV3 ...... **59** B4
Batsford Rd CV6 ..... **38** A4
Battalion Ct CV6 ..... **20** A1
Bawnmore Ct CV22 ... **89** A2
Bawnmore Inf Sch
CV22 .... **89** B1
Bawnmore Pk CV22 .... **89** B1
Bawnmore Rd CV22 .... **89** A1
Baxter Cl CV4 .... **36** B2
Bayley La CV1 .... **97** C2
Bayliss Ave CV6 ...... **22** A4
Bayton Rd CV7 .... **14** B3
Bayton Road Ind Est
CV7 .... **14** B4
Bayton Way CV7 ...... **14** C3
Bay Tree Cl CV2 ...... **23** A1
Beacon Rd CV6 .... **21** A3
Beaconsfield Ave CV22.. **90** A3
Beaconsfield Rd CV2 ... **40** C2
Beake Ave CV6 .... **29** C3
Beamish Cl CV2 ...... **33** B2
Beanfield Ave CV3 .... **59** A4
Beatty Dr CV22 .... **89** A4
Beauchamp Rd CV8.... **74** B2
Beaudesert Rd CV5 ... **38** B1
Beaufort Dr CV3 ..... **51** A3
Beaumaris Cl CV5 .... **27** A1
Beaumont Cres CV6 ... **38** B4
Beaumont Ct **9** CV6 ... **38** B4
Beaumont Rd CV7 .... **12** A2
Beausale Croft CV5 ... **36** B3
Beche Way CV5........ **27** C1
Beckbury Rd CV2 ..... **33** B2

Beckfoot Cl CV21 ...... **80** B2
Beckfoot Dr CV2 .... **23** C1
Bede Arc **2** CV12....... **6** B3
Bede Rd
Bedworth CV12 .... **6** A4
Coventry CV6 .... **29** C2
Bedford St CV1 .... **38** B2
Bedlam La CV6 .... **21** B2
BEDWORTH **6** B1
Bedworth Cl CV12 ...... **8** B2
BEDWORTH HEATH **5** B1
Bedworth La CV12 ..... **5** A4
Bedworth Rd
Bedworth CV12 .... **7** C2
Bulkington CV12 ...... **8** A2
Coventry CV6, CV7 .... **14** A1
Bedworth Sta CV12 .... **6** C2
Beechcroft CV12 ...... **5** C1
Beech Ct CV22 .... **91** C2
Beech Dr
Kenilworth CV8 ...... **67** C1
Rugby CV22 .... **88** C2
Thurlaston CV23 ...... **93** A1
Beecher's Keep CV8 ... **53** A1
Beeches The
Bedworth CV12 .... **5** B2
Clifton u D CV23 ...... **87** A3
Beechnut Cl CV4 ..... **35** B2
Beech Rd CV6 .... **29** C1
Beech Tree Ave CV4 ... **36** C2
Beechwood Ave CV5... **47** A4
Beechwood Croft CV8 .. **74** B2
Beechwood Ct
Coventry CV5 .... **47** A4
Rugby CV21 .... **85** A2
BEECHWOOD GARDENS
.... **46** C4
Beechwood Rd CV12 ... **7** A4
Beehive Hill CV8 ...... **66** C3
Beeston Cl CV3 ...... **51** A4
Belgrade Theatre CV1 . **96** B3
Belgrave Dr CV21 ..... **86** B4
Belgrave Rd CV2 ..... **41** C4
Belgrave Sq CV2 ..... **41** C4
Bellairs Ave CV12 ..... **5** B1
Bellbrooke Cl CV6 .... **22** B1
Bell Dr CV7 .... **13** B3
BELL GREEN **31** C4
Bell Green Rd CV6 .... **31** B4
Bellview Way CV6 ..... **22** B1
Bell Wlk CV21 .... **92** A2
Belmont Mews CV8.... **74** B4
Belmont Rd
Coventry CV6 .... **31** B3
Rugby CV22 .... **90** A3
Belvedere Rd CV5 .... **47** B4
Benches Furlong CV23.. **80** B3
Benedictine Ct CV1 ... **96** C3
Benedictine Rd CV3 ... **48** A4
Benedict Sq CV2...... **32** A4
Bennett Ct CV8 ...... **65** A3
Bennett's Rd CV7 .... **19** C4
Bennett's Road N CV7 .. **11** B3
Bennett's Road S CV6.. **19** C2
Bennett St CV21 ..... **85** A1
Bennfield Rd CV21 .... **85** B1
Benn Rd CV12 .... **8** B2
Benn St CV22 .... **90** C4
Benson Rd CV6 ...... **20** A1
Benthall Rd CV6 ..... **21** C2
Bentley Ct CV6 ...... **20** C4
Bentley Rd CV7 ...... **6** A1
Bentree The CV3 ..... **49** C4
Beresford Ave CV6.... **21** B1
Berkeley Rd CV8 ..... **66** C2
Berkeley Rd N CV5.... **38** B1
Berkeley Rd S CV5.... **47** B4
Berkett Rd CV6 ...... **20** B2

Berkswell Rd CV6 ..... **22** B2
BERMUDA **2** C4
Bermuda Bsns Pk CV12.. **2** C4
Bermuda Ind Est CV10... **3** A4
Berners Cl CV4 ...... **35** C2
Berry St CV1 .... **39** C4
Bertie Rd CV8 .... **74** C4
Berwick Cl CV5 ...... **36** C4
Berwick Ho CV8 ...... **74** C3
Berwyn Ave CV6 ..... **20** A1
Best Ave CV8 .... **68** A3
Beswick Gdns CV22... **89** A1
Bettman Cl CV3 ..... **48** C2
Bevan Ct CV3 .... **48** B3
Beverly Dr CV4 ...... **58** B2
Bevington Cres CV6 ... **28** C1
Bexfield Cl CV5 ...... **27** B2
Biart Pl CV21 .... **86** B2
Bideford Rd CV2 ..... **32** A3
Bigbury Cl CV3 ...... **48** C1
Biggin Hall Cres CV3... **40** C2
Bilberry Rd CV2 ..... **23** A2
Billesden Cl CV3 ..... **50** C4
Billing Rd CV5 .... **37** B3
Billinton Cl CV2 ..... **41** C2
BILTON **88** C1
Bilton CE Jun Sch CV22 **94** B4
Bilton Grange Sch CV22 **94** C2
Bilton High Sch CV22... **88** B3
Bilton Ind Est CV22 ... **40** A1
Bilton Inf Sch CV22.... **88** C1
Bilton La
Dunchurch CV22 ...... **94** B2
Long Lawford CV22, CV23 . **83** C1
Bilton Rd CV22 ...... **89** B4
BINLEY **50** C4
Binley Ave CV3 ...... **51** A3
Binley Bsns Pk CV3 ... **42** B1
Binley Gr CV3 .... **51** A3
Binley Ind Est CV3 .... **51** B4
Binley Rd CV2, CV3 .... **41** B1
BINLEY WOODS **52** A3
Binley Woods Prim Sch
CV3 .... **52** C3
Binns Cl CV4 .... **45** A4
Binswood Cl CV2 ..... **23** A2
Binton Rd CV2........ **23** A2
Birch Cl
Bedworth CV12 .... **7** A4
Coventry CV6 .... **27** A2
Birch Dr CV22 .... **88** B4
Birches La CV8 ...... **75** A3
Birches The CV12 ..... **8** B4
Birchfield Rd CV6..... **29** A4
Birchgrave Cl CV6 ... **31** B3
Birchwood Rd CV3.... **52** A3
Bird Grove Ct CV1 ... **30** B1
Bird St CV1........... **96** C3
Birkdale Cl CV6....... **20** B4
Birmingham Rd
Allesley CV5 .... **26** C3
Kenilworth CV8........ **66** A4
Stoneleigh CV8........ **69** C2
Birstall Dr CV21 ..... **86** B4
Birvell Ct CV12 ...... **7** A3
Bishopgate Bsns Pk
CV1 .... **30** B1
BISHOPGATE GREEN .. **30** B1
Bishopgate Ind Est CV1. **30** B1
Bishop St CV1........ **96** B3
Bishops Wlk CV5 .... **47** C4
Bishopton Cl CV5..... **36** C3
Bishop Ullathorne RC Sch
CV3 .... **59** A4
Bishop Wulstan RC Sch
CV22 .... **90** A3
BLACK BANK **6** A1
Black Bank CV7 ...... **6** B1

Blackberry Cl CV23 .... **80** B2
Blackberry La
Coventry, Neal's Green
CV7 .... **12** C1
Coventry, Wyken Green
CV2 .... **32** A2
Blackburn Rd CV6 .... **21** C3
Black Horse Rd CV6,
CV7 .... **14** B2
Blackman Way CV21... **85** A2
Black Prince Ave CV3 .. **48** C2
Blackshaw Dr CV2 .... **33** A2
Blackthorn Cl CV4 .... **46** B1
Blackthorne Rd CV8 ... **74** C3
Blackwatch Rd CV6.... **30** A4
Blackwell Rd CV6...... **30** C4
Blackwood Ave CV22 .. **89** A4
Blair Dr CV12......... **5** A1
Blake Cl CV22 .... **88** C4
Blandford Dr CV2..... **33** A1
Bleaberry CV21 ...... **80** A1
Blenheim Ave CV6 .... **20** C2
Blenheim Wlk CV6.... **20** B4
Bletchley Dr CV5 .... **36** C4
Blind La CV8 .... **57** A1
Bliss Cl CV4 .... **35** C3
Blockley Rd CV12...... **6** C4
Blondvil St CV3....... **48** B3
Bloxam Gdns CV22.... **89** C4
Bloxam Pl **6** CV21.... **85** B1
Bluebell Cl CV23...... **80** B2
Bluebell Dr CV12 ..... **5** B2
Bluebell Wlk CV6 .... **36** A1
Blundells The CV8 ... **67** B1
Blyth Cl
Bedworth CV12......... **4** C1
Cawston CV22......... **88** A2
Blythe Rd CV1 .... **39** C4
Boar Croft CV4 ...... **36** A2
Bockendon Rd CV4 ... **44** C1
Bodmin Rd CV2....... **33** A1
Bodnant Way CV8 .... **68** A2
Bohun St CV4 .... **36** A1
Bolingbroke Rd CV3 ... **40** B1
Bolton Cl CV3 .... **48** C1
Bonds Hospl CV1 ..... **96** A3
Bond St
Coventry CV1 .... **96** B3
Rugby CV21........... **85** A1
Bonington Dr CV12.... **6** A4
Bonnington Cl CV21... **92** B3
Booths Fields CV6 .... **21** B2
Borrowdale CV21...... **80** A2
Borrowdale Cl CV6.... **29** B4
Borrowell La CV8 .... **74** A4
Borrowell Terr CV8 ... **74** A4
Boston Pl CV6 .... **30** B4
Boswell Dr CV2....... **33** B3
Boswell Rd CV22 ..... **89** B1
Bosworth Cl CV8 .... **60** C2
Botoner Rd CV1 ..... **40** A2
Bott Cl CV5 .... **46** B4
Boughton Leigh Inf Sch
CV21 .... **80** A1
Boughton Leigh Jun Sch
CV21 .... **80** A1
Boughton Rd CV21.... **86** A4
Boughton Road Ind Est
CV21 .... **85** C4
Boundary Rd CV21, CV22. **91** A4
Bourne Rd CV3........ **41** A1
Bow Ct CV5 .... **46** B4
Bowden Way CV3...... **42** A1
Bowen Rd CV22 ...... **91** A3
Bow Fell CV21 .... **80** B1
Bowfell Cl CV5 ...... **36** C4
Bowling Green La CV7,
CV12 .... **13** B4

Bowls Ct CV5 . . . . 38 A3
Bowness Cl CV6 . . . . 29 B4
Boxhill The CV3 . . . . 40 C1
Boyce Way CV23 . . . . 83 C3
Boyd Cl CV2 . . . . 33 B4
Bracadale Cl CV3 . . . . 42 B2
Bracken Cl CV22 . . . . 89 B3
Bracken Dr CV22 . . . . 89 B3
Brackenhurst Rd CV6 . . . 29 B3
Brackley Cl CV6 . . . . 29 A3
Bracknell Wlk 1 CV2 . . . 33 B3
Braddock Cl CV3 . . . . 42 B1
Brade Dr CV2 . . . . 33 C3
Bradfield Cl CV5 . . . . 28 A1
Bradney Gn CV4 . . . . 44 C3
Bradnick Pl CV4 . . . . 36 A1
Braemar Cl CV2 . . . . 32 C2
Brafield Leys CV22 . . . . . . 95 B4
Braids Cl CV21 . . . . 86 B2
Bramble St CV1 . . . . 39 C2
Brambling Cl CV23 . . . . . . 80 A2
Brampton Way CV12 . . . . .8 B3
Bramston Cres CV4 . . . . . 36 A1
Bramwell Gdns CV6 . . . . . 13 C1
Brandfield Rd CV6 . . . . 29 A4
BRANDON 53 A1
Brandon Cl CV3 . . . . 51 B3
Brandon La CV3, CV8 . . . . 52 A1
Brandon Marsh Nature
Reserve★ CV3 . . . . 63 B4
Brandon Marsh Visitor
Ctr★ CV3 . . . . 63 C4
Brandon Rd
  Bretford CV23 . . . . 54 B3
  Coventry CV3 . . . . 51 B4
Brandon Wood Farm★
CV8 . . . . 52 B1
Branksome Rd CV6 . . . . . . 28 C2
Bransdale Ave CV6 . . . . . 21 A3
Bransford Ave CV4 . . . . . . 46 B1
Branstree Dr CV6 . . . . 21 A2
Brathay Cl CV3 . . . . 48 B2
Braunston Pl CV22 . . . . . . 91 A2
Brayford Ave CV3 . . . . 48 A2
Bray's La CV2 . . . . 40 B3
Braytoft Cl CV6 . . . . 20 C2
Brazil St CV4 . . . . 35 C2
Bredon Ave CV3 . . . . 51 A4
Bree Cl CV5 . . . . 27 B3
Brentwood Ave CV3 . . . . . 60 A3
Brentwood Gdns CV3 . . . 60 A3
BRETFORD 54 B4
Bretford Rd CV2 . . . . 22 C1
Bretts Cl CV1 . . . . 96 D4
Brewer Rd CV12 . . . . .9 A2
Brewers Cl CV3 . . . . 42 B1
Brewster Cl CV2 . . . . 41 C2
Briansway CV6 . . . . 21 B3
Briardene Ave CV12 . . . . . .6 B2
Briars Cl
  Coventry CV2 . . . . 41 A2
  Long Lawford CV23 . . . . . . 83 C2
Brick Hill La CV5 . . . . 26 C4
Brick Kiln Way CV12 . . . . .7 A3
Bridal Path The CV5 . . . . . 27 C2
Bridgeacre Gdns CV3 . . . 42 A2
Bridgecote CV3 . . . . 50 C2
Bridgeman Rd CV6 . . . . . . 38 C4
Bridge St
  Coventry CV6 . . . . 31 B3
  Kenilworth CV8 . . . . 67 A1
  Rugby CV21 . . . . 86 A1
Bridget St CV21 . . . . 85 A1
Bridge View CV3 . . . . 60 B3
Bridle Brook La CV5,
CV7 . . . . 18 A3
Bridle Rd CV21 . . . . 84 C1

Bridport Cl CV2 . . . . 42 B4
Brierley Rd CV2 . . . . 32 A4
Brightmere Rd CV6 . . . . . 38 C4
Brighton St CV2 . . . . 40 A3
Bright St CV6 . . . . 30 C2
Brightwalton Rd CV3 . . . 48 B3
Brill Cl CV4 . . . . 46 A1
Brindle Ave CV3 . . . . 41 A2
Brindley Paddocks CV1 . 96 B4
Brindley Rd
  Bedworth CV7 . . . . 14 B4
  Rugby CV21 . . . . 92 B3
Brinklow Rd CV3 . . . . 42 B2
Brisbane Cl CV3 . . . . 48 C2
Brisbane Ct 2 CV12 . . . . .6 A2
Briscoe Rd CV6 . . . . 21 A4
Bristol Rd CV5 . . . . 38 A2
Britannia St CV2 . . . . 40 A3
Briton Rd CV2 . . . . 40 B4
Brixham Dr CV2 . . . . 32 A3
Brixworth Cl CV3 . . . . 50 C4
Broadgate CV1 . . . . 96 B3
Broad Heath Com Prim Sch
  CV6 . . . . 30 C2
Broad La CV5 . . . . 35 B4
Broadlands Cl CV5 . . . . . . 37 A2
Broadmead Ct CV5 . . . . . 37 A2
Broadmere Rise CV5 . . . . 36 B2
Broad Park Rd CV2 . . . . . 32 B4
Broad St CV6 . . . . 30 C3
Broad Street Jetty CV6 . 30 C3
Broadwater CV5 . . . . 47 B4
Broadway CV5 . . . . 38 B1
Broadway Mans CV5 . . . . 38 B1
Broadwell Ct CV4 . . . . . . 45 A2
Broadwells Cres CV4 . . . 45 B1
Brockenhurst Way CV6 . 14 B2
Brockhurst Dr CV4 . . . . . 35 B2
Bromleigh Dr CV2 . . . . . . 41 A2
Bromleigh Villas CV8 . . . 61 A2
Bromley Cl CV8 . . . . 66 C2
Bromwich Cl CV3 . . . . 51 A4
Bromwich Rd CV21 . . . . . 91 C3
Bronte Cl CV21 . . . . 86 B1
Brook Cl CV1 . . . . 39 C4
Brooke Ct CV21 . . . . 85 A1
Brooke Rd CV8 . . . . 75 A4
Brooke Sch CV22 . . . . . . 89 B1
Brooke Specl Sch CV22 . 89 C3
Brookford Ave CV6 . . . . . 20 A3
Brooklea CV12 . . . . .5 C2
Brooklime Dr CV23 . . . . . 80 C2
Brooklyn Rd CV1 . . . . 30 B2
Brookshaw Way CV2 . . . 33 A4
Brookside Ave
  Coventry CV5 . . . . 37 A3
  Kenilworth CV8 . . . . 74 A4
Brookside Cl CV22 . . . . . . 90 A4
Brook St
  Bedworth CV12 . . . . 3 A1
  Wolston CV8 . . . . 65 B3
Brookstray Flats CV5 . . . 36 C3
Brookvale Ave CV3 . . . . . 41 C1
Brook View CV22 . . . . 94 A1
Broom Cl CV22 . . . . 89 B3
Broome Croft CV6 . . . . . . 20 B3
Broomfield Pl CV5 . . . . . . 38 B2
Broomfield Rd CV5 . . . . . 38 B1
Broomybank CV8 . . . . 67 C2
Browett Rd CV6 . . . . 29 B1
Browning Rd
  Coventry CV2 . . . . 41 A3
  Rugby CV21 . . . . 92 B2
Brownshill Ct CV6 . . . . . . 29 A4
BROWNSHILL GREEN . . 18 C2
Brownshill Green Rd
  CV6 . . . . 19 B1
Brown's La CV5 . . . . 18 C1

BROWNSOVER 80 A2
Brownsover Com Inf Sch
  CV23 . . . . 80 B2
Brownsover La CV21 . . . 79 C2
Brownsover Rd
  Rugby CV21 . . . . 79 A1
  Rugby CV21 . . . . 79 B1
Bruce Rd
  Bedworth CV7 . . . . 13 C3
  Coventry CV6 . . . . 29 C4
Bruce Williams Way
  CV22 . . . . 90 B4
Brudenell Cl CV22 . . . . . . 88 A2
Brunel Cl CV2 . . . . 40 A3
Brunes Ct CV21 . . . . 80 B1
Brunswick Cl CV21 . . . . . 86 A4
Brunswick Rd CV1 . . . . . . 38 C2
Bruntingthorpe Way
  CV3 . . . . 50 C4
Brunton Cl CV3 . . . . 42 C1
Bryanston Cl CV2 . . . . . . 42 B4
Bryant Rd CV7 . . . . 14 A3
Brympton Rd CV3 . . . . . . 41 A2
Bryn Jones Cl CV3 . . . . . . 51 A3
Bryn Rd CV6 . . . . 31 A3
Bryony Cl CV12 . . . . .5 B1
BUBBENHALL 72 B1
Bubbenhall Rd CV8 . . . . . 61 A1
Buccleuch Cl CV22 . . . . . 94 A2
Buchanan Rd CV22 . . . . . 89 B3
Buckfast Cl CV3 . . . . 48 C1
Buckhold Dr CV5 . . . . 27 C1
Buckingham Rise CV5 . . . 36 C4
Buckland Rd CV6 . . . . 20 B2
Buckler's Yd 5 CV12 . . . .6 A2
Buckley Ho CV5 . . . . 38 A1
Bucknill Cres CV21 . . . . . 92 B1
Buckwell La CV23 . . . . . . 87 C4
Budbrooke Cl CV2 . . . . . . 23 A2
BULKINGTON 8 B1
Bulkington Rd
  Bedworth CV12 . . . . 7 A2
  Shilton CV7 . . . . 17 B2
Bullfield Ave CV4 . . . . 35 C1
Bullimore Gr CV8 . . . . 74 C2
Bull's Head La CV3 . . . . . . 40 C2
Bull Yd CV1 . . . . 97 B2
Bulwer Rd CV6 . . . . 29 B2
Bulwick Cl CV3 . . . . 42 C1
Bunkers Hill La CV23 . . . 54 C2
Burbages La CV6 . . . . 21 A4
Burbury Cl CV12 . . . . .6 C4
Burges CV1 . . . . 96 B3
Burlington Rd
  Coventry CV2 . . . . 40 A4
  Nuneaton CV10 . . . . 3 A3
Burnaby Rd CV6 . . . . 20 B1
Burnham Rd CV3 . . . . 49 B2
Burnsall Gr CV5 . . . . 46 B4
Burnsall Rd CV5 . . . . 46 B4
Burnside
  Coventry CV3 . . . . 42 B2
  Rugby CV22 . . . . 89 C4
Burns Rd CV2 . . . . 40 C3
Burns Wlk CV12 . . . . .6 C1
Burrow Hill La CV7 . . . . . 11 A3
Burton Cl CV5 . . . . 18 C2
BURTON GREEN 56 A4
Bury Ho CV4 . . . . 36 A3
Busby Cl CV3 . . . . 51 A3
Bushbery Ave CV4 . . . . . . 36 A2
Bush Cl CV4 . . . . 36 A3
Bush Ct CV2 . . . . 31 C2
Bushelton Cl CV1 . . . . 97 C1
Butcher's La CV5 . . . . 28 A2
Butler Cl CV8 . . . . 68 A3
Butlers Cres CV7 . . . . .6 A1
Butlers Leap CV21 . . . . . . 86 B3

Butlers Leap Ind Est
  CV21 . . . . 86 B2
Butlin Rd
  Coventry CV6 . . . . 20 C4
  Rugby CV21 . . . . 86 B1
Buttercup Way CV21 . . . .5 A2
Buttermere CV21 . . . . 80 B1
Buttermere Cl CV3 . . . . . . 51 A3
Butterworth Dr CV4 . . . . 45 B2
Butt La CV5 . . . . 27 C3
Butts CV1 . . . . 38 B2
Butts Pk Arena CV1 . . . . 38 B2
Butts Rd CV1 . . . . 38 C2
Byfield Rd CV6 . . . . 28 C1
Byron Ave CV12 . . . . .7 A2
Byron St CV1 . . . . 96 C4
Bywater Cl CV3 . . . . 47 C1

C

Cadden Dr CV4 . . . . 36 C2
Cadman Cl CV12 . . . . .6 C3
Caesar Rd CV8 . . . . 74 A3
Caithness Cl CV5 . . . . 36 B4
Calcott Ho CV3 . . . . 49 C1
Caldecote Rd CV6 . . . . . . 30 A1
Caldecott Pl CV21 . . . . . . 90 C4
Caldecott St CV21, CV22 . 90 C4
Calder Cl
  Bulkington CV12 . . . . .8 B2
  Coventry CV3 . . . . 48 C3
Calgary Cl CV3 . . . . 42 B2
Callier Cl CV22 . . . . 88 B2
Calmere Cl CV2 . . . . 33 A4
Caludon Castle Sch
  CV2 . . . . 41 C4
Caludon Lodge CV2 . . . . . 32 C1
Caludon Park Ave CV2 . . 32 C1
Caludon Rd CV2 . . . . 40 B4
Calvert Cl
  Coventry CV3 . . . . 48 B2
  Rugby CV21 . . . . 80 C1
Calverstone Pl CV22 . . . . 88 A1
Calvestone Rd CV22 . . . . 88 B2
Calvestone Sq CV22 . . . . 88 B2
Cambridge Cl CV21 . . . . . 86 A1
Cambridge St
  Coventry CV1 . . . . 30 C1
  Rugby CV21 . . . . 86 A1
Camden St CV2 . . . . 40 B4
Camellia Rd 1 CV2 . . . . . 22 B2
Camelot Gr CV8 . . . . 68 A1
Cameron Cl CV5 . . . . 27 B3
Campbell St CV21 . . . . . . 84 C1
Campion Cl CV3 . . . . 48 B2
Campion Way
  3 Bedworth CV12 . . . . 5 A2
  Rugby CV23 . . . . 80 B2
Campling Cl CV12 . . . . . . .8 B2
Camville CV3 . . . . 42 B2
Canal Rd CV6 . . . . 31 A4
Canalside CV6 . . . . 14 B2
Canberra Ct 2 CV12 . . . .5 C2
Canberra Rd CV2 . . . . 22 C4
Canford Cl CV3 . . . . 60 A3
CANLEY 46 A3
Canley Ford CV4, CV5 . . . 46 C3
CANLEY GARDENS 46 C4
Canley Rd CV5 . . . . 46 B4
Canley Sta CV5 . . . . 37 B1
Cannes Ct CV4 . . . . 46 B2
Cannocks La CV4 . . . . 46 B2
Cannon Cl CV4 . . . . 47 A2
Cannon Hill Rd CV4 . . . . . 46 B1

Cannon Park District Ctr
CV4................... **46** A2
Cannon Park Prim Sch
CV4................... **46** B1
Cannon Park Rd CV4... **46** C1
Canon Dr CV7 .... **13** A2
Canon Evans CE Inf Sch
CV12..................... **6** A2
Canon Hudson Cl CV3... **50** A2
Canon Maggs CE Jun Sch
CV12.....................**6** B2
Canterbury Cl CV8...... **75** B3
Canterbury St CV1..... **96** D3
Cantlow Cl CV5........ **36** B3
Capmartin Rd CV6..... **30** A3
Capulet Cl
Coventry CV3 .... **50** A2
Rugby CV22........... **94** C4
Caradoc Cl CV2........ **32** B3
Caradoc Hall CV2...... **32** B3
Cardale Croft 1 CV3.. **51** A4
Cardiff Cl CV3 .... **50** B1
Cardigan Rd CV12......**4** C1
Cardinal Newman RC Sch
& Com Coll CV6 .... **19** C2
Cardinal Wiseman RC Sch
CV2................... **23** B1
Carding Cl CV5........ **36** A4
Carew Wlk CV22........ **88** C3
Carey St CV6 .... **31** C4
Cargill Cl CV6 .... **13** C1
Carlton Cl CV12........**8** B3
Carlton Ct CV5 .... **38** A2
Carlton Gdns CV5...... **47** B4
Carlton Rd
Coventry CV6 .... **21** C1
Rugby CV22........... **89** A3
Carmelite Rd CV1...... **39** C2
Carnation Way CV10....**2** C4
Carnbroe Ave CV5..... **51** A3
Carnegie Cl CV3....... **49** C1
Carolyn Lane Ct CV21... **85** A2
Carrie Ho CV1 .... **97** A2
Carsal Cl CV7.......... **13** A1
Carter Rd CV3 .... **49** B4
Carthusian Rd CV3 .... **48** A3
Cartmel Cl CV5 .... **36** B4
Carvell Cl CV5........ **18** B1
Carver Cl CV2 .... **41** C2
Cascade Cl CV3........ **48** C2
Cashmore Rd
Bedworth CV12.........**5** B1
Kenilworth CV8....... **75** B4
Cash's Bsns Ctr CV1.... **30** B1
Cash's La CV1 .... **30** B2
Casita Gr CV8 .... **75** B4
Caspian Way CV2...... **33** B4
Cassandra Cl CV4..... **58** B3
Castle Cl CV3.......... **48** B2
Castle Ct CV8.......... **67** B2
Castle Gn CV8 .... **66** B1
Castle Gr CV8 .... **74** A4
CASTLE GREEN **66** B2
Castle Hill CV8 .... **66** C1
Castle Mound Way
CV23................. **80** B4
Castle Place Ind Est
CV1................... **96** D4
Castle Rd CV8 .... **66** C1
Castle St
Coventry CV1 .... **96** D4
Rugby CV21........... **85** C1
Catesby Rd
Coventry CV6 .... **29** C4
Rugby CV22........... **91** A3

Cathedral Lanes Sh Ctr
CV1................... **96** B3
Catherine St CV2 ...... **40** A3
Catherine Ward Hall
CV12....................**3** A1
Cavans Cl CV3........ **51** B4
Cavans Way CV3....... **51** B4
Cave Cl CV22.......... **88** A2
Cavendish Cl CV2..... **88** A3
Cavendish Rd CV4 .... **35** C2
Cawnpore Rd CV6 .... **20** B2
CAWSTON **88** B2
Cawston Grange Dr
CV22................. **88** A2
Cawston Grange Prim Sch
CV22................. **88** B2
Cawston Ho CV22..... **93** C4
Cawston La CV22 ..... **93** C3
Cawston Way CV22 ... **88** C2
Cawthorne Cl 1 CV1 .. **39** C4
Cecily Rd CV3 .... **48** C3
Cedar Ave CV8 .... **63** C1
Cedar Ct CV5.......... **27** B2
Cedars Ave CV6 ...... **29** A1
Cedars Rd CV7 ....**6** B1
Cedric Cl CV3 .... **50** A1
Celandine CV23....... **80** C2
Celandine Rd CV2 .... **23** A2
Celandine Way CV12....**5** B2
Centaur Rd CV5 ...... **38** A2
Centenary Rd CV4.... **46** B3
Central Ave CV2 ...... **40** B2
Central Bldgs
Coventry CV3 .... **97** B1
8 Rugby CV21......... **85** C1
Central Bvd CV6, CV7... **12** A1
Central City Ind Est CV6 **31** A1
Central Park Dr CV21... **80** B4
Central Six Ret Pk CV1 . **97** A1
Chace Ave CV3 .... **50** A2
Chaceley Cl CV2...... **33** B4
Chace Prim Sch CV3 .. **50** A2
Chadwick Cl CV5 ..... **36** C3
Chalfont Cl
Bedworth CV12.......... **6** A4
Coventry CV5 .... **36** C4
Challenge Bsns Pk CV1. **30** B1
Challenge Cl CV1..... **96** C4
Chamberlaine St CV1...**6** B3
Chamberlain Rd CV21... **92** B2
Chamberlain's Gn CV6.. **29** A3
Chancellors Cl CV4 ... **58** B4
Chandos St CV2 ...... **40** B3
Channel Way CV6..... **14** B2
Chantries The CV1 .... **30** C1
Chapel Farm Cl CV3 .. **50** A2
CHAPEL FIELDS **37** C3
Chapel La
Barnacle CV7 .... **16** B2
Ryton-on-D CV8 .... **63** C2
Chapel St
Bedworth CV12........ **6** C3
Coventry CV1 .... **96** B3
Long Lawford CV23 .... **83** B2
Rugby CV21........... **85** B1
Chard Rd CV3 .... **50** B4
Chariot Way CV21 .... **79** B1
Charity Rd CV7 .... **12** A3
Charlecote Rd CV2 ... **20** A2
Charles Eaton Rd CV12..**5** C3
Charlesfield Rd CV22 ... **90** A2
Charles Lakin Cl CV7... **16** C1
Charles St
Coventry CV1 .... **96** D4
Rugby CV21........... **85** A1
Charles Warren Cl
CV21................. **85** C1
Charlewood Rd CV6 ... **20** B2

Charlotte St CV21...... **85** C1
Charminster Dr CV3 ... **60** B4
Charter Ave CV4...... **45** C3
Charter Ho CV4....... **45** B3
Charterhouse Rd CV1... **39** C2
Charter Prim Sch (Harris
Site) CV4............. **45** A3
Charter Prim Sch (Parkes
Site) CV4............. **46** A4
Charter Rd CV22...... **91** B2
Charwelton Dr CV21... **86** C4
Chatham Cl CV1...... **50** A4
Chatsworth Gr CV8 ... **68** A1
Chatsworth Rise CV3 .. **48** C2
Chaucer Rd CV22..... **95** A4
Chauntry Pl CV1...... **96** C3
Cheadle Cl CV2....... **22** A4
Cheam Cl CV6........ **22** A1
Cheetah Rd CV1...... **97** C1
Chelmarsh CV6....... **30** A2
Chelney Wlk CV3 ..... **42** B1
Chelsey Rd CV2....... **32** C4
Cheltenham Cl CV12.....**6** B4
Cheltenham Croft CV2.. **33** A3
Chelveston Rd CV6 ... **28** C1
Chelwood Gr CV2..... **23** C1
Chenies Cl CV5 .... **36** C3
Chepstow Cl CV3..... **50** A1
Chequer St CV12.......**8** C2
Cheriton Cl CV5 ...... **37** B4
Cherrybrook Way CV2 . **22** C1
Cherry Cl CV6 .... **21** A2
Cherry Gr CV22....... **89** B2
Cherry Orch CV8 ..... **67** B1
Cherry Way CV8 ..... **67** B1
Cherrywood Gr CV5 ... **27** A1
Cherwell Way CV23... **83** C2
Chesford Cres CV6.... **22** B2
Cheshire Cl CV22 ..... **88** C2
Chesholme Rd CV6.... **20** B2
Cheshunt Sch CV1..... **97** B1
Chesils The CV3 ...... **48** B2
Chester St
Coventry CV1 .... **38** C3
Rugby CV21........... **86** A2
Chesterton Rd CV6 ... **29** B3
Chestnut Ave CV8 .... **74** B3
Chestnut Ct CV3...... **49** C4
Chestnut Field CV21 ... **85** B1
Chestnut Gr
Coventry CV4 .... **36** B2
Wolston CV8 .... **65** B3
Chestnut Rd CV12.......**7** A4
Chestnuts The CV12.....**5** B2
Chestnut Tree Ave CV4 . **36** B2
Cheswick Cl CV6 ..... **31** B3
Chetton Ave CV6 ..... **30** A2
Chetwode Cl CV5..... **36** C4
Cheveral Ave CV6..... **29** C2
Cheveral Rd CV12 ......**6** A3
Cheviot The CV4 ..... **46** B2
CHEYLESMORE **48** C3
Cheylesmore CV1..... **97** B2
Chicory Dr CV23...... **80** B2
Chideock Hill CV3 .... **47** B2
Chiel Cl CV5.......... **36** A4
Chillaton Rd CV6 ..... **20** B2
Chiltern Ct 2 CV6 .... **29** B1
Chiltern Ho CV5...... **35** B4
Chiltern Leys 2 CV6... **38** B4
Chilterns The CV5 .... **36** C4
Chingford Rd CV6 .... **22** A4
Chorley Way CV6..... **30** A2
Christchurch Rd CV6 ... **29** B1
Christopher Hooke Ho
CV6.................. **30** C4
Christ the King RC Inf Sch
CV6.................. **29** A2

Christ the King RC Jun Sch
CV6.................. **29** A3
Chudleigh Rd CV2 .... **32** C3
Church Cl CV8........ **63** C2
Church Ct CV6........ **19** C1
Church Dr CV8 .... **67** A1
CHURCH END **41** A4
Churchill Ave
Coventry CV6 .... **30** C4
Kenilworth CV8....... **67** B2
Churchill Rd CV22 .... **90** A3
Church La
Ash Green CV7 .... **13** B3
Corley CV7 .... **10** B3
Coventry, Middle Stoke
CV2 .... **40** C3
Coventry, Upper Eastern Green
CV5 .... **26** A1
Stoneleigh CV8 .... **70** A2
CHURCH LAWFORD ... **55** C2
Church Lawford Bsns Ctr
CV23................. **55** B3
Church Park Cl CV6.... **19** C1
Church Rd
Baginton CV8 .... **61** A2
Bubbenhall CV8....... **72** A2
Church Lawford CV23.... **82** A3
Ryton-on-D CV8 ...... **63** C2
Shilton CV7 .... **17** B1
Church St
Bulkington CV12....... **8** C2
Clifton u D CV23...... **87** B3
Coventry CV1 .... **96** C4
Rugby CV21........... **85** B1
Church Way CV12.......**6** B2
Church Wlk
Allesley CV5 .... **28** A2
Rugby, Bilton CV22 .... **89** A2
Rugby CV21, CV22 .... **90** A4
Thurlaston CV23 ...... **93** A1
City Arc CV1.......... **97** B2
City Coll Coventry (Butts
Ctr) CV1.............. **38** B2
City Coll Coventry
(Maxwell Ctr) CV1 .... **38** C1
City College Coventry (Tile
Hill Ctr) CV4.......... **36** A1
Clara St CV2.......... **40** B2
Clare Ct CV21......... **85** A1
Claremont Cl CV12......**8** B4
Claremont Rd CV21.... **86** A1
Claremont Wlk CV5.... **28** A2
Clarence Rd CV21 .... **84** C1
Clarence St 5 CV1 ... **39** C4
Clarendon Ct 10 CV21.. **85** C1
Clarendon Rd CV8 .... **74** C3
Clarendon St CV5..... **38** A1
Clarke's Ave CV8 .... **74** C3
Clark St CV6.......... **22** A1
Claverdon Rd CV5 .... **36** C3
Clayhill La CV23 ..... **83** A4
Clay La CV2 .... **40** B4
Clayton Rd CV6....... **28** C1
Clement Ho CV5 ..... **67** B1
Clements Cl CV8...... **67** B1
Clements St CV2...... **40** B3
Clement Way CV22 ... **88** A2
Clennon Rise CV2 .... **32** B4
Cleveland Rd
Bulkington CV12........**8** B3
Coventry CV2 .... **40** B4
Clifden Gr CV8 .... **68** A2
Clifford Bridge Prim Sch
CV3.................. **42** B3
Clifford Bridge Rd CV3.. **42** A4
Clifton Rd CV21....... **86** B1
Clifton St CV1........ **96** D4

CLIFTON UPON DUNMORE 87 B4
Clifton-upon-Dunsmore
CE Prim Sch CV23 .... 87 A3
Clinton Ave CV8 .... 66 B2
Clinton La CV8 .... 66 B2
Clinton Prim Sch CV8 .. 74 A3
Clinton Rd CV6 .... 21 C2
Clipstone Rd CV6........ 28 C2
Clock Towers Sh Ctr The
CV21 .... 85 B1
Cloister Croft CV2 ...... 33 A2
Close The
Brandon CV8.......... 53 A1
Kenilworth CV8........ 67 B2
Cloud Gn CV4 .... 46 B1
Clovelly Gdns CV2 ..... 32 A1
Clovelly Rd CV2 .... 31 C1
Clover Cl CV23 .... 80 B2
Cloverdale CV6 .... 20 B4
Clover Way CV12 ....5 A2
Clyde Rd CV12..........8 A2
COALPIT FIELD 7 A1
Coalpit Fields Rd CV12....6 C1
Coat Of Arms Bridge Rd
CV3 .... 47 B2
Cobbs Rd CV8 .... 66 B2
Cobden St CV6 .... 30 C1
Coburg Ho CV5 .... 37 C3
Cockerills Mdw CV21 ... 92 A2
Coldwells Ct CV22...... 90 A4
Colebrook Cl CV3....... 42 A2
Coleby Cl CV4 .... 44 B3
Coleman St CV4 .... 36 A3
Coleridge Rd CV2...... 41 A3
Colina Cl CV3.......... 50 A1
Colledge Rd CV6 ...... 21 A1
Collett Wlk **2** CV1 ..... 38 C3
Colliery La CV7..........6 B1
Colliery La N CV7.........6 B1
Collingwood Ave CV22... 89 A3
Collingwood Rd CV5..... 38 B2
Collins Gr CV4......... 46 B1
COLLYCROFT 2 C1
Columbia Gdns CV12 ....7 B2
Columbine Way CV12....5 B1
Colyere Cl CV7 .... 12 C2
Common La CV8........ 67 C3
Common Way CV2...... 31 B2
Compass Ct **4** CV1 ... 38 C3
Compton Ct
  Coventry CV6 .... 21 A2
  Rugby CV22.......... 93 C4
Compton Rd CV6 .... 21 A2
Comrie Cl CV2......... 33 A2
Congleton Cl CV6...... 21 B2
Congreve Wlk **3** CV12 ....6 B3
Conifer Cl CV12..........6 C4
Conifer Paddock CV3... 41 C1
Conifers The CV8 ...... 75 A3
Coniston Cl
  Bulkington CV12 ...... 8 C3
  Rugby CV21.......... 86 B4
Coniston Dr CV5....... 35 B4
Coniston Grange CV8... 67 A1
Coniston Rd CV5 ...... 38 A1
Conrad Cl CV22........ 95 A4
Conrad Rd CV6........ 29 B3
Constable Cl CV12.......2 C1
Constable Rd CV21 ..... 92 B3
Constance Cl CV12 ..... 13 C4
Consul Rd CV21........ 85 B4
Convent Cl CV8........ 67 B3
Conway Ave CV4....... 44 B4
Cook Cl CV21.......... 80 A1
Cooke Cl CV6.......... 22 A4
Cook St CV1........... 96 B3

Coombe Abbey Ctry Pk★
  CV3 .... 43 C3
Coombe Abbey Visitor
  Ctr★ CV3 .... 43 C4
Coombe Ave CV3 ...... 51 A3
Coombe Cl CV3 .... 42 B2
Coombe Dr CV3 .... 52 C3
Coombe Park Rd CV3... 42 A2
Coombe St CV3........ 40 C2
Co-Operative St CV2 ... 22 B3
Coopers Wlk CV8...... 72 A1
Cope Arnolds Cl CV6.... 21 C4
Copeland CV21......... 80 A1
Cope St CV1........... 96 C3
Copland Pl CV4........ 35 C1
Copperas St CV2 ...... 22 B2
Copper Beech Cl CV3 ... 21 B1
Copperfield Rd CV2..... 40 C3
Coppice Cl CV8........ 73 C4
Coppice The CV3 ...... 49 C4
Copse The CV7 .... 14 A4
Copsewood Terr CV3.... 41 A2
Copthall Ho CV1....... 97 B1
Copthorne Lo CV6...... 29 A4
Copthorne Rd CV6..... 29 A4
Copt Oak Cl CV4...... 44 A2
Coral Cl CV5.......... 37 A2
Corbet Rd CV6 .... 30 A3
Corbett St CV21....... 86 A2
Cordelia Way CV22 .... 94 C4
Corfe Cl CV2.......... 33 A1
Corinthian Pl CV2 ..... 32 B2
CORLEY 10 B3
CORLEY ASH 10 A4
Corley (Coventry) Sch
  CV7 .... 10 B2
Corley View CV7 ...... 12 C2
Cornelius St CV3 ...... 48 B4
Cornerstone Ho CV1.... 96 C4
Cornfield The CV3 ..... 41 A1
Cornflower Dr CV23 .... 80 B2
Cornhill Gr CV8........ 68 A1
Corn Mdws CV12........6 C2
Cornwalls Rd CV22..... 88 C4
Cornwall Rd CV1 ...... 39 C1
Coronation Rd
  Church Lawford CV23..... 55 C2
  Coventry CV1 .... 40 A4
Coronel Ave CV6...... 21 B4
Corporation St
  Coventry CV1 .... 96 B3
  Rugby CV21.......... 85 B1
Corpus Christi RC Sch
  CV3 .... 50 B3
Cosford La
  Rugby CV21.......... 79 A2
  Rugby CV21.......... 79 B4
Cotman Cl CV12........6 A4
Coton Park Dr CV23 ... 80 A2
Coton Rd CV21........ 92 A3
Cotswold Dr CV3 ...... 60 A3
Cottage Farm Lodge
  CV6................. 20 A1
Cottage Farm Rd CV6... 20 A2
Cottage Leap CV21 .... 86 B3
Cotterell Rd CV21...... 85 A4
Cottesbrook Cl CV3..... 41 C1
Cotton Dr CV8........ 68 A2
Cotton Park Dr CV23.... 80 A3
COUNDON 29 A2
Coundon Court Sch & Com
  Coll CV6............ 28 C2
Coundon Gn CV6...... 28 C4
COUNDON GREEN 28 C4
Coundon Prim Sch CV6. 28 C1
Coundon Rd CV1...... 38 C3
Coundon St CV1....... 96 A4

Coundon Wedge Dr CV5,
  CV6................. 28 B3
Countess's Croft The
  CV3 .... 48 B3
Courtaulds Way CV6.... 30 B2
Courthouse Croft CV8 .. 75 B4
Courthouse Green Prim
  Sch CV6............ 31 B4
Courtland Ave CV6..... 29 A1
Court Leet CV3 .... 52 B3
Court Leet Rd CV3..... 48 C3
COVENTRY 97 C1
Coventry Airport CV8... 61 C2
Coventry Blue Coat CE Sch
  The CV1............ 40 B1
Coventry Bsns Pk CV5.. 37 B1
Coventry Canal Basin
  Warehouse CV1...... 96 B4
Coventry Cath Church of St
  Michael★ CV1 .... 96 C3
Coventry Gram Sch
  CV5................ 38 A1
Coventry Muslim Sch
  CV6................ 30 C4
Coventry Prep Sch CV3. 47 C4
Coventry Railway Ctr
  CV8................ 61 B3
Coventry Rd
  Baginton CV8........ 61 A2
  Barnacle CV7, CV12 .... 16 A4
  Bedworth CV12........6 B2
  Bedworth, Hawkesbury
  CV2 .... 15 B2
  Bulkington CV12.......8 B1
  Cawston CV22........ 88 A1
  Church Lawford CV23... 54 C3
  Dunchurch CV22...... 93 C1
  Kenilworth CV8....... 67 B3
  Long Lawford CV23 ... 82 C2
  Nuneaton CV10........3 B3
  Stoneleigh CV8, CV3.... 70 A3
Coventry Ret Mkt CV1 .. 97 B2
Coventry Road Exhall
  CV7 .... 14 A4
Coventry St CV2 ...... 40 B4
Coventry Sta CV1 ..... 97 B1
Coventry Toy Mus★
  CV1 .... 97 C2
Coventry Transport Mus★
  CV1 .... 96 B3
Coventry Univ CV1 .... 97 C2
Coventry University Tech
  Pk CV1.............. 97 C1
Coventry Walsgrave
  Triangle Bsns Pk CV2.. 24 A1
Coventry & Warwickshire
  Hospl CV1........... 96 C4
Cove Pl CV2.......... 32 A3
Coverley Pl CV22 ...... 84 C1
Cowan Cl CV22........ 88 C3
Cowley Rd CV2 .... 41 B4
Cox Cres CV22........ 94 A2
Cox St CV1........... 96 C3
Cozens Cl CV12........6 A4
Crabmill La CV6....... 31 A3
CRACKLEY 67 C3
Crackley Cotts CV8 .... 67 C4
Crackley Cres CV8..... 67 C4
Crackley Hall Sch CV8.. 67 C3
Crackley La
  Coventry CV4 .... 57 A3
  Kenilworth CV8....... 67 B3
Crackthorne Dr CV23... 80 B3
Craigends Ave CV3 .... 50 C2
Crakston Cl CV2....... 41 C2
Cramper's Field CV6.... 29 B1
Cranborne Chase CV2 .. 33 B1
Craner's Rd CV1....... 40 A4

Cranford Rd CV5 ...... 37 B4
Crathie Cl CV2........ 33 A2
Craven Ave CV3 ...... 52 B3
Craven Ct CV3........ 42 A2
Craven Rd CV21...... 86 A2
Craven St CV5........ 38 A2
Crecy Rd CV3......... 48 C3
Crescent Ave CV3..... 41 A2
Crescent Sch CV22 .... 89 A2
Crescent The
  Cawston CV22....... 88 B2
  Keresley CV7 .... 11 C2
Cressage Rd CV2 ..... 33 B2
Cresswell Ho CV6..... 29 C3
Creswell Pl CV22 ..... 88 A3
Crew La CV8 .... 68 C2
Cricket Cl CV5........ 38 A3
Critchley Dr CV22..... 94 B1
Croft Fields CV12.......6 B2
Croft Pool CV12........5 C2
Croft Rd
  Bedworth CV12....... 5 C2
  Coventry CV1 .... 97 A2
Croft The
  Bulkington CV12.......8 B2
  Coventry CV6 .... 21 C4
  Rugby CV21.......... 92 A2
Cromarty Cl CV5...... 27 B1
Cromes Wood CV4..... 35 B1
Cromwell La CV4, CV8... 44 A2
Cromwell Rd CV22..... 90 C3
Cromwell St CV6 ..... 31 A2
Crondal Rd CV7 ...... 14 B3
Croome Cl CV6....... 38 A4
Crosbie Rd CV5....... 37 C3
Cross Cheaping CV1... 96 B3
Crossley Ct CV6 ...... 31 A3
Cross Point Bsns Pk
  CV2 .... 33 C4
Cross Rd
  Coventry CV6 .... 31 A4
  Keresley CV7 .... 11 C2
Cross Road Ind Est CV6. 31 A3
Cross St
  Coventry CV1 .... 96 C4
  Long Lawford CV23 ... 83 B3
  Rugby CV21.......... 86 A2
Crossway Rd CV3...... 59 C4
Crowmere Rd CV2 .... 33 A3
Crown Gn CV6........ 21 B2
Crown Ho CV5........ 37 C3
Crowsfurlong CV23 .... 80 B3
Crow Thorns CV21 .... 86 B4
Croxhall St CV12........6 C3
Croydon Cl CV3........ 48 C2
Crummock Cl CV6..... 21 A3
Cryfield Grange Rd CV4,
  CV8 .... 58 A2
Cryfield Hts CV4...... 58 B2
Cryfield Village CV4.... 57 C4
Cubbington Rd CV6.... 22 A2
Cuckoo La CV1....... 96 C3
Culworth Cl CV21..... 80 C1
Culworth Ct CV6...... 30 C3
Culworth Row CV6.... 30 C4
Cumbernauld Wlk **7**
  CV2 .... 33 B3
Cumbria Cl CV1 ...... 38 B3
Cunnery The CV8 ..... 76 C3
Cunningham Way N
  CV22 .... 88 C3
Cunningham Way S
  CV22 .... 88 C3
Curie Cl CV21 .... 86 B1
Curriers Cl CV4....... 44 B3

Curtis Rd CV2 .... 32 B2
Curzon Ave CV6 .... 30 C4
Cygnet Ct CV1......... 96 C4
Cymbeline Way CV22 ... 94 B4
Cypress Croft CV3 ..... 51 A4

D

Daffern Rd CV7..........6 A1
Daffodil Dr 4 CV12.....5 A2
Dahlia Wlk CV10........2 C4
Daimler Rd CV6 .... 30 A1
Daintree Croft CV3 .... 48 A3
Daisy Croft CV12.......5 A2
Dalby Cl CV3 .... 50 C4
Dalehouse Flats CV8... 67 C2
Dalehouse La CV8 ..... 68 B3
Dale St CV21 .... 85 B2
Daleway Rd CV3 .... 59 C4
Dalkeith Ave CV22 ..... 89 A1
Dallington Rd CV6 ..... 28 C2
Dalmeny Rd CV4....... 44 B3
Dalton Cl CV23 .... 55 C3
Dalton Gdns CV2 ...... 42 A4
Dalton Rd
  Bedworth CV12........ 6 A2
  Coventry CV5 .... 38 C1
Dalwood Way CV6 ..... 22 B4
Dame Agnes Gr CV6 ... 31 C4
Dane Rd CV2 .... 40 C4
Daneswood Rd CV3.... 52 C3
Daphne Cl CV2 .... 22 C3
Darfield Ct CV8........ 72 A1
Dark La
  Bedworth CV12........ 5 A1
  Coventry CV1 .... 96 B4
Darnford Cl CV2 ...... 33 A3
Darrach Cl CV2 .... 23 B1
Dartmouth Rd CV2..... 32 A1
Dartmouth Sch CV2 ... 32 B1
Darwin Cl CV3......... 33 B2
Darwin Ct 1 CV12......6 A2
Datchet Cl CV5 .... 37 A4
D'aubeny Rd CV4 ..... 46 A4
Davenport Lodge Sch
  CV5.................. 47 C4
Davenport Rd CV5..... 47 C4
Daventry Rd CV3 ...... 48 B3
David Rd
  Bedworth CV7........ 13 C4
  Coventry CV1 .... 40 A2
  Rugby CV22........... 89 A2
Davies Rd CV7........ 13 C3
Davy Ct CV23......... 80 A4
Dawes Cl CV2 .... 40 B3
Dawley Wlk 9 CV2 ... 33 B3
Dawlish Dr CV3....... 48 B1
Dawson Rd CV3 ...... 40 B1
Days Cl CV1 .... 39 C3
Day's La CV1 .... 40 A3
Deacon Cl CV22 ...... 90 C3
Deane Par CV21 ...... 92 A2
Deane Rd CV21 .... 92 B2
Dean St CV2 .... 40 B3
Deanston Croft CV2 ... 23 C1
Deans Way CV7........ 13 A2
Deasy Ho CV3 .... 49 C1
Deasy Rd CV1 .... 97 C1
De-Compton Cl CV7 ... 12 A3
Deedmore Rd CV2..... 23 A1
Deedmore Sch CV2.... 32 A4
Deegan Cl CV2 .... 31 B1
Deepmore Rd CV22.... 89 A2
Deerdale Terr 8 CV3 .. 51 A4
Deerdale Way CV3..... 51 A4

Deerhurst Mews CV22 .. 94 A1
Deerhurst Rd CV6 ..... 20 B2
Deerings Rd CV21 ..... 92 A2
Deer Leap The CV8 .... 67 C2
Deighton Gr CV3 ...... 50 A2
Delage Cl CV1......... 22 B4
Delamere Rd CV12......5 C2
Delaware Rd CV3....... 48 A1
Delf Ho CV2........... 23 A1
Delhi Ave CV6 .... 21 A1
Delius St CV4......... 35 C3
Dell Cl CV3 .... 50 A1
De Montfort Rd CV8 ... 66 C2
De Montfort Way CV4... 46 B1
Dempster Rd CV12......6 A4
Denbigh Rd CV6 ...... 28 C1
Dencer Dr CV8 .... 75 B4
Denemoor Ct CV8 ..... 67 C1
Denewood Way CV8 ... 68 A2
Denham Ave CV5 ..... 37 A4
Dennis Rd CV2 .... 31 C2
Denshaw Croft CV2.... 33 B4
Denton Cl CV8........ 66 B2
Dering Cl CV2 .... 32 B4
Deronda Cl CV12 ......6 A3
Derry Cl CV8 .... 65 B3
Dersingham Dr CV6 ... 22 B2
Derwent Cl
  Coventry CV5 .... 35 C4
  Rugby CV21........... 86 A4
Derwent Rd
  Bedworth CV12........ 6 A2
  Coventry CV6 .... 20 A2
Despard Rd CV5 ...... 35 B4
Devereux Cl CV4....... 35 A1
Devon Gr CV2 .... 31 C2
Devonshire Cl CV22.... 88 B3
Devoran Cl CV7........ 14 B4
Dewar Gr CV21 .... 91 B4
Dew Cl CV22 .... 94 A1
Dewis Ho 4 CV2 ..... 22 B1
Dewsbury Ave CV3..... 47 C1
Dial House La CV5 .... 36 A4
Diana Dr CV2......... 23 B1
Dickens Rd
  Coventry CV6 .... 29 B4
  Rugby CV22........... 95 A4
Dickinson Ct CV22.... 90 A3
Didsbury Rd CV7 ......6 A1
Digbey Cl CV5 .... 27 C2
Dilcock Way CV4 ..... 45 A3
Dillam Cl CV6 .... 22 A4
Dillotford Ave CV3..... 48 B2
Dingle Cl CV6 .... 29 B2
Dingley Rd CV12.......8 B2
Discovery Way CV3 ... 51 C3
Ditton Cl CV22........ 88 C3
Dodgson Cl CV6...... 22 A4
Doe Bank La CV1 ..... 38 B3
Dogberry Cl CV3...... 50 A2
Dolomite Ave CV4 .... 37 B1
Doncaster Cl CV2..... 32 B3
Done Cerce Cl CV22 ... 94 A1
Donegal Cl CV4...... 45 B3
Donnington Ave CV6... 28 C1
Doone Cl CV2 .... 32 C2
Dorchester Way CV2.... 42 B4
Dorlecote Pl CV10......3 B4
Dorlecote Rd CV10 .....3 B4
Dormer Harris Ave CV4 . 36 A1
Dorney Cl CV5......... 46 C4
Dorothy Powell Way
  CV2.................. 23 C1
Dorset Cl CV22........ 88 B3
Dorset Rd CV1......... 30 A1
Douglas Ho CV1....... 96 D4
Douglas Rd CV21 ..... 86 A4
Doulton Cl CV2....... 23 B1

Dove Cl CV12..........5 B3
Dovecote Cl CV6...... 28 B1
Dovecotes The CV5 .... 27 C1
Dovedale CV21 .... 80 A1
Dovedale Ave CV6 .... 21 C2
Dover St CV1 .... 96 A3
Dowley Croft CV3..... 42 C1
Downderry Way CV6... 31 B2
Downing Cres CV12......6 C4
Downton Cl CV2....... 33 B4
Dowty Ave CV12.......5 A1
Doyle Dr CV6 .... 21 C3
Drake St CV6 .... 30 B3
Draper Cl CV8 .... 75 B4
Drapers Ct CV1....... 96 B4
DRAPER'S FIELDS 96 B4
Draper's Fields CV1 ... 96 B4
Draycott Rd CV2...... 32 A3
Drayton Cres CV5..... 26 B1
Drayton Leys CV22.... 90 A1
Drayton Rd CV12.......7 A2
Drew Cres CV8 ...... 74 C4
Dreyer Cl CV22 ...... 88 C4
Drinkwater Ho 7 CV1 . 38 C2
Drive The
  Coventry CV2 .... 41 C3
  Dunchurch CV22 ...... 94 C2
Dronfield Rd CV2...... 40 C3
Droylsdon Park Rd CV3 . 59 C3
Dr Phillips Sh Ctr The
  CV2.................. 23 A1
Druid Rd CV2......... 40 C3
Drummond Cl CV6..... 29 A3
Drury La CV21 .... 85 B1
Dryden Cl CV8........ 74 B3
Dryden Pl CV22....... 84 C1
Dryden Wlk CV22...... 84 C1
Dudley Rd CV8 ...... 74 B2
Dudley St CV6 .... 22 A1
Dudley Terr CV8 ..... 69 C2
Duffy Pl CV21........ 92 A2
Dugdale Rd CV6...... 29 C2
Duke Barn Field CV2 .. 31 B1
Dukes Jetty 8 CV21 .. 85 B1
Duke St
  Coventry CV5 .... 38 A2
  Rugby CV21.......... 85 B2
Dulverton Ave CV5.... 37 B4
Dulverton Ct CV5 .... 37 B4
Duncan Dr CV22...... 94 B4
DUNCHURCH 94 B1
Dunchurch Boughton CE
  Jun Sch CV22 .... 94 A1
Dunchurch Hall CV22 .. 94 A1
Dunchurch Highway
  CV5................. 36 B4
Dunchurch Inf Sch
  CV22................ 94 A1
Dunchurch Rd CV22 ... 89 C1
Duncroft Ave CV6..... 29 A3
Dunhill Ave CV4 ..... 35 C3
Dunkirk Pl CV3....... 51 A3
Dunnerdale CV21..... 80 B1
Dunnose Cl CV6...... 30 C4
Dunrose Cl CV2...... 41 C2
Dunsmore Ave
  Coventry CV3 .... 50 A2
  Rugby CV22.......... 91 B2
Dunsmore Bsns Ctr
  CV21................ 85 C1
Dunsmore Heath CV22.. 94 A1
Dunster Pl CV6....... 21 A3
Dunsville Dr CV6..... 33 A4
Dunvegan Cl
  Coventry CV3 .... 42 B2
  Kenilworth CV8....... 75 B4
Durbar Ave CV6...... 30 B4
Durham Cl CV7........ 19 C4

Durham Cres CV5 ..... 27 C3
Durrell Dr CV22....... 88 A1
Dutton Rd CV2 .... 23 A3
Dyer's La CV8 .... 65 C3
Dymond Rd CV6 ...... 21 A3
Dysart Cl CV1 .... 39 C4
Dyson Cl CV21........ 91 C3
Dyson St CV4......... 35 C3

E

Eacott Cl CV6......... 20 A3
Eagle Ho CV1......... 30 B1
Eagle La CV8 .... 74 B3
Eagle St E CV1........ 30 B1
Eagle St CV1 .... 30 B1
Earl Place Bsns Pk CV4 . 36 C1
Earl's Croft The CV3 ... 48 B3
EARLSDON 38 B1
Earlsdon Ave CV5..... 47 B4
Earlsdon Ave N CV5... 38 A1
Earlsdon Ave S CV5... 47 B4
Earlsdon Ho CV5 .... 47 B4
Earlsdon Prim Sch CV5. 38 B1
Earlsdon St CV5 ..... 47 A4
Earl St
  Bedworth CV12........ 6 C2
  Coventry CV1 .... 97 C2
  Rugby CV21.......... 85 C1
Earl's Wlk CV3 ...... 52 B3
Easedale Cl CV3 ..... 47 C2
East Ave
  Bedworth CV12........ 7 A2
  Coventry CV2 .... 40 B2
Eastbourne Cl CV6.... 28 C2
Eastcotes CV4 .... 36 C1
Eastern Green Jun Sch
  CV5................. 26 B1
Eastern Green Rd CV5 . 36 A4
Eastfield Pl CV21 ..... 85 B1
Eastlands Gr CV5 .... 37 C4
Eastlands Pl CV21 .... 86 B1
Eastlands Prim Sch
  CV21................ 91 A4
Eastlands Rd CV21.... 91 A4
Eastleigh Ave CV5 .... 47 A3
East St
  Coventry CV1 .... 39 C3
  Rugby CV21.......... 86 B2
East Union St CV22 ... 90 A4
Eastwood Gr CV21 .... 92 C2
Easy La CV21 .... 85 A1
Eathorpe Cl CV2...... 22 C1
Eaton Rd CV1........ 97 B1
Ebbw Vale Terr CV3 ... 48 B3
Ebourne Cl CV8 ..... 74 C4
Ebro Cres CV3........ 42 A1
Eburne Rd CV2 ...... 22 C3
Eccles Cl CV2 .... 32 A4
Ecton Leys CV22..... 90 A1
Edale Way CV6 ...... 31 B3
Eddie Miller Ct CV12.....6 B2
Eden Croft CV8....... 75 A3
Eden Rd
  Coventry CV2 .... 33 B4
  Rugby CV21.......... 91 C3
Eden St CV6 .... 31 A3
Edgcote Cl CV21...... 91 C3
Edgefield Rd CV2..... 33 B4
Edgehill Pl CV4....... 35 A1
Edgwick Com Prim Sch
  CV6................. 30 C4
EDGWICK 31 A4
Edgwick Park Ind Est
  CV6................. 31 A4
Edgwick Rd CV6...... 31 A3
Edinburgh Villas CV8.. 61 A2
Edinburgh Way CV23 ... 83 C3

Edingale Rd CV2....... 33 A4
Edmonson Cl CV22.... 94 B2
Edmund Rd CV1....... 30 B1
Edward Bailey Cl CV3... 50 C3
Edward Ct 2 CV21..... 85 C1
Edward Rd
 Bedworth CV12......... 6 C3
 Coventry CV6......... 20 A3
Edwards Gr CV8....... 68 A1
Edward St
 Coventry CV6......... 30 C1
 Rugby CV21.......... 85 A1
Edward Tyler Rd CV7.....6 A1
Edwin Cl CV22........ 88 B1
Edyth Rd CV2......... 41 C4
Edyvean Cl CV22...... 94 C4
Egerton Cl CV21...... 85 A4
Egret Wlk CV2........ 22 B3
Elborow St 5 CV21.... 85 B1
Elderberry Way CV2 ... 31 C2
Elder Cl CV2......... 88 B3
Eld Rd CV6.......... 30 C3
Elgar Rd CV6......... 31 C4
Eliot Ct CV22........ 84 C1
Elizabeth Ct 8 CV6... 38 B4
Elizabeth Way
 Coventry CV2......... 33 A3
 Kenilworth CV8........ 66 C1
 Long Lawford CV23...... 83 C3
Elkington St CV6...... 31 A4
Ellacombe Rd CV2..... 32 B4
Ellerman Gdns CV6.... 21 C3
Ellesmere Rd CV12 .....6 A2
Elliott Ct CV5........ 37 A1
Elliott's Field Ret Pk
 CV21.............. 85 B4
Ellis Park Dr CV3 ..... 42 C1
Ellys Rd CV1......... 30 A1
Elmbank Rd CV8...... 66 C2
Elm Cl CV3.......... 52 A3
Elmdene Cl CV8...... 65 B4
Elmdene Rd CV8...... 75 B4
Elmhurst Rd CV6..... 22 A4
Elmore Cl CV3........ 50 B4
Elmore Rd CV22...... 89 C3
Elmsdale Ave CV6 .... 21 C2
Elms Dr CV22........ 91 C2
Elms Paddock The
 CV23.............. 87 A3
Elms The CV12........5 B2
Elm Tree Ave CV4 ..... 36 C2
Elm Tree Rd CV12.......9 A2
Elmwood Ave CV6.... 29 A1
Elmwood Cl CV1...... 96 B4
Elphin Cl CV6........ 20 A4
Elsee Rd CV21........ 85 C1
Elstop Ave CV23 ...... 80 B3
Elter Cl CV21........ 80 B1
Eltham Rd CV3....... 48 C3
Elwy Circ CV7........ 12 C2
Ely Cl CV2.......... 33 B2
Embassy Wlk CV2 ..... 32 B4
Emerson Rd CV2 ..... 41 A3
Emery Cl CV2........ 32 C3
Emily Smith Ho 2 CV2.. 22 B1
Emperor Way CV21..... 79 A1
Empire Rd CV4....... 35 C2
Emscote Rd CV3...... 41 A2
Ena Rd CV1......... 30 B1
Endemere Rd CV6..... 30 B3
Enfield Rd CV2....... 40 C3
Engleton Rd CV6..... 29 B2
English Martyrs RC Prim
 Sch CV21........... 92 A1
Ennerdale Cl CV21..... 80 A1
Ennerdale La CV2..... 42 A4
Ensign Bsns Ctr CV4... 45 A2
Ensign Cl CV4........ 35 B1

Epsom Cl CV12 ....6 B4
Epsom Dr CV3 .... 50 A2
Epsom Rd CV22....... 89 A3
Erica Ave CV12 ....5 C2
Eric Grey Cl CV2...... 31 B1
Erithway Rd CV3....... 59 C4
Ernesford Grange Prim Sch
 CV3.............. 41 C1
Ernesford Grange Sch &
 Com Coll CV3 ...... 50 B4
Ernest Richards Rd CV12..6 B4
Ernsford Ave CV3..... 40 C1
Esher Dr CV3........ 48 C3
Eskdale CV21........ 80 A2
Eskdale Wlk CV3 ..... 50 B3
Essex Cl
 Coventry CV5......... 36 C3
 Kenilworth CV8........ 74 A2
Essex St CV21........ 85 B2
Esterton Cl CV2...... 20 C2
Ethelfield Rd CV2..... 40 C3
Ettington Rd CV5 ..... 36 B3
Europark Ind Est CV23.. 81 C4
Eustace Rd CV12 ....9 A1
Euston Cres CV3...... 50 A2
Evans Cl CV12 ....6 C3
Evans Rd CV22....... 88 C4
Evelyn Ave CV6...... 21 C2
Evenlode Cres CV6 ... 29 A1
Everard Cl CV23...... 87 B3
Everdon Cl CV21...... 91 B2
Everdon Rd CV6...... 20 B2
Everest Rd CV22...... 89 B2
Eversleigh Rd CV6 ... 28 C3
Evesham Wlk CV4 .... 46 B1
Evreux Way CV21...... 85 B1
Exeter Cl CV3........ 50 B4
EXHALL............ 14 B3
Exhall Cedars Inf Sch
 CV7.............. 14 A4
Exhall Gn CV7........ 13 C3
Exhall Grange Sch &
 Science Coll CV7..... 12 C1
Exhall Rd CV7........ 12 A2
Exminster Rd CV3..... 48 C1
Exmouth Cl CV2...... 32 A3
Exton Cl CV7........ 12 C2
Eydon Cl CV21........ 86 C4

Fabian Cl CV3 .... 50 B3
Fairbanks Cl CV2..... 33 B3
Fairbourne Way CV6... 28 C4
Faircroft CV8........ 74 B3
Fairfax St CV1....... 96 C3
Fairfield Cl CV3...... 49 B3
Fairlands Pk CV4 ..... 46 C1
Fairmile Cl CV3...... 50 A4
Fairview Wlk CV6..... 21 B2
Fairway Ct CV21...... 86 B2
Fairway Rise CV8..... 68 A2
Fairways Cl CV5...... 27 B2
Falcon Ave CV3...... 51 A4
Falkener Ho CV6..... 30 C3
Falkland Cl CV4...... 44 B3
Fallowfields CV6..... 20 C4
Falstaff Dr CV22..... 94 B4
Falstaff Rd CV4...... 35 C1
Fancott Dr CV8...... 67 A2
Faraday Rd CV22..... 90 C3
Farber Rd CV2....... 33 B2
Farcroft Ave CV5..... 35 B4
Fareham Ave CV22.... 91 B2
Far Gosford St CV1.... 39 C2
Farlow Cl CV6....... 31 B2
Farman Rd CV5....... 38 B2
Farm Cl CV6......... 20 B3

Farmcote Lodge CV2 ... 22 B4
Farmcote Rd CV2..... 22 B4
Farmer Ward Rd CV8 ... 74 C3
Farm Gr CV22........ 90 C3
Farmhurst CV22..... 91 A3
Farm Rd CV8 .... 74 A2
Farmside CV3........ 50 B1
Farmstead The CV3 ... 49 C4
Farndale Ave CV6..... 21 A3
Farndon Cl CV12...... 8 B3
Farr Dr CV4......... 36 C2
Farren Rd CV2....... 32 C1
Farthing Wlk CV4..... 44 B2
Faseman Ave CV4 .... 36 A3
Faulconbridge Ave CV5. 35 C4
Fawley Cl CV3....... 50 A2
Fawsley Leys CV22.... 90 A1
Faygate Cl CV2...... 42 A3
Featherbed La
 Coventry CV4......... 45 B1
 Rugby CV21.......... 92 A3
Feilding Cl CV4...... 33 B2
Fein Bank CV4....... 35 A2
Fellows Way CV21 .... 91 C2
Felton Cl CV2....... 23 B1
Fennell Ho 10 CV1.... 38 C2
Fennyland La CV8..... 67 C3
Fenside Ave CV5...... 60 B4
Fenwick Dr CV21..... 92 A2
Fern Cl
 Coventry CV2......... 22 C2
 Rugby CV23.......... 80 B2
Ferndale Dr CV8..... 74 C2
Ferndale Rd CV2..... 52 B3
Ferndown Cl CV4..... 36 B3
Ferndown Ct CV22.... 89 B3
Ferndown Rd CV22.... 89 B3
Ferndown Terr CV22... 89 B3
Fern Gr CV12..........5 B2
Fernhill Cl CV8...... 66 C2
Ferrers Cl CV4....... 36 A2
Ferrieres Cl CV22..... 94 A1
Fetherston Cres CV8... 63 C1
Field Cl CV8........ 67 C1
Field Ct CV2........ 32 B3
Fieldfare Cl CV23..... 80 A2
Fieldgate La CV8..... 67 A2
Fieldgate Lawn CV8... 67 A2
Field Ho CV8........ 67 A1
Field March CV3...... 50 C1
Fieldside La CV3..... 42 A3
Field View CV22..... 88 B2
Field View Cl CV7..... 14 A4
Fife Rd CV5......... 38 A2
Finch Cl CV2........ 20 C2
Findon Cl CV12 ....8 C3
Fingal Cl CV3........ 50 A2
Fingest Cl CV5....... 36 C4
FINHAM........... 60 A3
Finham Cres CV8..... 67 C2
Finham Flats CV8..... 67 C2
Finham Gr CV3....... 60 A3
Finham Green Rd CV3 .. 59 C3
Finham Park Sch CV3 .. 59 B4
Finham Prim Sch CV3 .. 59 C3
Finham Rd CV8....... 67 C2
Finlay Rd CV1....... 97 C1
Finmere CV21....... 86 B4
Finnemore Cl CV3..... 47 C1
Firedrake Croft CV1 ... 40 B2
Fir Gr CV4..........9 A2
Firs Dr CV22........ 89 C4
First Ave CV3....... 41 A1
Firs The
 Bedworth CV12.........5 B2
 Coventry CV5......... 47 C4
Fir Tree Ave CV4 ..... 36 C2

Fir Tree Gr CV11.........3 C4
Fisher Ave CV22..... 91 B2
Fisher Rd CV6....... 30 C4
Fishponds Rd CV8.... 74 A3
Fitzalan Cl CV23..... 55 C3
Fitzroy Cl CV2....... 33 C2
Fivefield Rd CV7...... 11 B1
Flamboro' Cl CV3..... 51 A4
Flaunden Cl CV5..... 36 C4
Flecknose St CV3..... 50 A2
Fleet Cres CV21...... 91 B4
Fleet St CV1........ 96 B3
Fletchamstead Highway
 CV5.............. 46 B3
Fletchworth Gate CV5 .. 46 B4
Fletchworth Gate Ind Est
 CV4.............. 46 B4
Florence Cl CV12 ..... 13 C4
Florence Rd CV3..... 42 B2
Florin Cl CV4....... 44 C2
Florin Pl CV21....... 92 A2
Flowerdale Dr CV2 ... 31 C2
Flude Rd CV7....... 12 C2
Flynt Ave CV5....... 27 C2
FOLESHILL.......... 22 A2
Foleshill CE Prim Sch
 CV6.............. 22 A2
Foleshill Rd CV1, CV6.... 30 B2
Folkland Gn CV6..... 29 B3
Follager Rd CV21..... 85 A2
Fontmell Cl CV2..... 42 B4
Ford St CV1......... 96 C3
Fordwell Cl CV5...... 38 A3
Foreland Way CV6.... 20 A3
Forest Ct CV5....... 36 B4
Foresters Pl CV21..... 92 B1
Forester's Rd CV3.... 48 C2
Forfield Rd CV6...... 28 C1
Forge Rd CV8....... 67 B2
Forge Way CV6...... 20 C3
Forknell Ave CV2..... 32 A1
Fornside Cl CV21..... 80 B1
Forrest Rd CV8...... 74 A4
Forum Dr CV21...... 85 B4
Fosseway Rd CV3..... 59 C4
Fosterd Rd CV21..... 85 A4
Foster Rd CV6....... 29 C3
Founder Cl CV4...... 45 A3
Four Pounds Ave CV5... 38 A3
Fowler Rd CV6....... 38 C4
Fow Oak CV4....... 35 A2
Fox Cl CV21........ 92 B3
FOXFORD........... 14 A1
Foxford Cres CV2 .... 22 B4
Foxford Sch & Com Arts
 Coll CV6............ 14 A1
Foxglove Cl
 Bedworth CV12.........5 B1
 Coventry CV2......... 20 C2
 Rugby CV23.......... 80 C2
Foxons Barn Rd CV21... 86 A4
Foxton Rd CV3....... 41 C1
Foxwood Dr CV3..... 52 B3
Framlingham Gr CV8 ... 68 A2
Frampton Wlk CV2 ... 42 A4
Frances Cres CV12......6 A3
Frances Rd CV8...... 61 A3
Franciscan Rd CV3 ... 48 B4
Francis Dr CV22..... 88 A2
Francis St CV6....... 30 C3
Frankland Rd CV6..... 22 A1
Franklin Gr CV4..... 35 C1
Franklins Gdns CV3.... 42 C1
Frankpledge Rd CV3... 48 C3
Frankton Ave CV3 .... 48 A1

Frank Walsh Ho CV1 .... **96** C4
Frankwell Dr CV2....... **23** B1
Fraser Rd CV6.......... **20** A1
Frederick Bird Prim Sch
CV2 .... **31** A1
Frederick Neal Ave CV5. **35** B4
Frederick Press Way
CV21 .... **85** A1
Frederick St CV1........ **85** A1
Fred Lee Gr CV3 .... **60** B4
Freeburn Cswy CV4..... **46** A3
Freehold St CV1........ **40** A4
Freeman St CV6........ **31** A2
Freemantle Rd CV22.... **88** C4
Freshfield Cl CV5....... **18** C1
Fretton Cl CV6.......... **31** A3
Frevill Rd CV6 .... **31** C4
Friars Cl CV3 .... **52** C3
Friars' Rd CV1 .... **97** B2
Frilsham Way CV5 ...... **36** C4
Frisby Rd CV4 .... **35** C2
Friswell Dr CV6........ **31** A4
Friswell Ho 🟥 CV2..... **32** B4
Frobisher Rd
Coventry CV3 .... **48** A1
Rugby CV22............. **88** C4
Frogmere Cl CV5 ...... **28** A2
Frythe Cl CV8 .... **68** A2
Fuchsia Cl 🟥 CV2 ..... **22** B2
Fulbrook Rd CV2 ...... **22** C2
Fullers Cl CV6 .... **29** A3
Fullwood Cl CV3 .... **23** B2
Furlong Rd CV1 .... **97** C1
Furnace Cl CV12....... **7** A3
Furnace Rd CV12 ...... **7** A4
Furness Cl CV21 .... **80** B1
Furrow Cl CV21 .... **86** B2
Fylde Ho CV2........... **41** B4
Fynford Rd CV6........ **29** C1

Gable Cl CV22 .... **89** A2
Gabor Cl CV21 .... **86** A4
Gainford Rise CV3 ...... **42** B3
Gainsborough Cres
CV21 .... **92** B3
Gainsborough Dr CV12... **6** A4
Galey's Rd CV3 .... **48** B4
Gallagher Bsns Pk CV6 . **13** B1
Gallagher Rd CV12...... **6** A2
Gallagher Ret Pk CV6 .. **31** A4
Galliards The CV4...... **58** B4
Galmington Dr CV3 .... **47** C2
Garard Ct 🟥 CV22 ..... **88** A2
Garard Pl 🟥 CV22 ..... **88** A2
Garard Row 🟥 CV22 ... **88** A2
Garden Flats CV5....... **26** B1
Garden Gr CV12 .... **13** C4
Gardenia Dr CV5 ...... **27** C2
Gardens The
Kenilworth CV8........ **74** C3
Rugby CV22............ **88** C1
Thurlaston CV23....... **93** A1
Gardner Ho 🟥 CV1 .... **38** C2
Gardner Way CV8...... **74** C2
Garlands Croft CV7 .... **12** A2
Garlick Dr CV8 .... **68** A2
Garratt Cl CV23........ **83** C3
Garrick Cl CV5......... **35** A4
Garth Cres CV3........ **50** B4
Garth Ho CV3.......... **50** B4
Garyth Williams Cl
CV22 .... **89** B2
Gas St CV21 .... **85** C1

Gatehouse Cl CV21 ..... **92** A2
Gatehouse La CV12 ...... **6** A2
Gateside Rd CV6........ **21** B2
Gaulby Wlk CV3 .... **42** B1
Gaveston Rd CV6 ...... **29** A2
Gaydon Cl CV6 .... **31** B4
Gayer St CV6 .... **22** A1
Gayhurst Cl CV3 ...... **50** C4
Gaza Cl CV2 .... **36** B1
Gazelle Cl CV1......... **96** D3
Gentian Way CV23 ..... **80** C2
Geoffrey Cl CV21 ...... **31** C1
George Eliot Ave CV12 .. **7** A2
George Eliot Com Sch
CV11 .... **3** C4
George Eliot Rd CV1.... **30** B1
George Hodgkinson Cl
CV4 .... **36** A3
George Marston Rd
CV3 .... **41** C1
George Park Cl CV2..... **22** C1
George Poole Ho 🟥
CV1 .... **38** C2
George Robertson Cl
CV3 .... **50** C3
George St
Coventry CV1 .... **30** C1
Rugby CV21............ **85** A1
George Street Ringway
CV12 .... **6** B3
Gerandria Ct CV22...... **91** B2
Gerard Ave CV4........ **45** C4
Gerard Rd CV22 .... **88** A2
GIBBET HILL **58** C2
Gibbet Hill Rd CV4..... **57** C3
Gibbons Cl CV4........ **36** A2
Gibbs Cl CV2 .... **33** C2
Gibson Cres CV12....... **6** A1
Gibson Dr CV21........ **92** A3
Gielgud Way CV2 ...... **33** C4
Gilbert Ave CV22....... **89** A4
Gilbert Cl
Bedworth CV12........ **6** B2
🟥 Coventry CV1....... **39** C3
Gilberts Rugby Football
Mus ★ CV21 .... **85** B1
Giles Cl CV6........... **20** C2
Gillians Wlk CV2....... **33** B4
Gilquart Way CV1...... **97** C1
Gingles Ct CV21 .... **92** A2
Gipsy La CV10, CV11 ..... **3** C3
Girdlers Cl CV3 .... **47** C1
Girtin Cl CV12 .... **6** A4
Givens Ho 🟥 CV1...... **38** C2
Glade The CV5......... **36** A3
Gladiator Way CV21.... **79** A1
Gladstone St CV21..... **85** A2
Glaisdale Ave CV6 ..... **21** B3
Glamorgan Cl CV3 ..... **50** B1
Glaramara Cl CV21 .... **80** B1
Glasshouse La CV8 .... **75** C4
Glebe Ave CV12........ **5** B1
Glebe Cl CV4 .... **45** B3
Glebe Cres
Kenilworth CV8........ **74** C3
Rugby CV21............ **84** C1
Glebefarm Gr CV3 ..... **42** A3
Glebe Farm Ind Est
CV21 .... **79** A1
Glebe Farm Rd CV21.... **79** A1
Glebe The CV7......... **10** C3
Glencoe Rd CV3 .... **40** C1
Glendale Ave CV8...... **67** B2
Glendale Way CV4..... **35** A2
Glendon Gdns CV12..... **8** C3
Glendower Ave CV5.... **37** B3
Gleneagles Rd CV2 .... **32** C2
Glenfern Gdns CV8 .... **62** C2

Glenmore Dr CV6....... **13** C1
Glenmount Ave CV6 .... **13** C1
Glenn St CV6 .... **21** A3
Glenridding Cl CV6 .... **13** C1
Glenrosa Wlk CV5 ..... **45** B3
Glenroy Cl CV2 .... **32** C2
Glentworth Ave CV6 ... **13** C1
Glenwood Gdns CV12.... **2** C1
Gloster Dr CV8 .... **67** A2
Gloucester St CV1 ..... **38** C3
Godiva Pl CV1 .... **96** D3
Godiva Trad Est CV6 ... **31** A4
Gold Ave CV22......... **88** B2
Golden Acres La CV3 ... **51** A3
Goldsmith Ave CV22 ... **95** A4
Goldthorn Cl CV5...... **35** B4
Goodacre Cl CV23 ..... **87** B3
Goode Croft CV4 ...... **36** A2
Goodman Way CV4 .... **35** A1
Good Shepherd RC Sch
CV6 .... **21** C1
Goodway Ho CV8 ...... **67** B1
Goodwood Cl CV3 ..... **50** A2
GOODYERS END **13** A4
Goodyers End La CV12... **13** A4
Goodyers End Prim Sch
CV12 .... **13** B4
Gordon Cl CV12 .... **6** C4
Gordon St CV1 .... **38** C2
Goring Rd CV2 .... **40** B4
Gorse Cl CV22 .... **89** B3
Gorseway CV5......... **37** A3
GOSFORD GREEN **40** A2
Gosford Ind Est CV1 ... **40** A2
Gosford Park Prim Sch
CV1 .... **40** A2
Gosford St CV1 .... **97** D2
Gospel Oak Rd CV6 ... **20** B4
Gosport Rd CV6 .... **30** C4
Gossett La CV8 .... **53** A3
Grafton Cl CV4 .... **45** C3
Grafton St CV1 .... **40** A2
Graham Cl CV6........ **22** B1
Graham Rd CV21 ...... **86** A2
Granborough Cl CV3... **51** A4
Grange Ave
Coventry, Binley CV3..... **51** A3
Coventry, Finham CV3.... **60** A3
Kenilworth CV8........ **66** C3
Grange Education Unit The
CV6 .... **19** B1
Grange Farm Prim Sch
CV3 .... **47** C1
Grangehurst Prim Sch
CV6 .... **22** B4
Grangemouth Rd CV6... **29** C3
Grange Rd
Coventry CV6 .... **14** B1
Rugby CV21............ **84** C4
Grange Wlk CV6....... **14** B1
Granoe Cl CV3......... **50** C4
Grantham St CV2 ..... **40** A3
Grant Rd
Bedworth CV7.......... **6** A1
Coventry CV3 .... **40** C2
Grapes Cl CV6 .... **29** C1
Grasmere Ave CV3..... **47** A2
Grasmere Cl CV21 ..... **86** B4
Grasmere Rd CV12..... **6** B2
Grasscroft Dr CV3 .... **48** C2
Gratton Ct CV3 .... **47** A2
Gravel Hill CV4 .... **36** A1
Graylands The CV3..... **60** A4
Grayswood Ave CV5 ... **37** B4
Great Borne CV21 ..... **80** A1
Great Central Walk ★
CV23 .... **81** A4

Great Central Walk Nature
Trail ★ CV22 .... **91** A1
Great Central Way CV21. **86** B3
GREAT HEATH **30** C2
Green Cl CV23......... **83** A2
Green Ct CV21......... **86** B2
Greendale Rd CV5 ..... **37** B3
Green Field The CV3 ... **49** C4
Greenhill Rd CV22 .... **89** C3
Green La
Church Lawford CV23..... **82** A3
Coventry CV3 .... **59** C4
Greenland Ave CV5.... **27** A1
Greenland Ct CV5 ..... **27** A1
GREEN LANE **47** C1
Greenleaf Cl CV5 ..... **36** B3
Greenodd Dr CV6...... **13** C1
Greensleeves Cl CV6... **20** B2
Greens Rd CV6 .... **20** A1
Greensward Cl CV8 .... **67** C2
Greensward The CV3... **42** B2
Greens Yd CV12....... **6** C3
Green The
Dunchurch CV22........ **94** A1
Long Lawford CV23 .... **83** B2
Rugby CV22............ **88** C2
Stoneleigh CV8......... **70** A2
Greenways CV4........ **35** A2
Greenwood Cl CV23 ... **83** B3
Gregory Ave CV3 ..... **47** B2
Gregory Hood Rd CV3.. **60** C4
Grendon Cl CV4 ...... **35** A1
Grendon Dr CV21...... **80** C1
Grenville Ave CV2 .... **40** C3
Grenville Cl CV22 ..... **88** C3
Gresham Rd CV10 ...... **3** A4
Gresham St CV2 ...... **40** B2
Gresley Rd CV2 .... **32** B3
Greswold Cl CV4...... **36** A1
Gretna Rd CV3........ **59** A4
Greville Rd CV6....... **74** B4
Greycoat Rd CV6 ..... **20** A2
Greyfriars Ct CV6..... **29** B3
Greyfriars La CV1..... **97** B2
Greyfriars Rd CV1 .... **97** B2
GRIFF **3** A2
Griffiths Ho CV21 ..... **80** A1
Griff La
Nuneaton CV10......... **2** C2
Nuneaton CV10......... **3** A2
Grimston Cl CV3....... **42** B2
Grindle Rd CV6 .... **21** C4
Grindley Ho 🟥 CV1 ... **38** C2
Grizebeck Dr CV5...... **27** B1
Grizedale CV21 .... **80** A1
Grosvenor Ho CV1 .... **97** A2
Grosvenor Rd
Coventry CV1 .... **97** A1
Rugby CV21............ **86** A1
Grove Ct CV5 .... **47** C4
Grovehurst Pk CV8 ... **77** A2
Grove La CV7.......... **11** C3
Grovelands Ind Est CV7. **14** A2
Grove Rd CV7 .... **25** A3
Grove St CV1 .... **96** C3
Grove The CV12........ **6** C3
Guardhouse Rd CV6 ... **29** C4
Guildford Ct CV6 ..... **30** B3
Guild Rd CV6......... **30** B3
Guilsborough Rd CV3... **50** C4
Guinea Cres CV4 ...... **44** C2
Gulson Hospl CV1 ..... **97** D2
Gulson Rd CV1 .... **39** C2
Gun La CV2........... **31** B1
Gunton Ave CV5 ...... **50** A2
Guphill Ave CV5 ...... **37** B2
Guphill La CV5 .... **37** B3
Gurney Cl CV4........ **35** C3

Gutteridge Ave CV6..... **20** A2
Guy Rd CV8........... **74** B2
Gypsy La CV8........... **74** B2

H

Haddon End CV3 .... **48** C2
Haddon St CV6 .... **31** B4
Hadfield Cl CV23 .... **87** B3
Hadleigh Rd CV3 .... **60** A4
Hadrians Way CV21..... **79** A1
Haig Ct CV22 .... **89** B3
Hales Park Ind Est CV6 . **21** B4
Hales St CV1 .... **96** C3
Halford La CV6 .... **20** A2
Halford Lodge CV6 ..... **20** A2
Halfway La CV22...... **93** C1
Halifax Cl CV5 .... **27** B3
Hallam Rd CV6 .... **20** B2
Hallams Cl CV8........ **53** A1
Hall Brook Rd CV6 .... **20** A4
Hall Cl CV8........... **69** C2
Hall Dr CV8........... **60** C3
HALL GREEN **22** A3
Hall Green Rd CV2, CV6.. **22** B2
Hall La CV2........... **33** A2
Hallway Dr CV7........ **17** B2
Hamilton Cl CV12......**4** C1
Hamilton Ct CV1....... **96** B4
Hamilton Rd CV2 ...... **40** B3
Hamlet Cl CV22....... **94** B4
Hammersley St CV12 ....**5** B1
Hammond Rd CV2..... **40** A4
Hammonds Terr CV8.... **66** B1
Hampden Way CV22 .... **88** C1
Hampshire Cl CV3 .... **51** A4
Hampton Cl CV6....... **31** A2
Hampton Rd CV6 ...... **31** A2
Hanbury Rd CV12.......**6** C4
Hancock Gn CV4...... **45** A4
Handcross Gr CV3 ..... **47** B1
Handley's Cl CV8 ...... **63** B1
Handsworth Cres CV5 . . **35** C4
Hanford Cl CV6........ **30** C2
Hanford Close Ind Est
CV6 .... **30** C2
Hanover Gdns CV21..... **85** C2
Hans Cl CV2........... **40** A4
Hanson Way CV6 ...... **22** A4
Hanwood Cl CV5....... **35** B4
Harborough Rd
  Coventry CV6 .... **20** B2
  Rugby CV23.......... **78** A2
Harbourne Cl CV8 ...... **67** B1
Harcourt CV3.......... **50** C1
Hardwick Cl CV5 ...... **36** B4
Hardwyn Cl CV3 .... **42** B1
Hardy Cl CV22......... **88** C4
Hardy Rd CV6 .... **29** B4
Harebell Way CV23 .... **80** B2
Harefield Ho CV2 ...... **40** C3
Harefield La CV12 ......**2** B4
Harefield Rd CV12 ..... **40** C3
Harewood Rd CV5 ..... **37** A2
Harger Ct CV8......... **74** B4
Harger Mews CV8 ..... **74** B4
Hargrave Cl CV3........ **42** B1
Harington Rd CV6 ..... **29** B1
Harlech Cl CV8 .... **68** A1
Harley St CV2 .... **96** B4
Harlow Wlk 8 CV2 .... **33** B3
Harmer Cl CV2 .... **33** B3
Harnall Ind Est CV1..... **96** C4
Harnall La CV1 .... **96** C4
Harnall La E CV1....... **39** C4
Harnall La W CV1...... **96** C4
Harnall Row
  Coventry CV1 .... **39** C2

Harnall Row continued
  Coventry CV1 .... **39** C3
Harold Cox Pl CV22 .... **94** C3
Harold Rd CV2......... **41** B2
Harpenden Dr CV5...... **27** B1
Harper Rd CV1 .... **39** C2
Harrington Ct CV3..... **42** A2
Harrington Way CV10....**2** C3
Harris Dr CV22 .... **89** C2
Harrison Cl CV21...... **92** B2
Harrison Cres CV12......**6** A2
Harris Rd CV2 .... **40** C2
Harris Sch CV22........ **89** C3
Harrow Cl CV6......... **22** A4
Harry Caplan Ho CV5 .. **27** C2
Harry Edwards Ho 2
CV2................... **32** B4
Harry Rose Rd CV2 .... **41** C3
Harry Salt Ho CV1 ..... **96** D3
Harry Stanley Ho CV6... **31** B4
Harry Truslove Cl CV6.. **29** B3
Harry Weston Rd CV3... **42** B1
Hart Cl CV21.......... **91** A4
Hartington Cres CV5.... **38** A1
Hartland Ave CV2 ..... **31** C1
Hartlepool Rd CV1..... **96** D4
Hartridge Wlk CV5..... **36** C4
Harvesters Cl CV3 ..... **42** B2
Harvey Cl CV5 .... **27** B3
Harvon Garth CV21 .... **86** A2
Haselbech Rd CV3 ..... **42** A1
Haseley Rd CV2........ **22** C1
Hasilwood Sq CV3 ..... **40** C2
Hastings Rd CV2 ...... **40** B4
Haswell Cl CV22....... **90** C4
Hathaway Rd CV4...... **35** B1
Hatters Ct CV12 ....**7** A2
Havendale Cl CV6 ..... **29** C1
HAWKESBURY **14** C1
Hawkesbury Fields Sch
CV2................... **22** C3
Hawkesbury La CV2.... **15** A1
HAWKES END **18** B2
Hawkeshead CV21..... **80** B1
Hawkes Mill La CV5.... **18** B2
Hawkesworth Dr CV8.. **67** B2
Hawkins Cl CV22 ...... **89** B3
Hawkins Rd CV5....... **38** B2
Hawksworth Dr 1 CV1. **38** B2
Hawlands CV21........ **86** B4
Hawthorn Cl CV4...... **35** C1
Hawthorne Cl CV8 ..... **65** B4
Hawthorn La CV8 ..... **35** C1
Hawthorn Way CV22.... **88** B4
Haydock Cl CV6 .... **22** B4
Hayes Cl CV21........ **80** B1
Hayes Green Rd CV12... **13** C4
Hayes La CV7.......... **14** A4
Hay La CV1............ **97** C2
Haynestone Rd CV6.... **28** C2
Haynes Way CV21...... **79** A2
Hayton Gn CV4 .... **45** A4
Haytor Rise CV2........ **32** A3
Hayward's Gn CV6..... **29** B3
Hazel Gr CV12 ....**7** A3
Hazel Rd CV6.......... **22** B1
Hazelwood Cl CV22.... **94** A1
Hazlemere Cl CV5 ..... **36** C4
Headborough Rd CV2... **31** B1
Headington Ave CV6... **20** A2
Headlands The CV5 .... **37** B4
Healey Cl CV21........ **80** A1
Health Centre Rd CV4... **58** A4
Hearsall Comm CV5 ... **38** A2
Hearsall Com Prim Sch
CV5 .... **38** A2
Hearsall Ct CV4........ **37** B2
Hearsall La CV5 .... **38** A2

HEATH **94** A2
Heath Ave CV12 ....**5** B1
Heathcote Ct CV6..... **29** B3
Heathcote St CV6..... **29** B3
Heath Cres CV2....... **31** B2
Heather Cl CV22...... **89** B3
Heather Dr CV12.......**5** B2
Heather Rd
  Binley Woods CV3..... **52** B3
  Coventry CV2 .... **22** C2
Heathfield Rd CV5 .... **37** A2
Heath Green Way CV4 . **45** A2
Heath Rd
  Bedworth CV12........ **5** C1
  Coventry CV2 .... **40** B4
Heath The CV22....... **94** A2
Heath Way CV22...... **91** A2
Heckley Rd CV7 .... **14** A3
Heddle Gr CV6 .... **31** C4
Hedgefield Way CV4... **45** A4
Hedgerow Wlk CV6.... **20** B4
Heera Cl CV6......... **30** B4
Helen St CV6......... **31** A2
Hele Rd CV3.......... **48** B2
Helmdon Cl CV21...... **86** B4
Helvellyn Way CV21.... **80** B1
Hemingford Rd CV2 ... **33** B4
Hemsby Cl CV4....... **45** B3
Hemsworth Dr CV12 ....**8** B2
Henderson Cl CV5 ..... **28** A3
Hendre Cl CV5........ **37** B2
Hen La CV6........... **21** A3
Henley Coll CV2 ...... **32** A4
Henley Ct CV2........ **32** B3
HENLEY GREEN **32** B4
Henley Mill La CV2.... **32** A3
Henley Park Ind Est
CV2................... **32** C3
Henley Rd CV2 .... **32** B3
Henley Wlk CV2 ...... **32** B4
Henrietta St CV6 ..... **30** C1
Henry Boteler Rd CV4... **45** C3
Henry Hinde Inf Sch
CV22................. **88** C3
Henry Hinde Jun Sch
CV22................. **88** B4
Henry St
  Coventry CV1 .... **96** B3
  Kenilworth CV8....... **67** B1
  Rugby CV21.......... **85** B1
Henson Rd CV12.......**5** B1
Hepworth Rd CV3 ..... **42** C1
Herald Ave CV5....... **37** B1
Herald Bsns Pk CV3 ... **51** A3
Herald Way CV3 ...... **51** B3
Herbert Art Gall & Mus★
CV1................... **97** C2
Herbert Gray Coll CV21. **85** B1
Herbert's La CV8 ...... **67** B1
Hereward Coll CV4 .... **36** A1
Heritage Ct
  Coventry CV4 .... **58** B3
  Kenilworth CV8....... **67** C3
Heritage Dr CV6....... **14** C2
Hermes Cres CV2...... **32** C2
Hermitage Rd CV2..... **41** B4
Hermitage Way CV8.... **74** C3
Hermit's Croft CV3 .... **48** B4
Heronbank CV4 .... **35** A2
Heron Ho CV1 .... **40** C2
Herrick Rd CV2........ **41** B3
Hertford Pl CV1....... **97** A2
Hertford St CV1....... **97** B2
Heslop Cl CV3......... **51** A4
Hewitt Ave CV6....... **38** C4
Hexby Cl CV2......... **33** B2
Hexworthy Ave CV3.... **47** C1
Heybrook Cl CV2 ..... **32** A3

Heycroft CV4 .... **58** B4
Heyford Cl CV2 .... **23** A3
Heyford Leys CV22..... **95** A4
Heyville Croft CV8 .... **75** B3
Heywood Cl CV6...... **31** B3
Hibberd Ct CV8....... **74** B4
Hibbert Cl CV22 ...... **90** A3
Hidcote Rd CV8 ...... **68** A2
High Ash Cl CV7 ..... **13** C3
High Beech CV5 ...... **27** B2
Highfield Cl CV8...... **74** A4
Highfield Rd CV2 ..... **40** A4
Highgrove
  Coventry CV4 .... **45** A1
  Rugby CV22.......... **89** A1
Highland Rd
  Coventry CV5 .... **38** A1
  Kenilworth CV8....... **68** A3
High Park Cl CV5 ..... **36** A3
High St
  Bedworth CV12........ **6** B2
  Coventry CV1 .... **97** C2
  Coventry, Keresley CV6 .. **19** C3
  Kenilworth CV8....... **66** C1
  Rugby CV21.......... **85** B1
  Rugby, Hillmorton CV21 .. **92** A2
  Ryton-on-D CV8 ...... **63** C1
High View Dr CV7...... **12** C3
Highwaymans Croft
CV4................... **46** B1
Hilary Rd CV4 .... **46** C2
Hillary Rd CV22....... **89** C2
Hill Farm Prim Sch CV6 **29** C3
Hillfield Rd CV22 ..... **88** C3
HILLFIELDS **39** C4
Hillfields Ho 1 CV1... **39** C3
Hill Fray Dr CV3 ...... **49** B1
Hilliard Cl CV2........ **33** B2
Hillman Ho CV1 ...... **96** B3
HILLMORTON **92** B2
Hillmorton La CV23.... **87** B2
Hillmorton Prim Sch
CV21................. **92** B2
Hillmorton Rd
  Coventry CV2 .... **22** C1
  Rugby CV22.......... **90** C4
Hill Rd CV7........... **11** C2
Hill Side CV2 .... **31** B2
Hillside N CV2 .... **31** B2
Hill St
  Bedworth CV12........ **3** A1
  Coventry CV1 .... **96** B3
  Rugby CV21.......... **85** B2
Hill Top CV1 .... **96** C3
Hilton Ct CV5......... **38** A2
Himley Rd 2 CV12......**5** A2
Hinckley Rd
  Ansty CV2, CV7....... **24** C2
  Coventry CV2 .... **33** B4
Hinde Cl CV21........ **80** A1
Hipswell Highway CV2... **41** B3
Hiron Croft CV3 ...... **48** A4
Hiron The CV3........ **48** A4
Hirst Cl CV23......... **83** B3
Hobley Cl CV22....... **89** A1
Hockett St CV3 ...... **48** B4
Hocking Rd CV2 ...... **41** C4
HOCKLEY **35** A4
Hockley La CV5....... **26** A1
Hodnet Cl CV8........ **67** C1
Hogarth Cl CV12......**6** A4
Holbein Cl CV12......**6** A4
Holborn Ave CV6...... **20** C4
Holbrook Ave CV21.... **85** C2
Holbrook La CV6 ...... **21** A2

Holbrook Park Est CV6 . **30** B4
Holbrook Prim Sch CV6 **21** B1
Holbrook Rd CV23 . . . . . **83** C3
HOLBROOKS **20** C3
Holbrook Way CV6. . . . . . **21** A1
Holcot Leys CV22 . . . . . . **90** A1
Holland Rd CV6. . . . . . . **29** B2
Hollies The CV23. . . . . . . **81** A3
Hollis La CV8 . . . . **66** C4
Hollis Rd CV3. . . . . **40** B2
Holloway Field CV6. . . . **29** B2
Hollow Cres CV6. . . . . . **29** C1
Hollowell Way CV21 . . . . **80** A1
Holly Bank CV5. . . . . . . **47** B4
Hollybush La CV6. . . . . . **22** A4
Holly Dr CV8 . . . . **63** C1
Hollyfast La CV7. . . . . . **18** C4
Hollyfast Prim Sch CV6. **28** C3
Hollyfast Rd CV6 . . . . . . **28** C2
Holly Gr
  Church Lawford CV23. . . . **55** C2
  Coventry CV4 . . . . **36** C2
HOLLYHURST **15** C4
Hollyhurst CV12 . . . . **5** C1
Holly Marie Ct CV5 . . . . **38** A1
Holly Wlk CV8 . . . . **60** C2
Holmcroft CV2 . . . . **33** A4
Holme Cl CV21 . . . . **86** A4
Holmes Ct CV8 . . . . **67** A1
Holmes Dr CV5 . . . . **26** B1
Holmewood Cl CV8. . . . **67** C1
Holmewood Ct CV8. . . . **67** C1
Holmfield Rd CV2. . . . . . **40** C3
Holmsdale Rd CV6. . . . **30** C3
Holroyd Ho CV4 . . . . . . **36** A2
Holy Cross Ct CV2 . . . . . **41** C4
Holy Family RC Prim Sch
  CV6 . . . . **20** B3
Holyhead Rd CV5. . . . . . **28** C1
Holyoak Cl
  Bedworth CV12. . . . . **5** C1
  Rugby CV22. . . . . **88** C2
Holywell Cl CV4 . . . . . . **35** B1
Home Cl CV8 . . . . **72** A2
Home Farm CV8 . . . . . . **76** C3
Homeward Way CV13 . . **42** B1
Honeybourne Cl CV5. . . **36** C3
Honeyfield Rd CV1. . . . . **30** B1
Honeysuckle Cl CV23 . . **80** B2
Honeysuckle Dr CV2 . . **22** B2
Honiley Ct CV2 . . . . **23** A1
Honiley Way CV2 . . . . . . **23** A1
Honiton Rd CV2 . . . . . . **32** A1
Hood St CV1. . . . . **39** C3
Hood's Way CV22 . . . . . . **89** A4
Hope Cl CV7. . . . . **12** A3
Hopedale Cl CV2 . . . . . . **41** C3
Hope St CV1. . . . . **38** C2
Hopkins Rd CV6 . . . . . . **38** B4
Hopton Cl CV5. . . . . . . **36** B4
Hornbeam Dr CV4 . . . . . **35** B1
Hornchuch Close Ind Est
  CV1 . . . . **97** B1
Hornchurch Cl CV1 . . . . **97** B1
Horndean Cl CV6. . . . . . **30** C4
Horne Cl CV21. . . . . **92** B2
Horninghold Cl CV3 . . . **50** C4
Hornsey Cl CV2. . . . . . . **32** C3
Horse Shoe Rd CV6. . . . **22** A4
Horsford Rd CV3 . . . . . . **48** C2
Horton Cl CV7. . . . . **13** C3
Horton Cres CV22. . . . . **90** B4
Hosiery St CV12 . . . . **6** C2

Hoskyn Cl CV21. . . . . . . **91** C2
Hospital La CV12 . . . . **4** B1
Hospital of St Cross
  CV22 . . . . **90** B3
Hotchkiss Way CV3 . . . . **51** B3
Hothorpe Cl CV3 . . . . . . **42** A1
Houldsworth Cres CV6. . **20** C4
Houston Rd CV21. . . . . . **86** A4
Hove Ave CV5 . . . . **35** C4
Hovelands Cl CV2. . . . . . **32** A4
Howard Cl
  Coventry CV5 . . . . **35** C4
  Dunchurch CV22. . . . . **94** B2
Howard St CV1 . . . . **96** C4
Howat Rd CV7. . . . . **11** C3
Howcotte Gn CV4. . . . . . **44** C4
Howells Cl CV12 . . . . **5** A1
Hudson Rd CV22. . . . . . **89** B3
Hugh Rd CV3 . . . . **40** B2
Hulme Cl CV3 . . . . **42** C1
Humber Ave CV1 . . . . . . **40** A1
Humber Rd CV3 . . . . . . **49** B4
Humberstone Rd CV6
  CV6 . . . . **29** B1
Humphrey Burton's Rd
  CV3 . . . . **48** A4
Humphrey-Davy Rd
  CV12 . . . . **13** A4
Hunters Cl CV3 . . . . **42** B2
Hunters La CV21. . . . . . . **85** B3
Hunters Lane Ind Est
  CV21 . . . . **85** B3
Hunter St CV21 . . . . **86** A2
Hunter Terr CV5 . . . . . . **46** B4
Huntingdon Rd CV5. . . . **47** B4
Hunt Paddocks CV8 . . . . **74** A1
Hunt Terr CV4 . . . . **45** C3
Hurn Way CV6. . . . . **22** B4
Hurst Rd
  Bedworth CV12. . . . . **6** B3
  Coventry CV6 . . . . **22** A4
Hurst Wlk CV6 . . . . **22** A4
Hyde Rd
  Coventry CV2 . . . . **41** C4
  Kenilworth CV8. . . . . **67** B1
Hypericum Gdns CV2 . . **41** A4

Ibex Cl CV3. . . . . **42** A1
Ibstock Rd CV6 . . . . **14** A1
Iden Rd CV1. . . . . **39** C4
Ilam Pk CV8. . . . . **68** A1
Ilford Cl CV12. . . . . **6** A3
Ilford Ct CV3 . . . . **52** B3
Ilford Dr CV3 . . . . **47** C1
Ilfracombe Gr CV3. . . . . **47** B1
Ilmer Cl CV21. . . . . **80** C1
Ilmington Cl CV3 . . . . . . **47** C1
Inca Cl CV3. . . . . **51** A4
Inchbrook Rd CV8. . . . . . **68** A3
Inchcape Cl CV22. . . . . . **88** B2
Ingram Rd CV5 . . . . **46** B4
Innis Rd CV3 . . . . **46** C4
Instone Rd CV6 . . . . **20** A1
Inveraray Cl CV8. . . . . . **75** B4
Inverness Cl CV5. . . . . . **36** B4
Invicta Rd CV3. . . . . **51** A4
Ireton Cl CV4 . . . . **35** A1
Ironbridge Way CV6 . . . **14** B2
Ironmonger Row CV1. . . **96** B3
Irving Rd CV1. . . . . **39** C2
Isambard Dr CV6 . . . . . . **13** C1

Ivor Rd CV6 . . . . **21** C2
Ivybridge Rd CV3 . . . . . . **48** B2
Ivy Farm La CV4 . . . . . . **46** B2

Jacker's Rd CV2 . . . . **22** B4
Jacklin Dr CV3 . . . . **60** A4
Jackson Cl CV7. . . . . **12** A3
Jackson Gr CV8 . . . . **75** B4
Jackson Rd
  Coventry CV6 . . . . **21** A1
  Rugby CV21. . . . . **92** A3
Jackwood Gn CV12 . . . . **12** C4
Jacob Dr CV4 . . . . **46** B2
Jacox Cres CV8. . . . . . . **68** A1
Jacquard Cl CV3. . . . . . . **60** B4
Jacquard Ho **3** CV1 . . . **39** C4
Jade Cl CV1 . . . . **96** D4
Jamescroft CV3 . . . . . . **50** C2
James Ct **4** CV21. . . . . . **85** C1
James Galloway Cl CV3. . **50** C3
James Green Rd CV4 . . . **36** A2
James Ho CV2. . . . . **32** A4
James St CV21 . . . . **85** C1
James Wlk **6** CV21. . . . . **85** C1
Jardine Cres CV4 . . . . . . **36** A2
Jasmine Gr CV8 . . . . . . **50** A4
Jedburgh Gr CV3 . . . . . . **59** B4
Jeffrey Cl CV12 . . . . **13** A4
Jeffrey Woods Cross
  CV1 . . . . **40** A4
Jeliff St CV1 . . . . **36** A2
Jenkins Ave CV5. . . . . . **36** A4
Jenkins Rd CV21. . . . . . . **92** A3
Jenner St CV1. . . . . **96** C4
Jephcott Ho **2** CV1. . . . **39** C3
Jephson Ct CV2 . . . . . . **22** C4
Jerome Ct CV21 . . . . . . **86** A1
Jesmond Rd CV1 . . . . . . **40** A4
Jim Forrest Cl **4** CV3 . . . **51** A4
Joanna Dr CV3 . . . . **60** A3
Joan of Arc Ho CV3 . . . . **48** C2
Joan Ward St CV3 . . . . . **48** B4
Job's La CV4 . . . . **36** B2
Joe OBrien Cl CV3. . . . . **50** A2
Joe Williams Cl **7** CV3. . **51** A4
John Grace St CV3. . . . . **48** B4
John Gulson Prim Sch
  CV1 . . . . **30** B1
John Haynes Cl CV7 . . . **14** A3
John Knight Rd CV12 . . . . **3** A1
John McGuire Cres CV3. **50** C2
John Nash Sq CV4 . . . . . **74** B3
John of Gaunt Ho CV3 . . **48** C2
John O'Gaunt Rd CV8 . . . **74** A3
John Rous Ave CV4 . . . . **45** C3
John Shelton Com Prim
  Sch CV6 . . . . **21** A4
John Shelton Dr CV6 . . . **21** A4
John Simpson Cl CV8. . . **65** B3
John Sinclair Ho CV1 . . . **96** B4
Johnson Ave CV22. . . . . **89** B4
Johnson Rd
  Bedworth CV12. . . . . **6** C3
  Coventry CV6 . . . . **31** B4
John St CV12. . . . . **6** A2
John Thwaites Cl CV22. . **90** A4
John Tofts Ho CV1 . . . . . **96** B4
Jonathan Rd CV2 . . . . . . **33** A4
Jones Rd CV7 . . . . **6** A1
Jordan Cl CV3. . . . . **75** A2
Jordans The CV5 . . . . . . **37** A4
Jordan Well CV1. . . . . . . **97** C2
Joseph Cash Prim Sch
  CV6 . . . . **30** A3
Joseph Creighton Cl
  CV3 . . . . **50** C3

Joseph Halpin Ho **3**
  CV1 . . . . **96** C4
Joseph Latham Ho **3**
  CV2 . . . . **22** B1
Joseph Luckman Rd
  CV12 . . . . **6** B4
Joyce Way CV22 . . . . . . **88** A2
Jubilee Cres CV6 . . . . . . **29** C3
Jubilee St CV21 . . . . . . **84** C2
Jubilee Terr CV12. . . . . . . **6** B4
Judd Cl CV12 . . . . **5** C3
Judds La CV6. . . . . **21** B4
Judge Cl CV23. . . . . **83** B3
Judith Way CV22 . . . . . . **88** A2
Julian Cl CV22 . . . . **33** A4
Juliet Dr CV22 . . . . **94** B4
Junction One Ret Pk
  CV21 . . . . **85** C4
Junction St CV1 . . . . **97** A2
Junewood Cl CV21. . . . . **80** B1
Juniper Cl CV12 . . . . **5** B2
Juniper Dr CV5 . . . . **27** A1

Kalfs Dr CV22. . . . . **88** B2
Kanzan Rd CV2 . . . . **22** B4
Kareen Gr CV3 . . . . **52** A3
Karlingford Cl CV5. . . . . **46** B4
Kathleen Ave CV12. . . . . . **5** B1
Kay Cl CV3 . . . . **80** A1
Keats Rd CV2. . . . . **41** B2
Kebull Gn CV4 . . . . **44** C4
Keeling Rd CV8. . . . . . . **67** C1
Keenan Dr CV12 . . . . **5** A1
Keepers Wlk CV12 . . . . . . **5** A1
Kegworth Cl CV6 . . . . . . **22** A4
Kele Rd CV4 . . . . **45** B3
Kelmscote Rd CV6. . . . . **29** A4
Kelsey's Cl CV8. . . . . . . **65** A3
Kelvin Ave CV2 . . . . **32** B1
Kelway CV3 . . . . **42** B2
Kempley Ave CV2 . . . . . **41** A2
Kendal Rise CV5. . . . . . . **37** A4
Kenderdine Montessori
  Sch CV5. . . . . **47** B4
Kendon Ave CV6. . . . . . **28** C2
Kendrick Cl CV6 . . . . . . **22** A4
Kenelm Ct CV3 . . . . **50** A1
Kenilcourt CV8 . . . . **66** B2
KENILWORTH **68** B1
Kenilworth Castle ★
  CV8 . . . . **66** B1
Kenilworth Ct CV3. . . . . **48** A4
Kenilworth Hall Mews
  CV8 . . . . **67** A1
Kenilworth Rd
  Coventry CV4 . . . . **58** C3
  Kenilworth CV8. . . . . **68** A4
Kenilworth Sch CV8 . . . **68** A1
Kenilworth Sch Castle Hall
  Sixth Form CV8 . . . . . . **74** B2
Kennedy Dr CV22 . . . . . **88** C4
Kennet Cl CV2 . . . . **32** A4
Kenpas Highway CV3 . . . **47** B1
Kensington Ct CV5. . . . . **38** B1
Kensington Rd CV5 . . . . **38** B1
Kent Cl CV3 . . . . **48** C2
Kenthurst Cl CV5 . . . . . . **35** A4
Kentmere Ct CV2 . . . . . . **23** B2
Kent The CV21. . . . . **92** A4
Kenwyn Gn CV7 . . . . . . **14** B4
Keppel Cl CV22 . . . . **88** C3
Keppel St CV1 . . . . **30** C1
KERESLEY **11** C1
Keresley Brook Rd CV6 . . **20** A2
Keresley Cl CV6 . . . . **20** A2

Keresley Grange Prim Sch
CV6 . . . . 19 C1
Keresley Green Rd CV6 . 19 C1
Keresley Newland Prim
Sch CV7 . . . . 11 C3
KERESLEY NEWLANDS
. . . . 12 B2
Keresley Rd CV6 . . . . 29 B4
Kerris Way CV3 . . . . 42 B1
Kerry's Ho **4** CV1 . . . . . 38 C2
Kestrel Croft **2** CV3 . . 51 A4
Keswick Dr CV1 . . . . 80 A2
Keswick Wlk CV2 . . . . 42 A4
Keviliok St CV3 . . . . 48 B2
Kew Cl CV8 . . . . 68 A1
Kew Ho CV4 . . . . 36 A3
Kew Rd CV21 . . . . 85 C2
Keyes Dr CV22 . . . . 88 C4
Kilburn Dr CV5 . . . . 38 A3
Kildale Cl CV1 . . . . 96 D3
Kilderkin Ct CV1 . . . . 97 C1
Kilsby La CV21 . . . . 92 C1
Kilworth Rd CV21 . . . . . . 92 B1
Kimberley Cl CV5 . . . . . . 36 A4
Kimberley Rd
  Baginton CV8 . . . . 61 A2
  Bedworth CV12 . . . . 6 C4
  Rugby CV21 . . . . 85 C2
Kimble Cl CV5 . . . . 36 C4
Kineton Rd
  Coventry CV2 . . . . 32 A2
  Kenilworth CV8 . . . . 75 B4
King Edward Rd
  Coventry CV1 . . . . 40 A4
  Rugby CV21 . . . . 85 C2
Kingfield Ind Est CV1 . . . 30 A2
Kingfield Rd CV1, CV6 . . . 30 B3
King George's Ave
  Bedworth CV12 . . . . 3 A1
  Coventry CV6 . . . . 21 C2
King George's Ct CV23 . . 83 B3
King Henry VIII Sch
CV3 . . . . 97 A1
King Richard St CV2 . . . . 40 A3
Kingsbury Rd CV6 . . . . . . 28 C1
Kingscote Gr CV3 . . . . . . 59 B4
Kingsford Rd CV6 . . . . . . 30 A3
Kings Gdns CV12 . . . . 6 C2
Kings Gr CV2 . . . . 40 C3
King's Hill La CV3 . . . . . . 59 C2
Kingsholm Cl CV3 . . . . . . 42 C1
Kingsland Ave CV5 . . . . . 38 A2
Kingsley Ave CV21 . . . . . 91 C3
Kingsley Cres CV12 . . . . . . 8 B3
Kingsley Ct CV3 . . . . 52 B2
Kingsley Orch CV21 . . . . . 91 B3
Kingsley Terr CV2 . . . . . . 32 C4
Kingsley Wlk CV2 . . . . . . 33 A3
Kingsmead Mews CV3 . . 50 B2
Kings Newnham La
CV23 . . . . 54 C4
Kings Newnham Rd
CV23 . . . . 55 C3
Kings Park Dr CV3 . . . . . . 42 C1
King St
  Bedworth CV12 . . . . 6 C2
  Rugby CV21 . . . . 85 B2
Kingston Ho CV12 . . . . . . 12 C4
Kingston Rd CV5 . . . . 38 A2
Kingsway
  Coventry CV2 . . . . 40 B3
  Rugby CV22 . . . . 90 A3
Kingsway Ho CV12 . . . . . . 6 C2
Kingswood Ave CV7 . . . . 10 B4
Kingswood Cl CV6 . . . . . . 21 A1
King William St CV1 . . . . 39 C4
Kinman Way CV21 . . . . . . 86 A4
Kintyre The CV2 . . . . 33 C3

Kinver Cl CV2 . . . . 23 B1
Kipling Rd CV6 . . . . 29 B4
Kirby Cl
  Brandon CV8 . . . . 53 A1
  Coventry CV1 . . . . 30 B2
Kirby Cnr CV4 . . . . 45 C1
Kirby Corner Rd CV4 . . . . 45 C2
Kirby Rd CV5 . . . . 38 A2
Kirkby Cl CV21 . . . . 86 C4
Kirkby Rd CV21 . . . . 91 C3
Kirkdale Ave CV6 . . . . . . 21 A3
Kirkstone CV21 . . . . 80 B1
Kirkstone Rd CV12 . . . . 6 A2
Kirton Cl CV6 . . . . 19 C1
Kitchener Rd CV6 . . . . . . 30 C4
Knight Ave CV1 . . . . 39 C1
Knightlow Ave CV3 . . . . . 50 A2
Knightlow Cl CV8 . . . . . . 75 B3
Knightsbridge Ave CV12 . 6 C4
Knights Templar Way
CV4 . . . . 36 B1
Knoll Croft CV3 . . . . 48 A2
Knoll Dr CV3 . . . . 48 A2
Knotting Way CV3 . . . . . . 41 A1
Knowle Hill CV8 . . . . 68 A2
Kwikform Bldg CV6 . . . . 21 B4
Kynner Way CV3 . . . . 51 C4

L

Laburnum Ave
  Coventry CV6 . . . . 29 A1
  Kenilworth CV8 . . . . 74 C4
Laburnum Cl CV12 . . . . 5 B2
Laburnum Gr CV22 . . . . . 89 B2
Ladbrook Rd CV5 . . . . . . 36 B4
LADYES HILLS 67 B3
Ladyfields Way CV6 . . . . 20 B4
Lady La
  Coventry CV6 . . . . 21 C4
  Kenilworth CV8 . . . . 74 B4
Lady Lane Mobile Home Pk
CV6 . . . . 21 C4
Ladymead Dr CV6 . . . . . . 20 B2
Ladysmock CV23 . . . . . . 80 B2
Lady Warwick Ave CV12 . . 7 A2
Lakeside CV12 . . . . 6 A2
Lake View Rd CV5 . . . . . . 38 A4
Lambeth Cl CV2 . . . . 32 C3
Lambourne Cl CV5 . . . . . 36 B4
Lamb St CV1 . . . . 96 B3
Lamerton Cl CV2 . . . . 32 A2
Lammas Ct CV8 . . . . 65 B3
Lammas Ho **6** CV6 . . . 38 B4
Lammas Rd CV6 . . . . 38 A4
Lancaster Pl CV8 . . . . 74 A2
Lancaster Rd CV21 . . . . . 85 B2
Lanchester Rd CV6 . . . . . 29 C2
Lancia Cl CV6 . . . . 22 B4
Lancing Rd CV12 . . . . 8 C2
Lancut Hill CV23 . . . . . . 80 B3
Landseer Cl CV21 . . . . . . 92 B3
Laneside CV3 . . . . 50 C2
Langbank Ave CV3 . . . . . 50 B3
Langbay Ct CV2 . . . . 33 A2
Langdale Ave CV6 . . . . . . 21 A3
Langdale Cl CV21 . . . . . . 80 A1
Langley Croft CV4 . . . . . . 36 B2
Langlodge Rd CV6 . . . . . 20 B2
Langnor Rd CV2 . . . . 32 A2
Langton Cl CV3 . . . . 50 C4
Langton Rd CV21, CV22 . . 91 B3
Langwood Cl CV4 . . . . . . 45 C3
Lansbury Cl CV2 . . . . 32 C3
Lansdowne Cl CV12 . . . . . . 6 A3
Lansdowne Pl CV21 . . . . 91 A4
Lansdowne St CV2 . . . . . 40 A3
Lapworth Rd CV2 . . . . . . 22 C1

Larch Cl CV22 . . . . 88 B4
Larches The CV7 . . . . 14 B4
Larchfields CV8 . . . . 65 B4
Larch Tree Ave CV4 . . . . . 36 B2
Larchwood Rd CV7 . . . . . . 6 B1
Larkfield Way CV5 . . . . . . 27 B2
Larkin Cl CV12 . . . . 8 B3
Larkin Gr CV2 . . . . 33 A2
Larkspur CV23 . . . . 80 C2
Larkspur Ct CV12 . . . . . . 12 C4
Larkspur Gr **5** CV12 . . . 5 A2
Latham Rd CV5 . . . . 38 B2
Latimer Cl CV8 . . . . 74 B2
Lauderdale Ave CV6 . . . . 21 A3
Lauderdale Cl CV23 . . . . 83 C2
Laurel Cl CV2 . . . . 23 B2
Laurel Ct CV5 . . . . 38 A1
Laurel Dr CV22 . . . . 88 B3
Laurel Gdns CV22 . . . . . . 89 C2
Laurels The
  Bedworth CV12 . . . . 5 B2
  Coventry CV4 . . . . 47 A2
Lavender Ave CV6 . . . . . . 29 A1
Lavender Cl
  Bedworth CV12 . . . . 5 B1
  Rugby CV23 . . . . 80 C2
Lawford Cl CV3 . . . . 41 C1
Lawford La CV22 . . . . . . 88 B3
Lawford Rd CV21, CV22 . 84 C1
Lawley Cl CV4 . . . . 36 B2
Lawns The CV12 . . . . 4 C2
Lawrence Gdns CV8 . . . . 67 B2
Lawrence Rd
  Bedworth CV7 . . . . 14 A4
  Rugby CV21 . . . . 86 B1
Lawrence Saunders Rd
CV6 . . . . 29 C1
Lawrence Sheriff Sch
CV21 . . . . 85 C1
Lawrence Sheriff St
CV22 . . . . 90 A4
Lea Cres CV21 . . . . 84 B4
Leacrest Rd CV6 . . . . 20 A2
Leaf Ct CV3 . . . . 60 B4
Leafield Cl CV2 . . . . 33 A4
Leaf La CV3 . . . . 48 C1
Leagh Cl CV8 . . . . 67 C3
Lealholme Ct CV5 . . . . . . 47 A4
Leam Gr CV4 . . . . 46 B1
Leamington Rd
  Coventry CV3 . . . . 48 A2
  Kenilworth CV8 . . . . 75 A2
  Ryton-on-D CV8 . . . . 73 B4
Leas Cl CV12 . . . . 6 A3
Leasowe's Ave CV3 . . . . . 59 A4
Lea Wlk CV8 . . . . 63 C1
Leeder Cl CV6 . . . . 20 C2
Leeming Cl CV4 . . . . 46 A2
Lee The CV5 . . . . 37 A4
Le Hanche Cl CV7 . . . . . . 12 A3
Leicester Cswy CV1 . . . . 30 B1
Leicester Ct CV12 . . . . 8 C2
Leicester Rd
  Bedworth CV12 . . . . 6 B4
  Rugby CV21 . . . . 85 C4
  Shilton CV7 . . . . 17 C2
Leicester Row CV1 . . . . . 96 B4
Leicester St
  Bedworth CV12 . . . . 6 B3
  Bulkington CV12 . . . . 8 C2
Leigh Ave CV3 . . . . 60 A3
Leigh CE Prim Sch CV4 . 44 B4
Leigh Rd CV21 . . . . 79 A2
Leigh St **4** CV1 . . . . . . 39 C4
Leighton Cl CV4 . . . . 58 B2
Lennon Cl CV21 . . . . 92 C1
Lennox Cl CV3 . . . . 50 C2
Lenton's La CV2 . . . . 23 B4

Leofric St CV6 . . . . 29 B1
Leonard Parkins Ho
CV12 . . . . 9 A2
Leopold Rd CV1 . . . . 40 A4
Lesingham Dr CV4 . . . . . 35 C1
Lesley Souter Ho CV21 . 90 B4
Lestock Cl CV22 . . . . 88 C4
Letchlade Cl CV2 . . . . . . 32 A4
Leven Way CV2 . . . . 33 B4
Lever Rd CV21 . . . . 92 A3
Levy Cl CV21 . . . . 85 A1
Lewis Rd CV1 . . . . 30 B1
Leyburn Cl CV6 . . . . 21 B2
Leycester Rd CV8 . . . . . . 74 C2
Leyes La CV8 . . . . 68 A1
Leyland Rd
  Bulkington CV12 . . . . 8 B2
  Coventry CV5 . . . . 37 B4
Leyside CV3 . . . . 50 C1
Leys Rd CV21 . . . . 92 C1
Leys The CV23 . . . . 81 B3
Library Rd CV4 . . . . 45 C1
Lichen Gn CV4 . . . . 46 B1
Lichfield Rd CV3 . . . . 48 B4
Lifford Way CV3 . . . . 51 B3
Light La CV1 . . . . 96 B4
Lilac Ave CV6 . . . . 29 A1
Lilac Dr CV22 . . . . 88 B4
Lilac Rd CV12 . . . . 3 C1
Lilacvale Way CV4 . . . . . 46 B1
Lilley Cl CV6 . . . . 20 C2
Lillington Rd CV2 . . . . . . 23 A1
Limbrick Ave CV4 . . . . . . 36 B1
Limbrick Wood Prim Sch
CV4 . . . . 36 A3
Lime Gr
  Coventry CV4 . . . . 36 C2
  Kenilworth CV8 . . . . 74 C4
Limes The
  Bedworth CV12 . . . . 5 B2
  Coventry CV6 . . . . 28 C1
Limestone Hall La CV23 . 55 B1
Lime Tree Ave
  Coventry CV4 . . . . 36 B2
  Rugby CV22 . . . . 88 B1
LIME TREE PARK 36 B2
Linaker Rd CV3 . . . . 50 A1
Lincoln St CV1 . . . . 96 C4
Lincroft Cres CV5 . . . . . . 37 C4
Lindale CV21 . . . . 80 B2
Linden Lea CV12 . . . . 6 A3
Lindfield The CV3 . . . . . . 50 A4
Lindisfarne Dr CV8 . . . . . 75 B4
Lindley Rd
  Bedworth CV12 . . . . 5 A2
  Coventry CV3 . . . . 40 C3
Lindsey Cres CV3 . . . . . . 74 C1
Linford Wlk CV2 . . . . 23 C1
Lingfield Ct CV6 . . . . 22 B4
Links Rd CV6 . . . . 29 C4
Linnell Rd CV21 . . . . 91 C4
Linnet Cl
  Coventry CV3 . . . . 50 B1
  Rugby CV23 . . . . 80 A3
Linstock Way CV6 . . . . . 22 B4
Linwood Dr CV2 . . . . 23 C1
Lion Fields Ave CV5 . . . . 27 C2
Lismore Croft CV2 . . . . . 33 C3
Little Church St
  1 Coventry CV1 . . . . . 96 C4
  Rugby CV21, CV22 . . . . . 85 B1
Little Cryfield CV4 . . . . . 58 A2
Little Elborow St CV21 . . 85 B1
Little Farm CV3 . . . . 50 B1
Little Field CV2 . . . . 31 B1

Little Gr CV22 . . . . 90 C3
LITTLE HEATH 21 C1
Little Heath Ind Est CV6 22 A2
Little Heath Prim Sch
CV6 . . . . 21 C1
Little London La CV23. . . 81 B3
Little Park St CV1. . . . . . . 97 C2
Little Pennington St
CV21 . . . . 85 A1
Little South St CV1 . . . . . . 39 C1
Littlethorpe CV3. . . . . 50 B2
Littleton CI CV8 . . . . 67 B3
Livingstone Ave CV23 . . . 83 A2
Livingstone Rd CV6. . . . . . 30 C3
Liza Ct CV21. . . . . 80 A2
Lloyd Cres CV2 . . . . 41 C3
Lloyd Rd CV21. . . . . 86 A4
Loach Dr CV2. . . . . 22 B4
Loch St CV3 . . . . 41 A1
Locke CI CV6. . . . . 20 A1
Lockhart CI CV8 . . . . 74 C4
Lockhurst La CV6. . . . . . . 30 B3
Locks The CV21. . . . . 92 B3
Loder CI CV4 . . . . 36 A3
Lodge Rd
Coventry CV3. . . . . 40 C1
Rugby CV22. . . . . 85 C2
Logan Rd CV2 . . . . 32 C3
Lole CI CV6. . . . . 22 A4
Lollard Croft CV3 . . . . 48 B4
Lomsey CI CV4 . . . . 36 B1
London Rd
Coventry, Cheylesmore
CV3 . . . . 48 C4
Coventry, Willenhall CV3. . 49 C1
Ryton-on-D CV8 . . . . 63 C1
Long Close Ave CV5 . . . . . 27 C2
Longfellow Rd CV2 . . . . . . 41 A3
Longfield Ho CV6. . . . . . . 31 B4
LONGFORD 21 C1
Longford Park Prim Sch
CV6 . . . . 22 A3
Longford Rd
Bedworth CV7. . . . . 14 A2
Coventry CV6 . . . . 22 A4
Longford Sq CV6 . . . . 22 A4
Long Furlong CV22 . . . . . . 89 C1
Long Hassocks CV23. . . . 80 C3
Long La CV5, CV7. . . . . . . 19 A2
LONG LAWFORD 83 B2
Long Lawford Prim Sch
CV23 . . . . 83 C3
Longrood PI CV22 . . . . 89 A1
Longrood Rd CV22. . . . . . . 89 A1
Long St CV12. . . . . .9 A2
Longstock Rd CV23 . . . . . 80 B3
Longville Ct CV3. . . . . 49 B2
Longwood CI CV4. . . . . . . 45 A2
Lonscale Dr CV3. . . . . 47 C1
Lord Lytton Ave CV2 . . . . 41 B2
Lord St CV5 . . . . 38 A2
Lorenzo CI CV3 . . . . 50 B2
Loudon Ave CV6 . . . . 29 B1
Lovell CI CV7 . . . . 14 A4
Lovell Rd CV12 . . . . .6 A3
Loverock Cres CV21 . . . . 91 B4
Lowe Rd CV6 . . . . 20 A2
LOWER EASTERN GREEN
. . . . 36 B3
Lower Eastern Green La
CV5 . . . . 36 A4
Lower End CV8 . . . . 72 A2
Lower Ford St CV1. . . . . . . 96 D3
Lower Hillmorton Rd
CV21 . . . . 91 A4

Lower Holyhead Rd
CV1 . . . . 96 A3
Lower Ladyes Hills CV8 . . 67 B2
Lower Prec CV1 . . . . 96 B3
Lower Rd CV7 . . . . 16 C2
Lower St CV21. . . . . 92 B2
LOWER STOKE 40 B1
Loweswater Rd CV3 . . . . . 41 C1
Lowfield Rd CV3. . . . . 41 A1
Lowry CI CV12. . . . . .6 A4
Lowther St CV2. . . . . 40 A4
Loxley CI CV21. . . . . 23 A2
Loxley Ct CV2. . . . . 23 A2
Lucas Ct CV21. . . . . 85 C2
Lucerne CI CV2. . . . . 22 C3
Lucian CI CV2 . . . . 33 C3
Ludlow Rd CV5. . . . . 38 B2
Luff CI CV3 . . . . 49 C4
Lulworth Pk CV8. . . . . 68 A2
Lumsden CI CV2. . . . . 33 A4
Lunar CI CV4 . . . . 46 B1
Lunn Ave CV8 . . . . 74 A3
Lunt The ★ CV8 . . . . 60 C3
Lupton Ave CV3 . . . . 48 A3
Luscombe Rd CV2 . . . . . . 32 C4
Luther Way CV5 . . . . 36 A4
Lutterworth Rd CV2 . . . . . 32 A1
Lydford Cl CV2 . . . . 32 A3
Lydgate Ct CV12. . . . . .6 A4
Lydgate Rd CV6 . . . . 29 C1
Lymesy St CV3. . . . . 48 B3
Lymington CI CV6 . . . . . . 30 B4
Lymington Dr CV6 . . . . . . 14 B2
Lymore Croft CV2. . . . . . . 33 B4
Lynbrook Rd CV5 . . . . 46 B4
Lynchgate CI CV4. . . . . . . 46 A2
Lynchgate Ho CV4. . . . . . 46 A2
Lynchgate Rd CV4 . . . . . . 46 A2
Lyndale CI CV5 . . . . 37 A3
Lyndale Rd CV5. . . . . 37 A3
Lynden Ho CV5. . . . . 47 C4
Lyndhurst CI CV6 . . . . 14 B2
Lyndhurst Croft CV5 . . . . 35 A4
Lyndhurst Rd CV21 . . . . . 91 C3
Lyne Ho ■ CV7 . . . . 32 B4
Lyng CI CV5 . . . . 36 B4
Lyng Hall Sch CV2. . . . . . 32 A2
Lynmouth Rd CV2 . . . . . . 32 C4
Lynton Rd CV6. . . . . 21 C1
Lythalls La CV6. . . . . 21 B2
Lythalls Lane Ind Est
CV6 . . . . 21 B1
Lytham Rd CV22 . . . . 89 B3
Lyttleton CI CV3 . . . . 42 B1

M

MacAulay Rd
Coventry CV2 . . . . 41 B4
Rugby CV22. . . . . 89 B1
Macbeth CI CV22 . . . . 94 C4
MacDonald Rd CV2 . . . . . 41 B3
McDonnell Dr CV6, CV7. . 13 C2
Macefield CI CV2 . . . . 23 A2
Mackenzie CI CV5 . . . . . . 27 B3
McKinnell Cres CV21 . . . 91 B4
McMahon Rd CV12 . . . . . 13 B4
Madden PI CV22. . . . . 88 C4
Madeira Croft CV5. . . . . . 37 C2
Maffey Ct CV22 . . . . 90 A4
Magnet La CV22 . . . . 88 C2
Magnolia CI CV3. . . . . 47 C1
Magpie Ho CV5. . . . . 26 B1
Maguire Ind Est CV4. . . . 45 A4
Maidavale Cres CV3 . . . . 60 A4
Maidenhair Dr CV23 . . . . 80 B2
Main Rd CV7 . . . . 25 A3

Main St
Clifton u D CV23 . . . . 87 A3
Long Lawford CV23 . . . . . 83 B3
Newton CV23 . . . . 81 B3
Rugby CV22. . . . . 88 C2
Rugby, Newbold on A
CV21 . . . . 78 B1
Thurlaston CV23. . . . . 93 A1
Wolston CV8 . . . . 65 B4
Malam CI CV4 . . . . 36 B1
Mallory Way CV6 . . . . 21 B4
Mallow Croft CV12. . . . . . .5 B2
Mallow Way CV23. . . . . . . 80 A2
Malmesbury Rd CV6 . . . . 20 A3
Malthouse La CV6 . . . . . . 66 C2
Malvern Ave CV22 . . . . . . 91 A3
Malvern Ho CV5 . . . . 35 B4
Malvern Rd CV5 . . . . 38 A4
Manderley CI CV5 . . . . . . 26 A1
Mandrake CI CV6 . . . . 21 A4
Manfield Ave CV2. . . . . . . 33 B3
Manning Wlk ■ CV21. . . 85 B1
Mann's CI CV8 . . . . 73 C4
Manor Ct CV8 . . . . 67 B2
Manor Est CV8 . . . . 67 B2
Manor Hall Mews CV3 . . 50 B2
MANOR HOUSE 22 C2
Manor House CI CV21. . . 78 B1
Manor House Dr CV1 . . . 97 B2
Manor La CV23 . . . . 87 B4
Manor Park Prim Sch
CV3 . . . . 48 B3
Manor Rd
Coventry CV1 . . . . 97 B1
Kenilworth CV8. . . . . 67 A2
Rugby CV21. . . . . 85 C2
Manor Terr CV8. . . . . 67 B2
Manor View CV8. . . . . 65 A3
Manse CI CV7 . . . . .6 A1
Mansel St CV6. . . . . 30 C4
Mantilla Dr CV3 . . . . 47 B1
Maple Ave CV7 . . . . .6 B1
Maplebeck CI CV5 . . . . . . 38 B3
Maple Gr CV21 . . . . 85 B2
Maples The CV12 . . . . .5 B2
Mapleton Rd CV6. . . . . . . 29 A4
Maple Wlk CV6. . . . . 13 C1
Mapperley CI CV2 . . . . . . 33 B4
March Ct CV22 . . . . 90 A3
March Way CV3 . . . . 50 B3
Mardol CI CV2 . . . . 32 B3
Margaret Ave CV12 . . . . . .6 B3
Margeson CI CV2 . . . . 41 C2
Margetts CI CV8 . . . . 74 B4
Marie Brock CI CV4 . . . . . 36 C1
Marigold Wlk CV10 . . . . . .2 C1
Marina CI CV4 . . . . 44 C3
Marion Rd CV6 . . . . 30 B3
Market Cnr CV8 . . . . 61 A2
MARKET END 5 A2
Market End CI CV12. . . . . .4 C2
Market Mall ■ CV21. . . . 85 B1
Market PI CV21. . . . . 85 B1
Market St CV21. . . . . 85 C2
Market Way CV1. . . . . 97 B2
Marlborough Rd
Coventry CV2 . . . . 40 B3
Rugby CV22. . . . . 89 B2
Marlcroft CV3 . . . . 50 C1
Marler Rd CV4 . . . . 45 A3
Marlissa Dr CV6. . . . . 21 B2
Marlow CI CV5 . . . . 36 C4
Marlston Wlk CV5 . . . . . . 36 C4
Marlwood CI CV6. . . . . . . 21 C4
Marner Cres CV6 . . . . 29 C1
Marner Rd CV12. . . . . .6 A3
Marnhull CI CV2. . . . . 42 A4
Marriners La CV5. . . . . . . 27 C1

Marriott Rd
Bedworth CV12. . . . . 5 A2
Coventry CV6 . . . . 38 B4
Marshall Rd CV7. . . . . 13 C4
Marshbrook CI CV2. . . . . 23 B3
Marshdale Ave CV6. . . . . 21 B3
Marshfield Dr CV4. . . . . . 58 B2
Marsh Ho CV2. . . . . 33 B3
MARSTON 65 C4
Marston La CV12 . . . . .3 C1
Martin CI CV5 . . . . 35 C3
Martindale Rd CV7 . . . . . 14 C4
Martin La CV22 . . . . 89 A1
Martins Rd CV12. . . . . .5 B1
Martyrs' CI The CV3. . . . . 48 B4
Mary Herbert St CV3. . . . 48 B3
Mary Slessor St CV3 . . . . 50 B3
Marystow CI CV5 . . . . 27 C4
Mason Gr CV8. . . . . 67 C1
Mason Rd CV6. . . . . 21 C1
Masser Rd CV6 . . . . 21 A4
Matlock CI CV21. . . . . 80 A1
Matlock Rd CV1 . . . . 30 B2
Matterson Rd CV6. . . . . . 29 B1
Maudslay Rd CV5. . . . . . . 37 C2
Maureen CI CV4 . . . . 35 A1
Mavor Dr CV12 . . . . .5 A1
Mawnan CI CV7 . . . . 14 B4
Max Rd CV6 . . . . 29 A1
Maycock Rd CV6 . . . . 30 B3
Mayfield CI CV12 . . . . .6 B3
Mayfield Dr CV8. . . . . 75 B4
Mayfield Rd CV5. . . . . 38 B1
Mayflower Dr CV2 . . . . . . 41 C2
May La CV22 . . . . 89 A3
Maynard Ave CV12. . . . . . 13 A4
Mayo Dr CV8 . . . . 74 C4
Mayor's Croft CV4 . . . . . . 45 C3
May St CV6. . . . . 30 C4
Meadfoot Rd CV3 . . . . 50 C2
Meadow CI CV7 . . . . 25 A3
Meadowcroft CI CV4. . . . 45 A4
Meadow Ho ■ CV1 . . . . . 38 C3
Meadow Rd
Coventry CV6 . . . . 20 B4
Rugby CV21. . . . . 84 C4
Wolston CV8. . . . . 65 B4
Meadows Sch The CV4 . . 35 C3
Meadow St CV1 . . . . 97 A2
Meadowsweet CV23 . . . . 80 A2
Meadway CV2 . . . . 31 C2
Meadway N CV2 . . . . 31 C2
Medhurst CI CV22 . . . . . . 94 A1
Medina Rd CV6 . . . . 21 B1
Medland Ave CV3. . . . . . . 47 A1
Melbourne Ct ■ CV12 . . .5 C2
Melbourne Rd CV5 . . . . . 38 B2
Melfort CI CV3. . . . . 42 A2
Mellish Ct CV22 . . . . 89 B3
Mellish Rd CV22 . . . . 89 B3
Mellor Rd CV21. . . . . 92 B2
Mellowdew Rd CV2 . . . . . 41 A4
Mellowship Rd CV5. . . . . 26 B1
Melrose Ave CV12 . . . . . . 13 A4
Melville CI
Bedworth CV7. . . . . 14 A4
Rugby CV22. . . . . 89 B3
Melville Rd CV1 . . . . 38 B3
Mercer Ave CV2 . . . . 31 B1
Mercer Ct ■ CV22 . . . . . . 91 C2
Mercers Mdw CV7 . . . . . . 12 A2
Mercia Ave CV8 . . . . 74 B4
Mercia Bsns Village
CV4 . . . . 45 A2
Mercia Ho CV1 . . . . 96 B3
Meredith Rd CV2 . . . . 41 B2
Meriden St CV1. . . . . 38 C3
Merlin CI CV23 . . . . 80 A2

Merrivale Rd CV5...... 37 C3
Merryfields Way CV2 ... 23 C1
Mersey Rd CV12........8 A3
Merttens Dr CV22..... 89 C4
Meryton Ave CV4..... 46 C1
Meschines St CV3 .... 48 B2
Mews The
Bedworth CV12..........6 B2
Kenilworth CV8....... 74 A3
3 Rugby CV21........ 92 A3
Michaelmas Rd CV3 .... 97 B1
Michel Ho CV1 ...... 96 C4
Michell Cl CV3 ...... 49 C4
Mickleton Rd CV5 .... 47 B4
Middleborough Rd CV1. 96 A4
Middlecotes CV4 ...... 36 C1
Middlefield Dr CV3 .... 42 C1
Middlefield Dr CV3 .... 42 B1
Middlemarch Bsns Pk
CV3 .... 62 A2
Middlemarch Rd CV6... 30 A3
Middle Ride CV3....... 50 C1
MIDDLE STOKE 40 B3
Midland Air Mus★ CV8 . 61 C3
Midland Oak Trad Est
CV6 .... 21 B2
Midland Rd CV6 ...... 30 C1
Midland Trad Est CV21 . 85 B4
Milburn Hill Rd CV4.... 45 C2
Mile La CV1 .... 97 C1
Miles Mdw CV6........ 22 B1
Milestone Dr CV22..... 89 C2
Milestone Ho **2** CV1... 38 C2
Mile Tree La CV3..... 15 C3
Milford Cl CV5....... 27 C2
Millais Cl CV12 ....6 A4
Mill Bank Mews CV8.... 67 C2
Millbeck CV21....... 80 B1
Mill Cl
Coventry CV2 .... 22 B3
Wolston CV8......... 65 A3
MILL END 67 B2
Mill End CV8 .... 67 B2
Millennium Pl CV1..... 96 B3
Millennium Way CV8... 65 A3
Millers Cl CV22...... 93 B1
Miller's Cl CV22 ..... 93 B2
Millers Dale Cl CV21 .... 80 A1
Mill Farm Cl CV22 ..... 94 A1
Millfields Ave CV21 .... 91 C2
Mill Furlong CV23 .... 80 B3
Mill Hill CV8......... 60 B3
Millhouse Ct CV6 ..... 31 A3
Mill La
Bulkington CV12 ...... 8 A3
Clifton u D CV23 ..... 86 C3
Coventry CV3 .... 42 A2
Mill Rd CV21 .... 86 A3
Mill Race La CV6 ..... 22 B3
Mill St
Bedworth CV12...........6 B3
Coventry CV1 .... 96 A3
Mill Terr CV12 ....3 A1
Milner Cl CV3 ....9 A2
Milner Cres CV2 ..... 23 B1
Milrose Way CV4 .... 45 A4
Milton Cl CV12 ....7 A1
Milton St CV2 .... 40 B4
Milverton Rd CV2..... 23 A2
Minster Rd CV1...... 38 C3
Minton Rd CV3 ..... 23 B1
Miranda Cl CV3...... 50 B3
Mitchell Ave CV4 .... 45 B3
Mitchell Ct CV23 .... 80 A4
Mitchell Ho CV4 ..... 45 B3
Mitchell Rd CV12 ......6 C2
Moat Ave CV3 ...... 47 A1
Moat Cl CV8........... 72 A2

Moat Farm Dr
Bedworth CV12.......... 12 C4
Rugby CV21........ 92 A1
Moat House La CV4..... 46 A3
Moat House Prim Sch
CV2 .... 23 A1
Modbury CV12 ...... 48 B1
Molesworth Ave CV3... 40 B1
Momus Bvd CV2 ..... 41 A2
Monks Cl CV22 ..... 88 A2
Monk's Croft The CV3... 48 A3
Monks Field Cl CV4.... 36 B1
MONKS PARK 20 C1
Monks Rd
Binley Woods CV3..... 52 A3
Coventry CV1 .... 40 A2
Monkswood Cres CV2 .. 32 B4
Monmouth Cl
Coventry CV5 .... 36 C3
Kenilworth CV8....... 67 A2
Monnington Ho CV8.... 67 A2
Montague Rd CV22 .... 94 B3
Montalt Rd CV3....... 48 C3
Montgomery Cl CV3... 62 A4
Montgomery Dr CV22... 88 C3
Montjoy Cl CV3....... 50 B3
Montpelier Ho CV8 .... 67 A1
Montpellier Cl CV3 .... 48 A2
Montrose Rd CV22..... 90 A3
Moore Cl CV6 ...... 14 A1
Moorfield The CV3..... 49 C4
Moorings Bsns Pk The
CV6 .... 14 A2
Moorlands Ave CV8.... 74 B3
Moorlands Lodge CV8 .. 74 B3
Moors La CV23 ..... 92 C3
Moor St CV5.......... 38 A1
Moreall Mdws CV4 .... 58 B3
Morfa Gdns CV6...... 28 B1
Morgans Rd CV5...... 35 A4
Morland Cl CV12.......9 A2
Morland Rd CV6...... 20 C2
Morningside CV5..... 47 C4
Morris Ave CV2...... 41 B4
Morris Cl CV21 ..... 85 A4
Morson Cres CV21.... 91 B4
Mortimer Rd CV8..... 74 B2
Morton Cl CV6...... 20 A1
Morton Ct CV22 ..... 91 C2
Morton Gdns CV21.... 90 C4
Mosedale CV21....... 80 A1
Moseley Ave CV6 .... 38 B4
Moseley Prim Sch CV6 . 38 B4
Moseley Rd CV8 ..... 75 A3
Moss Cl CV22....... 89 B3
Mossdale Cl CV6 .... 29 C2
Moss Gr CV8 .... 67 C3
Mottistone Cl CV3 .... 48 B2
Moultrie Rd CV21, CV22.. 85 C1
Mountbatten Ave CV8... 75 B3
Mount Dr CV12 ....6 A3
Mount Field Ct CV1... 96 D4
Mount Gdns CV5 ..... 47 C4
Mount Nod Prim Sch
CV5 .... 36 B3
Mount Nod Way CV5... 36 C3
MOUNT PLEASANT
Bedworth...............6 B3
Coventry........... 33 C4
Mount Pleasant Cotts
CV2 .... 33 B3
Mount Pleasant Rd CV12..6 A3
Mount St CV5........ 38 A2
Mount The CV3...... 48 C4
Mowbray St CV2..... 40 A3
Moyeady Ave CV22.... 91 B2
Moyle Cres CV5 ..... 35 B4
Much Park St CV1 .... 97 C2

Mulberry Ct CV8...... 74 B4
Mulberry Rd
Coventry CV6 .... 31 B3
Rugby CV22........ 88 B4
Mulliner St CV6 ..... 31 A1
Murrayfield Way CV3 .. 42 C1
Murrayian Cl CV21.... 85 C1
Murray Rd
Coventry CV6 .... 29 B3
Rugby CV21........ 85 C2
Mus of British Road
Transport★ CV1 96 B3
Myers Rd CV22 ..... 92 C2
Mylgrove CV3 .... 60 B3
Myrtle Gr CV5 ...... 38 A1

N

Nailcote Ave CV4 ...... 44 A4
Napier St CV1 .... 39 C3
Napton Ct CV22...... 93 C4
Napton Gn CV5...... 36 B3
Narberth Way CV3 .... 33 A4
Nares Cl CV22 ..... 89 B3
Narrowboat Cl CV6 ... 14 B2
Naseby Cl CV3....... 51 A4
Naseby Rd CV22 .... 90 C3
Naul's Mill Ho CV1..... 96 B4
Navigation Way CV6.... 31 B4
Nayler Cl CV21 ..... 86 A4
Neal Ct CV2 .... 33 B4
Neale Ave CV5....... 27 B2
Neale Cl CV12 ....8 C1
NEAL'S GREEN 13 A1
Nelson St **7** CV1 .... 39 C4
Nelson Way CV22..... 88 C3
Nene Cl CV3....... 50 B3
Nethermill Rd **1** CV6.. 29 B1
Newall Cl CV23 ..... 86 C3
New Ash Dr CV5..... 27 A1
NEW BILTON 84 C1
New Bldgs CV1 ..... 96 C3
Newbold Cl CV3 .... 42 A1
NEWBOLD ON AVON ... 78 A1
Newbold Quarry Ctry Pk★
CV21 84 C4
Newbold Rd
Rugby CV21......... 85 B2
Rugby, Newbold on A
CV21 .... 85 A4
Newbold Riverside Prim
Sch CV21........... 84 C4
Newby Cl CV3....... 48 C2
New Century Pk CV3 ... 41 A2
New Combe Cl CV22.... 94 A1
Newcombe Rd CV5 ... 38 B1
Newcomen Cl CV12... 13 A4
Newcomen Rd CV12....5 A1
Newdegate Cl CV12.....6 A4
Newdegate Rd CV12.... 6 A3
Newdigate Prim Sch
CV12 .... 4 C1
Newdigate Rd CV6.... 31 A2
Newey Ave CV12..... 13 A4
Newey Dr CV8....... 74 C2
Newey Rd CV2...... 41 B4
Newfield Ave CV8..... 75 A3
Newfield Rd CV1..... 30 A1
New Gate Ct CV1..... 97 C2
New Green Pk CV2 ... 32 B3
Newhall Rd CV2...... 32 B3
Newhaven Cl CV6.... 28 C2
Newington Cl CV6.... 28 B2
Newland La CV7..... 12 B3
Newland Rd CV1..... 30 B1
Newlands Ct CV3 .... 40 A2
Newland St CV22 .... 84 C1
Newman Cl CV12 ....6 B4

Newmarket Cl CV6..... 22 B4
Newnham Rd CV1 .... 31 A1
Newport Rd CV6..... 21 A1
New Rd
Ash Green CV7 ..... 12 B2
Coventry CV6 ...... 19 C1
New St
Bedworth CV12.......... 6 C2
Bulkington CV12 ..... 9 A2
Kenilworth CV8...... 67 A2
Rugby CV22........ 84 C1
Newstead Way CV3 ... 42 C1
NEWTON 81 B3
Newton Cl CV2 ..... 33 A3
Newton Manor La CV21,
CV23 .... 80 C1
Newton Rd CV23..... 81 B1
Newtown Bldgs CV12....6 B3
Newtown Rd CV12.......6 A2
New Union St CV1 .... 97 B2
Nicholas Chamberlaine Tec
Coll CV12............. 7 A3
Nicholas Cl CV12 ....6 C3
Nicholas Everton Cl
CV8 .... 53 B1
Nicholls St CV2...... 40 A4
Nickson Rd CV4 .... 35 C1
Nightingale Gdns CV3 . 80 A3
Nightingale La CV5 ... 46 C3
Niven Cl CV5....... 27 B2
Noble Dr CV22...... 88 A2
Nod Rise CV5....... 36 C3
Nolan Cl CV6....... 21 A4
Nordic Drift CV2..... 33 B2
Norfolk St CV1 ..... 38 C3
Norman Ashman Coppice
CV3 .... 52 A3
Norman Ave CV2 .... 23 C1
Norman Place Rd CV6 .. 29 A3
Norman Rd CV21 .... 85 A4
Northampton La CV22 .. 94 B2
North Ave
Bedworth CV12........ 7 A2
Coventry CV2 .... 40 B3
North Brook Rd CV6 ... 28 B4
Northcote Rd CV21 .... 85 A1
Northey Rd CV6 ..... 30 B4
Northfield Rd CV1 .... 40 A2
Northfolk Terr CV4.... 45 C3
Northlands Prim Sch
CV21 .... 85 C2
North Rd CV23...... 87 A4
North St
Coventry CV2 .... 31 C1
Rugby CV21........ 85 B1
Northumberland Rd
CV1 .... 38 B3
Northvale Cl CV8 .... 67 C2
North View CV2...... 24 A1
Northway **2** CV21 .... 85 B1
Norton Grange CV5.... 28 A2
Norton Hill Dr CV2.... 32 C2
Norton Leys CV22..... 95 A4
Norton St CV1...... 96 C3
Norwich Dr CV3..... 47 C1
Norwood Gr CV2 .... 23 B2
Nova Croft CV5...... 35 A4
Nuffield Rd CV6..... 31 B3
Nuneaton Rd
Bedworth CV12.........6 B4
Bulkington CV12 ....8 B4
Nunts La CV6....... 20 B3
Nunts Park Ave CV6 ... 20 B4
Nutbrook Ave CV4 .... 35 C2

O

Oak Cl
Baginton CV8 . . . . **61** A2
Bedworth CV12 . . . . **6** C4
Oak Ct CV3 . . . . **49** A3
Oakdale Rd CV3 . . . . **52** A3
Oakey Cl CV6 . . . . **21** C4
Oakfield Ho CV3 . . . . **42** B1
Oakfield Prim Sch CV22 **89** C4
Oakfield Rd
Coventry CV6 . . . . **29** A1
Rugby CV22 . . . . **89** C1
Oakford Dr CV5 . . . . **27** A2
Oakham Cres CV12 . . . .**9** A2
Oaklands Ct CV8 . . . . **74** C2
Oaklands The CV4 . . . . **36** B2
Oakley Ct CV12 . . . .**5** A1
Oakmoor Rd CV6 . . . . **22** A4
Oaks Pl CV6 . . . . **22** A3
Oaks Prec CV8 . . . . **74** A3
Oaks Rd CV8 . . . . **74** A2
Oak St CV22 . . . . **90** A4
Oaks The CV2 . . . .**5** C2
Oak Tree Ave CV3 . . . . . . **47** B2
Oak Tree Rd CV3 . . . . **51** B3
Oak Way CV4 . . . . **35** B2
Oakworth Cl CV2 . . . . **33** A4
Oatlands Cl CV6 . . . . **20** C4
Oban Rd CV6 . . . . **13** C1
Oberon Cl CV22 . . . . **94** B4
Occupation Rd CV2 . . . . . **41** A3
Oddicombe Croft CV3 . . **48** B1
Offa Dr CV8 . . . . **74** C4
Okehampton Rd CV3 . . . **48** C1
Okement Gr CV23 . . . . **83** C3
Olaf Pl CV2 . . . . **33** B3
Old Church Rd CV6 . . . . . **22** A1
Old Crown Mews CV2 . . . **15** A1
Oldfield Rd CV5 . . . . **37** C3
Oldham Ave CV2 . . . . **41** C4
Oldham Way CV23 . . . . . . **83** C2
Old House La CV7 . . . . **10** A3
Old Leicester Rd CV21 . . **79** B1
Old Meeting Yd ⬛ CV12 . .**6** B3
Old Mill Ave CV4 . . . . **46** B1
Old Penn's Yd ⬛ CV12 . . .**6** A2
Old Winnings Rd CV7 . . **11** C2
Old Yd The CV3 . . . . **33** A3
Olive Ave CV2 . . . . **32** B1
Oliver St
Coventry CV6 . . . . **31** A2
Rugby CV21 . . . . **85** A1
Olivier Way CV2 . . . . **33** C4
Olton Ave CV5 . . . . **35** C4
Omar Rd CV2 . . . . **41** B2
Omega Pl CV21 . . . . **85** C2
Onley Terr CV4 . . . . **46** A3
Oratory Dr CV3 . . . . **50** A2
Orchard Cres CV3 . . . . . . **48** A4
Orchard Ct CV3 . . . . **42** B1
Orchard Dr CV5 . . . . **35** A4
Orchard Ho CV6 . . . . **22** A4
Orchard La CV8 . . . . **75** B3
Orchard Ret Pk CV3 . . . . **62** B4
Orchard St CV12 . . . .**6** B4
Orchards The CV23 . . . . . **81** A3
Orchard Way
Bubbenhall CV8 . . . . **72** B1
Rugby CV22 . . . . **89** A2
Orchid Cl CV12 . . . .**5** B2
Orchid Way CV23 . . . . **80** B2
Ordnance Rd CV6 . . . . **30** C1
Orion Cres CV2 . . . . **23** B2

Orlando Cl CV22 . . . . **94** B4
Orlescote Rd CV4 . . . . **46** C2
Orpington Dr CV6 . . . . . . **21** A4
Orson Leys CV22 . . . . **89** C1
Orton Rd CV6 . . . . **21** A4
Orwell Cl CV23 . . . . **87** B3
Orwell Ct CV1 . . . . **96** C4
Orwell Rd CV1 . . . . **40** A1
Osbaston Cl CV5 . . . . **35** C4
Osborne Rd CV5 . . . . **47** B4
Osbourne Ho CV1 . . . . . . **97** A2
Oslo Gdns CV2 . . . . **33** B3
Osprey Cl CV2 . . . . **33** C2
Oswald Way CV22 . . . . **84** B1
Oswin Gr CV2 . . . . **41** A4
Othello Cl CV22 . . . . **94** B3
Our Lady of the
Assumption RC Prim Sch
CV4 . . . . **35** C1
Outermarch Rd CV6 . . . . **30** A3
Oval Rd CV22 . . . . **91** A2
Overberry Cl CV22 . . . . . . **23** A2
Overdale Rd CV5 . . . . **37** A3
OVERSLADE **89** B2
Overslade Cres CV6 . . . . . **28** C4
Overslade La CV22 . . . . . . **89** B2
Overslade Manor Dr
CV22 . . . . **89** C2
Over St CV6 . . . . **31** B4
Owenford Rd CV6 . . . . **30** A3
Ox Cl CV2 . . . . **31** B2
Oxendon Way CV3 . . . . . . **50** C4
Oxford St
Coventry CV1 . . . . **39** C3
Rugby CV21 . . . . **86** A1
Oxley Dr CV3 . . . . **60** A3

P

Packington Ave CV5 . . . . **27** C2
Packwood Ave CV21 . . . . **92** C2
Packwood Gn CV5 . . . . . . **36** B3
Paddocks Cl CV8 . . . . **65** B3
Paddocks The
Bulkington CV12 . . . .**8** B3
Kenilworth CV8 . . . . **67** C1
Paddock The CV23 . . . . . . **81** B3
Paddox Cl CV22 . . . . **91** C2
Paddox Prim Sch
Rugby CV22 . . . . **91** A2
Rugby CV22 . . . . **91** B2
Padstow Rd CV4 . . . . **44** C4
Page Rd CV4 . . . . **44** C3
Paget Ct CV2 . . . . **22** B3
Paget's La CV8 . . . . **72** B1
Pailton Cl CV2 . . . . **22** C2
Pake's Croft ⬛ CV6 . . . . . **29** B1
Palermo Ave CV3 . . . . **48** C2
Palmer La CV1 . . . . **96** B3
Palmer's Cl CV21 . . . . **92** B2
Palmerston Rd CV5 . . . . . **47** A4
Palm Tree Ave CV2 . . . . . . **22** C2
Pancras Cl CV2 . . . . **23** B1
Pandora Rd CV2 . . . . **32** C3
Pangbourne Rd CV2 . . . . **32** A4
Pangfield Pk CV5 . . . . **37** A4
Pantolf Pl CV21 . . . . **78** C1
Papenham Gn CV4 . . . . . . **45** B4
Paradise **31** A2
Paradise Ho ⬛ CV6 . . . . . . **31** A3
Paradise St
Coventry CV1 . . . . **97** C1
Rugby CV21 . . . . **86** A1
Paradise Way CV2 . . . . . . **24** B1
Paradise Works CV1 . . . . **31** A3
Paragon Pk CV1 . . . . **30** B2
Paragon Way CV7 . . . . **14** B4
Parbrook Cl CV4 . . . . **44** C4

Parisienne Ho CV5 . . . . . **37** C2
Park Ave CV6 . . . . **20** C3
Park Cl CV8 . . . . **67** C1
Park Ct CV5 . . . . **27** C2
Parkend CV21 . . . . **80** A1
Park Farm Cl CV22 . . . . . **89** A4
Parkfield Dr CV8 . . . . **67** C1
Parkfield Rd
Keresley CV7 . . . . **12** A2
Rugby CV21 . . . . **84** C3
Parkgate Prim Sch CV6 . **20** B3
Parkgate Rd CV6 . . . . **20** C3
PARK HILL **68** A2
Park Hill CV8 . . . . **67** C1
Parkhill Dr CV5 . . . . **27** B1
Park Hill Jun Sch CV8 . . **68** A1
Park Hill La
Allesley CV5 . . . . **27** B2
Coventry CV5 . . . . **27** B1
Park Hill Prim Sch CV5 . **36** B4
Parkland CV6 . . . . **20** C3
Park Paling The CV3 . . . . **48** C3
Park Rd
Bedworth CV12 . . . .**6** B2
Coventry CV1 . . . . **97** B1
Kenilworth CV8 . . . . **67** B2
Rugby CV21 . . . . **85** B2
Parkside CV1 . . . . **97** C2
Park St CV6 . . . . **30** C3
Parkstone Rd CV6 . . . . . . **21** C2
Parkview CV5 . . . . **97** A1
Park View CV3 . . . . **40** B2
Park View CV7 . . . . **14** A4
Parkville Cl CV6 . . . . **20** C3
Parkville Highway CV6 . . **20** B3
Parkway CV2 . . . . **33** C4
Parkwood Ct CV8 . . . . **67** C1
Park Wood La CV4 . . . . . . **44** B3
Parnell Cl CV21 . . . . **85** A1
Parrotts Gr CV2 . . . . **15** A1
Parry Rd CV2 . . . . **32** A3
Parson's Nook CV2 . . . . . **31** B1
Partridge Croft CV6 . . . . **22** A1
Patricia Cl CV4 . . . . **35** A1
Patterdale CV21 . . . . **80** B1
Pattison Coll CV3 . . . . . . **40** B2
Pauline Ave CV6 . . . . **22** B2
Paul Stacy Ho CV1 . . . . . **96** D4
Pavilion Way CV5 . . . . . . **38** A3
Paxmead Cl CV6 . . . . **20** A2
Paxton Rd CV6 . . . . **38** B4
Paynell Cl CV6 . . . . **20** B2
Paynes La CV21 . . . . **84** B1
Payne's La CV1 . . . . **40** A3
Peacock Ave CV2 . . . . **23** C1
Pearl Hyde Com Prim Sch
CV2 . . . . **33** B1
Pearl Hyde Ho ⬛ CV1 . . **96** C4
Pears Cl CV8 . . . . **67** A1
Pearson Ave CV6 . . . . **22** B2
Pear Tree Cl ⬛ CV2 . . . . . **22** B2
Pear Tree Way CV22 . . . . . **88** B3
Peat Cl CV22 . . . . **89** B3
Pebblebrook Way CV12 . . .**6** C1
Pebworth Cl CV5 . . . . **36** C3
Peckstone Cl CV1 . . . . **97** C1
Peel Cl CV6 . . . . **30** C2
Peel La CV6 . . . . **31** A1
Peel St CV6 . . . . **30** C2
Pegmill Cl CV3 . . . . **49** A4
Pembroke Cl CV12 . . . .**4** C1
Pembrook Rd CV6 . . . . . . **20** C2
Pembury Ave CV6 . . . . . . **22** A3
Penarth Gr CV3 . . . . **51** A3
Pencraig Cl CV8 . . . . **68** A1
Pendenis Cl CV6 . . . . **31** B4
Penderel Ct CV6 . . . . **20** C3
Pendred Rd CV22 . . . . **84** C1

Penn Ho CV4 . . . . **36** A[?]
Pennington Mews CV21 . **85** A[?]
Pennington St CV21 . . . . . **85** A[?]
Pennington Way CV6 . . . . **30** C[?]
Penny Park La CV6 . . . . . . **20** A[?]
Penrith Cl CV6 . . . . **20** C[?]
Penrose Cl CV4 . . . . **45** B[?]
Penryhn Cl CV8 . . . . **68** A[?]
Pensilva Way ⬛ CV1 . . . . **39** C[?]
Pepper La CV1 . . . . **97** B[?]
Pepys Cnr CV4 . . . . **35** C[?]
Perchfoot Cl CV1 . . . . **97** C[?]
Percival Rd CV22 . . . . **91** A[?]
Percy Cres CV8 . . . . **74** A[?]
Percy Rd CV1 . . . . **74** A[?]
Percy St CV1 . . . . **96** A[?]
Peregrine Dr CV5 . . . . **27** B[?]
Perkins Gr CV21 . . . . **91** C[?]
Permian Cl CV21 . . . . **86** A[?]
Pershore Pl CV4 . . . . **46** C[?]
Perth Rise CV5 . . . . **36** B[?]
Peterlee Wlk ⬛ CV2 . . . . **33** B[?]
Peters Wlk CV6 . . . . **22** A[?]
Petitor Cres CV2 . . . . **22** C[?]
Pettiver Cres CV21 . . . . . . **91** C[?]
Petunia Cl CV10 . . . .**2** C[?]
Peveril Dr CV3 . . . . **47** C[?]
Peyto Cl CV6 . . . . **20** C[?]
Pheasant Cl CV12 . . . .**5** A[?]
Pheasant Oak CV4 . . . . . . **35** A[?]
Philip Ct CV21 . . . . **85** C[?]
Phillip Docker Ct CV12 . . . .**8** B[?]
Phipps Ave CV21 . . . . **91** C[?]
Phoenix Pk Ind Est CV7 . **14** B[?]
Phoenix Way CV6 . . . . . . **21** B[?]
Pickard Cl CV21 . . . . **80** C[?]
PICKFORD . . . . **26** C[?]
Pickford Grange La
CV5 . . . . **26** A[?]
PICKFORD GREEN . . . . . **26** A[?]
Pickford Green La CV5 . . **26** A[?]
Pickford Way CV5 . . . . . . **27** C[?]
Pikers La CV7 . . . . **18** A[?]
Pilgrims La CV23 . . . . **81** A[?]
Pilgrims Wlk CV6, CV7 . . **12** B[?]
Pilkington Rd CV5 . . . . . . **46** B[?]
Pilling Cl CV2 . . . . **33** A[?]
Pinders Ct ⬛ CV21 . . . . . **85** C[?]
Pinders La CV21 . . . . **85** C[?]
Pine Ct CV5 . . . . **35** A[?]
Pine Gr CV21 . . . . **92** A[?]
Pines The
Bedworth CV12 . . . .**5** B[?]
Coventry CV4 . . . . **44** B[?]
Pine Tree Ave CV4 . . . . . . **36** B[?]
Pine Tree Ct CV12 . . . .**6** C[?]
Pine Tree Rd CV12 . . . .**7** A[?]
Pinewood Dr CV3 . . . . **52** A[?]
Pinewood Gr CV5 . . . . **47** C[?]
Pinfold St CV21 . . . . **84** C[?]
PINKETT'S BOOTH . . . . **26** A[?]
PINLEY . . . . **49** C[?]
Pinley Fields CV3 . . . . **49** C[?]
PINLEY GDNS . . . . **49** B[?]
Pinner's Croft CV2 . . . . . . **31** B[?]
Pinnock Pl CV4 . . . . **36** A[?]
Pioneer Ho CV1 . . . . **96** D[?]
Pipers Ct CV3 . . . . **59** A[?]
Piper's La CV8 . . . . **67** B[?]
Pipewell Cl CV22 . . . . **88** C[?]
Pipit Wlk CV23 . . . . **80** A[?]
Pipkin Ct CV1 . . . . **97** D[?]
Pit Hill CV8 . . . . **72** A[?]
Plantagenet Dr CV22 . . . **94** C[?]
Planter Cl CV22 . . . . **88** A[?]
Plants Hill Cres CV4 . . . . **35** C[?]
Plexfield Rd CV22 . . . . **88** C[?]
Pleydell Cl CV3 . . . . **50** A[?]

Plomer Cl CV22 . . . . 88 C2
Plowman St CV21 . . . . . . 85 A1
Plymouth Cl CV2 . . . . . . 32 A3
Poitiers Rd CV3 . . . . 48 B2
Polperro Dr CV5 . . . . 27 B1
Pomeroy Cl CV4 . . . . 44 B3
Pond Farm Mews CV5 . . 26 C1
Pondthorpe CV3 . . . . 50 C2
Pontypool Ave CV3 . . . . 51 A2
Pool Cl CV22 . . . . 89 A2
Poole Rd CV6 . . . . 29 B2
Poolside Gdns CV3 . . . . 47 B1
Pope St CV22 . . . . 84 C1
Poplar Ave CV12 . . . . .7 A2
Poplar Gr
  Rugby CV21 . . . . 85 B2
  Ryton-on-D CV8 . . . . . . 63 C1
Poplar Ho CV12 . . . . .7 A2
Poplar Rd CV5 . . . . 38 A1
Poppy Cl CV10 . . . . .2 C4
Poppy Ct CV3 . . . . 50 B2
Poppy Dr CV23 . . . . 80 C2
Poppyfield Ct CV4 . . . . . 58 B3
Porchester Cl CV3 . . . . . 42 B2
Porlock Cl CV3 . . . . 48 C1
Porter Cl CV4 . . . . 44 C4
Portland Pl CV21 . . . . . . 91 A4
Portland Rd CV21 . . . . . . 91 A4
Portree Ave CV3 . . . . 42 A2
Portsea Cl CV3 . . . . 48 B2
Portway Cl CV4 . . . . 44 C4
Portwrinkle Ave CV6 . . 31 B2
Postbridge Rd CV3 . . . . 48 B1
POTTER'S GREEN 23 B1
Potters Green Prim Sch
  CV2 . . . . 23 B1
Potters Green Rd CV2 . . 23 B1
Potters Rd CV12 . . . . .5 B1
Potton Cl CV3 . . . . 50 C2
Potts Cl CV8 . . . . 75 B4
Poultney Rd CV6 . . . . . . 29 B2
Powell Rd CV2 . . . . 40 B4
Powis Gr CV8 . . . . 68 A1
Poyser Rd CV10 . . . . .3 C3
Prentice Cl CV23 . . . . . . 83 C3
Prescelly Ct CV8 . . . . . . 67 A1
President Kennedy Sch &
  Com Coll CV6 . . . . 20 B4
Preston Cl CV4 . . . . 45 A3
Pretorian Way CV21 . . . . 79 B1
Pridmore Rd CV6 . . . . . . 30 B3
Primary Wlk CV22 . . . . . 88 B2
Primrose Cl CV23 . . . . . . 80 C2
Primrose Dr CV12 . . . . . . .5 B1
Primrose Hill St CV1 . . 96 C4
Prince Of Wales Rd
  CV5 . . . . 37 C3
Princes Cl CV3 . . . . 49 C4
Princes Ct CV21 . . . . 85 B2
Princes Dr
  Coventry CV6 . . . . 22 B1
  Kenilworth CV8 . . . . 67 C3
Princess St CV6 . . . . 31 A3
Princes St CV21 . . . . 85 B2
Princethorpe Way CV3 . 50 C4
Prince William Cl CV6 . 28 C2
Prior Deram Wlk CV4 . . 46 A3
Priors Field Prim Sch
  CV8 . . . . 66 B3
Priorsfield Rd
  🔟 Coventry CV6 . . . . . . 38 B4
  Kenilworth CV8 . . . . 66 B2
Priorsfield Rd N 🔟 CV6 . 38 B4
Priorsfield Rd S CV6 . . 38 B4
Priors Harnall CV1 . . . . 96 D4
Priors The CV12 . . . . .6 C4
Priory Ct CV5 . . . . 38 B1

Priory Ho CV8 . . . . 74 B4
Priory Pl CV1 . . . . 96 C3
Priory Rd
  Kenilworth CV8 . . . . 74 C4
  Wolston CV8 . . . . 65 C4
Priory Row CV1 . . . . 96 C3
Priory St CV1 . . . . 96 C3
Priory Visitors Ctr★
  CV1 . . . . 96 C3
Privet Rd CV2 . . . . 22 B2
Proffitt Ave CV6 . . . . 22 A1
Progress Cl CV3 . . . . 51 B3
Progress Way CV3 . . . . . 51 B4
Projects Dr CV21 . . . . . . 86 A4
Prologis Pk CV6 . . . . 12 B1
Prospect Way CV21 . . . . 86 B3
Providence St CV5 . . . . . 47 A4
Provost Williams CE Prim
  Sch CV8 . . . . 63 B1
Puma Way CV1 . . . . 97 C1
Pumphouse Cl CV6 . . . . 14 B2
Purcell Rd CV6 . . . . 31 C4
Purefoy Rd CV3 . . . . 48 B4
Purlieu La CV8 . . . . 66 B1
Pytchley Rd CV22 . . . . . . 90 C3
Pyt Pk CV5 . . . . 37 B4

Q

Quadrant The CV1 . . . . . . 97 B2
Quarry Cl CV21 . . . . 79 A1
Quarryfield La CV1 . . . . 97 D1
Quarry Rd CV8 . . . . 66 C2
Quarrywood Gr CV2 . . . 40 B4
Queen Isabel's Ave CV3 . 48 B4
Queen Margaret's Rd
  CV4 . . . . 46 A4
Queen Mary's Rd
  Bedworth CV12 . . . . .3 B1
  Coventry CV6 . . . . 30 C4
Queen Philippa St CV3 . 48 B2
Queensferry Cl CV22 . . 88 C2
Queensland Ave CV5 . . 38 A2
Queensland Gdns 🔟
  CV12 . . . . .5 C2
Queens Rd CV23 . . . . . . 54 C4
Queen's Rd
  Coventry CV1 . . . . 97 A2
  Kenilworth CV8 . . . . 74 B3
Queen St
  Bedworth CV12 . . . . 6 C2
  Coventry CV1 . . . . 96 C4
  Rugby CV21 . . . . 85 B1
Queenswood Ct CV7 . . . 19 A4
Queen Victoria Rd
  Coventry CV1 . . . . 96 B3
  Coventry CV1 . . . . 97 B2
Queen Victoria St CV21 . 86 A1
Quilletts Cl CV6 . . . . 22 A1
Quinn Cl CV3 . . . . 49 C3
Quinton Flats CV3 . . . . . 48 B3
Quinton Par CV3 . . . . . . 48 B3
Quinton Pk CV3 . . . . 48 B3
Quinton Rd CV1 . . . . 97 C1
Quorn Way CV3 . . . . 50 C3

R

Race Leys Inf Sch CV12 . .6 B4
Race Leys Jun Sch CV12 . .6 B4
Radcliffe Rd CV5 . . . . . . 47 A4
RADFORD 29 C3
Radford Circ 🔟 CV6 . . . 38 B4
Radford Ho CV6 . . . . 29 B3
Radford Prim Sch CV6 . . 29 C1
Radford Rd CV1, CV6 . . . 29 C1
Radnor Wlk CV2 . . . . 33 A4

Raglan Ct 🔟 CV1 . . . . . . 39 C3
Raglan Gr CV8 . . . . 67 C1
Raglan St CV1 . . . . 96 D3
Railway St CV23 . . . . . . 83 B2
Railway Terr
  Bedworth CV12 . . . . 6 C2
  Rugby CV21 . . . . 85 C2
Rainsbrook Ave CV22 . . 91 C2
Raleigh Rd CV2 . . . . 40 C2
Ralph Rd CV6 . . . . 29 A1
Ramsay Cres CV5 . . . . . . 27 C3
Ranby Rd CV2 . . . . 40 A4
Randall Rd CV8 . . . . 74 B3
Randle St CV6 . . . . 29 C1
Rangemoor CV3 . . . . 50 B2
Rankine Cl CV21 . . . . . . 78 B1
Rannock Cl CV3 . . . . 42 A2
Ransom Rd CV6 . . . . 30 C4
Ranulf Croft CV3 . . . . . . 48 A3
Ranulf St CV3 . . . . 48 A3
Raphael Cl CV5 . . . . 37 A3
Rathbone Cl
  Keresley CV7 . . . . 11 C2
  Keresley CV7 . . . . 12 A2
  Rugby CV21 . . . . 92 A2
Ratliffe Rd CV22 . . . . . . 89 C1
Raven Cragg Rd CV5 . . . 46 C4
Ravenglass CV21 . . . . . . 80 B1
Ravensdale Prim Sch
  CV2 . . . . 41 B4
Ravensdale Rd CV2 . . . . 41 B3
Ravensholt CV4 . . . . 46 B2
Ravensthorpe Cl CV3 . . 50 C4
Rawnsley Dr CV8 . . . . . . 68 A2
Raymond Cl CV6 . . . . . . 13 C1
Raynor Cres CV12 . . . . . . .5 A1
Reading Cl CV2 . . . . 22 B3
Read St CV1 . . . . 39 C3
Recreation Rd CV6 . . . . 22 A3
Rectory Cl
  Allesley CV5 . . . . 28 A2
  Bedworth CV7 . . . . 6 A1
Rectory Dr CV7 . . . . .6 A1
Rectory La CV5 . . . . 28 A2
Redcap Croft CV6 . . . . . 21 A4
Redcar Rd CV1 . . . . 30 C1
Red Deeps CV11 . . . . .3 C4
Redditch Wlk 🔟 CV2 . . 33 B3
Redesdale Ave CV6 . . . . 29 A1
Redfern Ave CV8 . . . . . . 67 B2
Redgrave Cl CV2 . . . . . . 33 C4
Red La
  Burton Green CV8 . . . . . 56 A2
  Coventry CV6 . . . . 31 A1
  Kenilworth CV8 . . . . 66 B4
Redland Cl CV2 . . . . 23 B2
Redland La CV8 . . . . 63 B3
Red Lodge Dr CV22 . . . . 89 B2
Redruth Cl CV6 . . . . 31 B4
Redthorne Gr CV8 . . . . . 67 C4
Rees Dr CV3 . . . . 60 B4
Reeve Dr CV8 . . . . 74 C4
Regency Ct CV5 . . . . 47 A4
Regency Dr
  Coventry CV3 . . . . 47 A1
  Kenilworth CV8 . . . . 74 B3
Regent Pl CV21 . . . . 85 B1
Regent St
  Bedworth CV12 . . . . 6 C4
  Coventry CV1 . . . . 97 A2
  Rugby CV21 . . . . 85 B1
Regiment Ct CV6 . . . . . . 20 A1
Regina Cres CV3 . . . . . . 33 B3
Regis Wlk CV2 . . . . 33 A3
Relton Mews CV6 . . . . . 31 A2
Rembrandt Cl CV5 . . . . . 37 A3
Remembrance Rd CV3 . . 50 B2
Renfrew Wlk CV4 . . . . . . 45 B4

Renison Rd CV12 . . . . .5 B1
Renolds Cl CV4 . . . . 37 A2
Renown Ave CV5 . . . . . . 37 A1
Repton Dr CV6 . . . . 22 B2
Reservoir Rd CV21 . . . . . 86 A4
Rex Cl CV4 . . . . 44 B4
Reynolds Cl CV21 . . . . . 92 B3
Reynolds Rd CV12 . . . . . .6 A4
Ribble Cl CV12 . . . . .8 B2
Ribble Rd CV3 . . . . 40 A2
Richard Joy Cl CV6 . . . . 20 C2
Richard Lee Prim Sch
  CV2 . . . . 41 C3
Richards Cl CV8 . . . . 67 A1
Richardson Way CV2 . . 33 C4
Richmond Rd CV21 . . . . 91 A4
Richmond St CV2 . . . . . 40 B3
Ricoh Arena (Coventry City
  FC) CV6 . . . . 21 B3
Riddings The CV5 . . . . . 46 C3
Ridge Ct CV5 . . . . 27 B2
Ridge Dr CV21 . . . . 86 B2
Ridgethorpe CV3 . . . . . . 50 C2
Ridgeway Ave CV3 . . . . 48 A2
Ridgley Rd CV4 . . . . 44 C4
Rigdale Cl CV2 . . . . 41 C2
Riley Cl CV8 . . . . 75 C4
Riley Ct CV5 . . . . 86 A1
Riley Ho CV1 . . . . 97 B2
Riley Sq CV2 . . . . 22 B1
Ringway Hill Cross CV1 . 96 A3
Ringway Queens CV1 . . 97 A2
Ringway Rudge CV1 . . . 97 A2
Ringway St Johns CV1 . 97 C2
Ringway St Nicholas
  CV1 . . . . 96 B3
Ringway St Patricks
  CV1 . . . . 97 B1
Ringway Swanswell
  CV1 . . . . 96 C3
Ringway Whitefriars
  CV1 . . . . 96 C3
Ringwood Highway CV2 . 23 B2
Ripon Cl CV5 . . . . 27 C4
Risborough Cl CV5 . . . . 37 A3
River Cl CV12 . . . . .5 C1
River Ct 🔟 CV1 . . . . 38 C3
Riverford Croft CV4 . . . 58 B4
Riverside CV8 . . . . 71 C1
Riverside Cl CV3 . . . . . . 49 B3
Riverslea Rd CV3 . . . . . . 41 A1
River Wlk CV2 . . . . 22 C2
Roadway Cl CV12 . . . . . . .6 B2
Robbins Ct 🔟 CV22 . . . 91 C2
Robert Cl CV3 . . . . 62 A4
Robert Cramb Ave CV4 . . 45 A4
Robert Hill Cl CV21 . . . 92 A3
Robert Rd CV7 . . . . 13 C4
Robertson Cl CV23 . . . . 87 B3
Robin Hood Rd CV3 . . . 50 A2
Robinson Rd CV12 . . . . . 13 A4
Robotham Cl CV21 . . . . . 85 A4
Rocheberie Way CV22 . . 89 C2
Rochester Rd CV5 . . . . . 46 C4
Rock Cl CV6 . . . . 22 B1
Rocken End CV6 . . . . 30 B4
Rock La CV7 . . . . 10 C3
Rocky La CV8 . . . . 75 C2
Rodhouse Cl CV4 . . . . . . 35 B1
Rodney Cl CV22 . . . . 88 C3
Rodway Dr CV5 . . . . 35 B4
Rodyard Way CV1 . . . . . 97 C1
Rokeby Cl CV22 . . . . 89 B1
Rokeby Inf Sch CV22 . . 90 A2
Rokeby Jun Sch CV22 . . 90 A2

Rokeby St CV21........ **86** B1
Roland Ave CV6 .... **20** C3
Roland Mount CV6...... **20** C3
Rollason Cl CV6 .... **30** A4
Rollason Rd CV6........ **29** C4
Rollason's Yd CV6 ...... **22** A3
Roman Rd CV2 .... **40** C3
Roman Way
 Coventry CV3 .... **60** B3
 Rugby CV21............ **79** B1
Romford Rd CV6........ **20** B2
Romsley Rd CV6........ **30** A2
Ro-Oak Rd CV6......... **29** A1
Rookery La CV6 .... **20** B4
Roosevelt Dr CV4 ...... **35** C2
Roper Cl CV21......... **92** A2
Rosaville Cres CV5..... **27** B2
Rose Ave CV6 .... **29** A1
Roseberry Ave CV2 ..... **22** C1
Rose Cottage Flats CV5 . **26** B1
Rose Croft CV8 .... **66** C2
Rosegreen Cl CV3 ..... **48** C2
Rosehip Dr CV2 .... **31** C2
Roseland Rd CV8....... **74** B3
Roselands Ave CV2 ..... **32** B4
Rosemary Cl CV4 ...... **35** C3
Rosemary Hill CV8...... **67** A1
Rosemary Mews CV8 .... **67** A1
Rosemount Cl CV2...... **32** C3
Rosemullion Cl CV7 ... **14** B4
Rosewood Ave CV22 .... **90** A2
Ross Cl CV5 .... **27** B1
Ross Ct CV21.......... **86** B1
Rosslyn Ave CV6....... **28** C2
Rotherham Rd CV6 ..... **20** C2
Rothesay Ave CV4 ..... **36** C2
Rothley Dr CV21...... **80** C1
Roughknowles Rd CV4.. **44** B2
Round Ave CV23 .... **83** B3
Round House Rd CV3 ... **49** C4
Rounds Gdns CV21..... **85** A2
Rounds Hill CV8 .... **74** A2
Round St CV21........ **85** A1
Rover Rd CV1 .... **97** B2
Rowan Cl CV3 .... **52** B3
Rowan Dr CV22........ **88** B4
Rowan Gr CV2......... **23** B2
Rowans The CV12....... **5** B2
Rowcroft Rd CV2 ...... **33** B2
Rowe Cl CV21 .... **92** C1
Rowington Cl CV6 .... **28** B1
Rowland St CV21 ..... **85** A1
Rowley Dr CV3 .... **61** C4
Rowley La CV3 .... **62** B3
Rowley Rd CV3, CV8.... **61** C3
ROWLEY'S GREEN **21** C3
Rowley's Green La CV6 . **21** B4
Rowleys Green Lane Ind
 Est CV6 .... **21** B4
Rowse Cl CV21 .... **80** A1
Row The CV7 .... **25** A3
Royal Cres CV3 .... **50** A1
Royal Oak La CV7, CV12.. **12** C3
Royal Oak Yd CV12....... **6** B4
Royston Cl CV3 .... **42** B3
Rubens Cl CV5 .... **37** A3
Rudgard Rd CV6....... **22** A4
RUGBY **90** B3
Rugby High Sch CV22 .. **94** B4
Rugby Rd
 Binley Woods CV3..... **52** B4
 Brandon CV8.......... **53** B1
 Bulkington CV12......... **9** A2
 Church Lawford CV23.... **82** A3
 Clifton u D CV23 ...... **87** A3

Rugby Rd *continued*
 Dunchurch CV22........ **94** B2
 Long Lawford CV23 .... **83** C2
 Wolston CV8........... **54** A1
Rugby Sch CV22....... **90** A4
Rugby Sta CV21........ **86** A2
Runcorn Wlk **10** CV2 ... **33** B3
Rupert Brooke Rd CV22. **89** B1
Rupert Rd CV6 .... **29** C4
Rushmoor Dr CV5 .... **38** A3
Rushton Hall Sch CV7 . **13** A1
Ruskin Cl
 Coventry CV6 .... **28** B2
 Rugby CV22............ **95** A4
Russell Ave CV22 ..... **94** B2
Russell St N **2** CV1 .... **96** C4
Russell St CV1......... **96** C4
Russelsheim Way CV22 . **90** A4
Russet Gr CV4......... **58** B3
Rutherglen Ave CV3 ... **49** B2
Rutland Croft **3** CV3 .. **51** A4
Rydal Cl
 Allesley CV5 .... **27** C4
 Rugby CV21............ **86** B4
Rye Hill CV5.......... **27** B2
Rye Hill Office Pk CV5.. **27** B3
Rye Piece Ringway CV12..6 C3
Ryhope Cl CV12 ....4 C1
Ryley St CV1........... **96** A3
Rylston Ave CV6....... **20** A1
RYTON 9 A2
Ryton Cl CV14 .... **45** C4
RYTON-ON-DUNSMORE

.... **63** C2
Ryton Organic Gdns★
 CV8 .... **64** C1
Ryton Pools Ctry Pk★
 CV8 .... **72** C1
Ryton Pools Visitor Ctr★
 CV8 .... **72** C1

S

Sackville Ho **1** CV1.... **96** D4
Sacred Heart RC Prim Sch
 CV2 .... **40** B3
Saddington Rd CV3.... **50** C4
Sadler Gdns CV12 ....6 C2
Sadler Rd CV6......... **29** B4
Saffron Cl CV23...... **80** C2
St Agatha's Rd CV2.... **86** B1
St Andrews Benn CE Prim
 Sch CV21............ **86** B1
St Andrew's CE Inf Sch
 CV5 .... **26** A1
St Andrews Cres CV22 . **90** A2
St Andrew's Ct CV21... **85** B2
St Andrew's Rd CV5 .... **47** A4
St Anne's RC Prim Sch
 CV3 .... **50** A2
St Anne's Rd CV22 .... **89** B3
St Ann's Rd CV2 ...... **40** B3
St Augustine's RC Prim Sch
 CV6 .... **29** B3
St Augustine's RC Prim
 Sch CV6.............. **66** C3
St Augustine's Wlk CV6. **29** B3
St Austell Rd CV2...... **41** C3
St Bartholemews Cl
 CV3 .... **42** B2
St Bartholomew's CE Prim
 Sch CV3............. **50** A2
St Bernard's Wlk CV3... **50** B2
St Catherine's Cl CV3 .. **49** C4
St Catherine's Lodge **7**
 CV6 .... **38** B4
St Christian's Croft CV3. **48** C4
St Christian's Rd CV3 ... **48** C4

St Christopher Prim Sch
 CV5 .... **37** B4
St Clements Ct CV2.... **32** B4
St Columba's Cl CV1.... **96** B4
St Davids Orch CV3 .... **51** A3
St Davids Way CV10......2 C2
St Elizabeth's RC Prim Sch
 CV6 .... **30** C3
St Elizabeth's Rd CV6... **30** C3
St Francis RC Prim Sch
 CV12 .... 6 C3
St Georges Ave CV22.... **89** C2
St George's Rd CV1.... **40** A2
St Georges Way CV10....3 A1
St Giles Jun Sch CV7... **13** C4
St Giles Rd CV7........ **13** A2
St Gregory's RC Prim Sch
 CV2 .... **41** C3
St Helen's Way CV5..... **27** C4
St Ives Rd CV2........ **41** C3
St James CE Jun Sch
 CV12 .... 8 C2
St James Ct CV3....... **50** C2
St James Gdns CV12.... **8** C2
St James' La CV3 ..... **50** B2
St John Fisher RC Prim
 Sch CV2............. **32** B1
St Johns Ave CV22 .... **91** B2
St John's Ave CV8 ..... **74** C3
St John's CE Prim Sch
 CV5 .... **37** A4
St John's Flats CV8 .... **74** C3
St John's La CV23 ..... **83** B3
St John's Prim Sch CV8 **74** B2
St John's St
 Coventry CV1 .... **97** C2
 Kenilworth CV8......... **74** C3
St John St CV21 ...... **85** B2
St John the Divine CE Prim
 Sch CV3............. **50** A1
St John Vianney RC Prim
 Sch CV5............. **36** C3
St Jude's Cres CV3 .... **50** B2
St Lawrence's Rd CV6 .. **21** C1
St Leonard's Wlk CV8... **63** B1
St Luke's Rd CV6 ..... **21** A3
St Margaret Rd CV1.... **40** A2
St Marie's RC Inf Sch
 CV22 .... **90** A4
St Marie's RC Jun Sch
 CV22 .... **89** C4
St Mark's Annexe (Coventry
 & Warwickshire Hospl)
 CV1 .... **96** C4
St Mark's Ave CV22 .... **88** C1
St Mark's Ct CV22 ..... **89** A2
St Martin's Rd CV3 .... **60** A2
St Mary & St Benedict RC
 Prim Sch CV1 .... **39** C4
St Mary's Ct CV8...... **74** B2
St Mary St CV1 .... **97** C2
St Matthew's Bloxam CE
 Prim Sch CV22 .... **89** B4
St Matthews St **7** CV21. **85** B1
St Michael's CE Prim Sch
 CV12 .... 7 A3
St Michael's Rd CV2 ... **40** B3
St Nicholas Ave CV8 ... **74** B3
St Nicholas CE Com Prim
 Sch CV8............. **67** A1
St Nicholas Cl CV1...... **30** A1
St Nicholas Ct
 3 Coventry, Edgwick
 CV6 .... **31** A3
 Coventry, Radford CV6 ... **29** C2
St Nicholas St CV1..... **96** B4
St Osburg's RC Prim Sch
 CV1 .... **96** A3

St Osburg's Rd CV2..... **40** B3
St Oswalds CE Prim Sch
 CV22 .... **84** B1
St Patrick's RC Prim Sch
 CV2 .... **23** A1
St Patrick's Rd CV1..... **97** B2
St Paul's Rd CV6....... **30** C2
St Peter's Ct CV1 ..... **96** D4
St Peters Rd CV21 ..... **86** A1
Saint's Peter & Paul RC
 Prim Sch CV2 .... **33** A3
St Thomas More RC Prim
 Sch CV3............. **48** B3
St Thomas' Rd CV6..... **22** A3
St Thomas's Ct **13** CV1 .. **38** C2
St Thomas's Ho **12** CV1.. **38** C2
Salcombe Cl CV3 ..... **50** B2
Salemorton Ct CV22 ... **93** C4
Salford Cl CV2......... **31** B1
Salisbury Ave CV3 .... **48** A2
Salisbury Cl CV8....... **65** A3
Salt La CV1........... **97** B2
Sam Gault Cl CV3...... **50** C3
Sammons Way CV4 .... **35** B1
Sampson Cl CV2....... **32** A4
Samuel Hayward Ho **5**
 CV2 .... **22** B1
Samuel Vale Ho CV1 ... **96** B4
Sanby Cl CV12..........6 A4
Sanders Rd CV6 ...... **14** B2
Sandford Cl CV2...... **23** B3
Sandford Way CV22.... **94** A1
Sandgate Cres CV2 ... **41** C2
Sandhurst Gr CV6 .... **29** C1
Sandilands Cl CV2..... **41** C4
Sandown Ave CV6 .... **21** C2
Sandown Rd CV21 .... **86** A2
Sandpiper Cl CV23..... **80** A3
Sandpiper Rd CV2 .... **22** B3
Sandpits La CV6 ...... **19** C2
Sandpits The CV12.......8 C2
Sandringham Cl CV4.... **45** A1
Sandwick Cl CV3 ..... **51** A4
Sandy La
 Coventry CV1 .... **30** A1
 Rugby CV21............ **84** C1
Sandy Lane Bsns Pk
 CV1 .... **30** A1
Sandythorpe CV3...... **50** C2
Santos Cl CV3 .... **51** A4
Sapcote Gr CV2 ...... **22** B4
Sapphire Gate CV2 ... **41** A2
Sarawak Pl CV22 ..... **88** B2
Saunders Ave CV12......6 B2
Saunton Cl CV5........ **27** C4
Saunton Rd CV22 ..... **89** C3
Saville Gr CV8........ **68** A1
Saxon Cl
 Binley Woods CV3...... **52** B3
 4 Cawston CV22....... **88** A2
Saxon Rd CV2 .... **40** C4
Scafell CV21.......... **80** B1
Scafell Cl CV5 .... **36** B4
Scarborough Way CV4.. **45** A3
Scarman Rd CV4 ..... **45** C1
Scholars Dr CV22...... **88** B2
Scholfield Rd CV7 .... **12** A2
School Cl CV3 .... **40** A2
Schoolfield Gr **1** CV21.. **85** B1
School Gdns CV21..... **92** A3
School House La CV2 ... **33** B2
School La
 Bedworth CV7........ **13** C3
 Kenilworth CV8........ **67** A1
School Rd CV12 ....8 C2
School St
 Church Lawford CV23..... **55** C2

School St *continued*
Dunchurch CV22 . . . . 94 A1
Long Lawford CV23 . . . . . 83 B2
Rugby CV21 . . . . 92 A3
Wolston CV8 . . . . 65 C4
Scotfold The CV6 . . . . 20 A1
Scots Cl CV22 . . . . 88 C1
Scots La CV6 . . . . 29 A2
Scott Rd CV18 . . . . 74 A2
Seabroke Ave CV22 . . . . . 85 A1
Seaford Cl CV6 . . . . 22 B4
Seagrave Rd CV1 . . . . 97 D1
Sealand Dr CV12 . . . . 6 A3
Seathwaite CV21 . . . . 80 A1
Sebastian Cl CV3 . . . . 49 C1
Second Ave CV3 . . . . 41 A1
Sedgemoor Rd CV3 . . . . . 49 C1
Sedlescombe Lodge
CV22 . . . . 89 B1
Sedlescombe Pk CV22 . . 89 C2
Seed Field Croft CV3 . . . 48 C3
Seekings Dr CV8 . . . . 75 A4
Sefton Rd CV4 . . . . 46 C2
Selborne Rd CV22 . . . . . . 89 A2
Selina Dix Ho CV1 . . . . . . 96 C4
Selsey Cl CV3 . . . . 62 A4
Selside CV21 . . . . 80 B1
Selworthy Rd CV6 . . . . . . 21 B3
Seneschal Rd CV3 . . . . . . 48 C3
Sephton Dr CV6 . . . . 14 C2
Servite Ho CV8 . . . . 74 B3
Seven Stars Ind Est CV3 49 B3
Severn Rd
Bulkington CV12 . . . . 8 A3
Coventry CV1 . . . . 40 A1
Sevilla Cl CV3 . . . . 42 B2
Sewall Ct CV6 . . . . 31 B4
Sewall Highway CV2 . . . 31 C2
Seymour Cl CV3 . . . . 50 A1
Seymour Ho CV3 . . . . 48 A4
Seymour Rd CV21 . . . . . . 86 A4
Shadowbrook Rd CV6 . . . 29 B1
Shaftesbury Ave CV7 . . . 12 A3
Shaftesbury Rd CV5 . . . . 47 A4
Shakespeare Ave CV12 . . . 7 A2
Shakespeare Gdns
CV22 . . . . 89 B1
Shakespeare St CV2 . . . . 40 C4
Shakleton Rd CV5 . . . . . . 38 B2
Shanklin Rd CV3 . . . . 61 C4
Shap Fell CV21 . . . . 80 B1
Sharp Cl CV6 . . . . 20 C2
Sharpley Ct CV2 . . . . 33 B4
Sharratt Rd CV12 . . . . 6 A2
Shearwater Dr CV23 . . . . 80 A3
Sheen Ho CV2 . . . . 32 B4
Sheep St CV21 . . . . 85 B1
Sheldrake Cl CV3 . . . . . . 42 B1
Shelfield Cl CV5 . . . . 36 C3
Shelley Cl CV12 . . . . 7 A1
Shelley Rd CV2 . . . . 41 A3
Shellon Cl CV3 . . . . 51 A4
Shelton Sq CV1 . . . . 97 B2
Shenstone Ave CV22 . . . 91 B3
Shepherd Cl CV4 . . . . 36 A3
Sherbourne Arc CV1 . . . . 97 B2
Sherbourne Cres CV5 . . . 37 C4
Sherbourne Ct CV1 . . . . . 97 B1
Sherbourne Fields Sch
CV6 . . . . 28 B1
Sherbourne St CV1 . . . . . 38 B2
Sheridan Cl CV22 . . . . . . 89 C1
Sheriff Ave CV4 . . . . 45 C3
Sheriff Rd CV21 . . . . 86 B1
Sheriffs Orch CV1 . . . . . . 97 B2
Sherington Ave CV5 . . . . 37 A4
Sherlock Rd CV5 . . . . 37 B3

Sherwood Jones Cl
CV6 . . . . 29 C2
Shetland Cl CV5 . . . . 36 B4
Shevlock Way CV6 . . . . . . 31 B2
Shillingstone Cl CV2 . . . 42 B4
SHILTON 17 C1
Shilton & Ansty CE Fst Sch
CV7 . . . . 17 B1
Shilton Ind Est CV7 . . . . . 17 B3
Shilton La
Barnacle CV2, CV7 . . . . . . 24 B4
Bulkington CV12 . . . . 9 A1
Coventry CV2 . . . . 23 C3
Shilton CV7, CV12 . . . . . . 17 A4
Shipston Rd CV2 . . . . 32 A2
Shirebrook Cl CV2 . . . . . . 23 A2
Shire Cl CV6 . . . . 22 B1
Shires The CV23 . . . . 55 C3
Shirlett Cl CV2 . . . . 22 B3
Shirley Rd CV2 . . . . 33 B3
Shorncliffe Rd CV6 . . . . . 28 C2
Shortlands CV7 . . . . 13 A2
Shortley Rd CV3 . . . . 49 A4
Short St CV1 . . . . 97 C2
Shottery Cl CV5 . . . . 36 C3
Shrubberies The CV4 . . . 58 C4
Shuckburgh Cres CV22 . . 91 A2
Shulman's Wlk CV2 . . . . 32 B3
Shultern La CV4 . . . . 46 B2
Shuna Croft CV2 . . . . 33 C3
Shuttle St CV6 . . . . 31 C4
Shuttleworth Rd CV23 . . 87 A3
Sibree Rd CV3 . . . . 61 C4
Sibton Cl CV2 . . . . 22 C1
Sidbury Rd CV6 . . . . 30 A2
Siddaway Ho CV21 . . . . . 80 A1
Siddeley Ave
Coventry CV3 . . . . 40 C1
Kenilworth CV8 . . . . 74 A3
Sidings The CV21 . . . . . . 85 C2
Sidmouth Cl CV2 . . . . 32 A3
Sidney Rd CV22 . . . . 91 A2
Sidney Stringer Com Tech
Coll CV1 . . . . 96 C3
Silksby St CV3 . . . . 48 B4
Silver Birch Ave CV12 . . . 5 B2
Silver Birch Cl CV3 . . . . . 52 B3
Silverdale Cl CV2 . . . . . . 22 B4
Silver St
Coventry CV1 . . . . 96 B3
Newton CV23 . . . . 81 B3
Silverstone Dr CV6 . . . . . 13 B1
Silverton Rd CV6 . . . . 31 A3
Silver Trees Dr CV12 . . . . . 8 B4
Simon Ct CV7 . . . . 14 A4
Simon Stone St CV6 . . . . 31 A4
Simpson Gr CV3 . . . . 50 A2
Sinclair Dr CV6 . . . . 14 C2
Singer Cl CV6 . . . . 31 C4
Sir Frank Whittle Bsns Ctr
CV21 . . . . 86 B3
Sir Frank Whittle Prim Sch
CV2 . . . . 33 A4
Sir Henry Parkes Rd
CV5 . . . . 46 B3
Sir Thomas White's Rd
CV5 . . . . 38 A2
Sir William Lyons Rd
CV4 . . . . 46 A2
Sir Winston Churchill Pl
CV3 . . . . 52 A3
Siskin Cl CV23 . . . . 80 A2
Siskin Dr CV3 . . . . 62 A4
Siskin Parkway E CV3 . . . 62 A1
Siskin Parkway W CV3 . . . 62 A2
Skiddaw CV21 . . . . 80 A1
Skipton Gdns CV2 . . . . . . 31 C2
Skipton Lodge CV2 . . . . 31 C2

Skipworth Rd CV3 . . . . . . 42 B1
Sky Blue Way CV1 . . . . . . 39 C3
Skydome The CV1 . . . . . . 97 A2
Slade Rd CV21, CV22 . . . . 90 C4
Sleath's Yd CV12 . . . . 6 B3
Sledmere Cl CV2 . . . . 22 B3
Sleets Yd CV12 . . . . 6 A2
Smalley Pl CV8 . . . . 74 B4
Smarts Rd CV12 . . . . 5 C1
Smercote Cl CV12 . . . . 5 A1
Smithford Way CV1 . . . . . 96 B3
Smiths Orch CV21 . . . . . . 86 A1
Smith St
Bedworth CV12 . . . . 5 B1
Coventry CV6 . . . . 31 A1
Smithy La CV23 . . . . 55 C3
Smorrall La CV12 . . . . 4 C2
Snape Rd CV2 . . . . 33 A1
Snowdrop Cl CV12 . . . . . . 5 B1
Soden Cl CV3 . . . . 50 B2
Soden's Ave CV8 . . . . 63 B1
Solent Dr CV2 . . . . 23 C1
Somerly Cl CV3 . . . . 51 A4
Somerset Pl CV22 . . . . . . 88 B3
Somerset Rd CV1 . . . . . . 30 A1
Somers Rd
Keresley CV7 . . . . 12 A2
Rugby CV22 . . . . 84 B1
Sommerville Rd CV2 . . . . 41 A4
Soredale Croft CV3 . . . . . 42 B1
Sorrel Cl CV4 . . . . 44 C4
Sorrel Dr CV23 . . . . 80 B2
Sorrell Pl CV10 . . . . 3 C4
Sorrell Rd CV10 . . . . 3 C4
Southam Cl CV4 . . . . 44 C3
South Ave CV2 . . . . 40 B2
Southbank Ct CV8 . . . . . . 74 B4
Southbank Rd
Coventry CV6 . . . . 28 C1
Kenilworth CV8 . . . . 74 B4
Southbrook Rd CV22 . . . . 90 A3
Southcott Way CV2 . . . . . 23 C1
Southey Rd CV22 . . . . 89 B1
Southfield Dr CV8 . . . . . . 67 B2
Southfield Rd CV22 . . . . . 90 C3
Southfields Prim Sch
CV1 . . . . 39 C3
Southleigh Ave CV5 . . . . 47 A3
Southport Cl CV3 . . . . . . 49 C1
South Rd CV23 . . . . 87 B3
South Ridge CV5 . . . . 36 C4
South St
Coventry CV1 . . . . 39 C3
Rugby CV21 . . . . 86 B1
South View Rd CV23 . . . . 83 A2
Sovereign Cl CV8 . . . . 74 B1
Sovereign Rd CV5 . . . . . . 38 B2
Sovereign Row CV5 . . . . 38 B2
Sowe Valley Prim Sch
CV3 . . . . 50 B3
Sparkbrook St CV1 . . . . . 40 A3
Sparkbrook Workshops
CV1 . . . . 40 A3
Sparta Cl CV21 . . . . 85 B4
Speedway La CV8 . . . . . . 53 A3
Speedwell Cl
6 Bedworth CV12 . . . . . . 5 A2
Rugby CV23 . . . . 80 C1
Spencer Ave CV5 . . . . 38 B1
SPENCER PARK 97 A1
Spencer Rd CV5 . . . . 97 A1
Sphinx Dr CV3 . . . . 40 C1
Spicer Pl CV22 . . . . 89 A3
Spindle St CV1 . . . . 30 B2
Spinney Cl CV3 . . . . 52 C3
Spinney The
Coventry CV4 . . . . 58 B3
Long Lawford CV23 . . . . . 83 B3

Spitfire Cl CV5 . . . . 37 A1
SPON END 38 B3
Spon End CV1, CV5 . . . . . 38 B3
Spon Gate Ho CV1 . . . . . 38 B2
Spon Gate Prim Sch
CV1 . . . . 38 B3
Spon St CV1 . . . . 96 A3
Spottiswood Cl CV22 . . . 88 A2
Spring Cl 6 CV1 . . . . 39 C3
Spring Ct CV8 . . . . 72 A1
SPRINGFIELD 6 B2
Springfield Cres CV12 . . . 6 B2
Springfield Pl CV1 . . . . . . 96 C3
Springfield Rd CV1 . . . . . 96 C4
Spring Hill CV8 . . . . 72 A1
Springhill Houses CV22 . 90 C2
Spring La CV8 . . . . 67 B1
Spring Rd
Barnacle CV7 . . . . 16 B2
Coventry CV6 . . . . 21 C1
Spring St CV21 . . . . 85 C1
Spruce Rd 5 CV2 . . . . . . 22 B2
Square The
Coventry CV2 . . . . 33 B3
Dunchurch CV22 . . . . 94 B1
Kenilworth CV8 . . . . 74 B4
Squires Croft CV2 . . . . . . 23 C1
Squires Way CV4 . . . . . . 46 B2
Stacey Ct CV22 . . . . 94 A3
Stadium Cl CV6 . . . . 21 A2
Stafford Cl CV12 . . . . 8 C2
Staircase La CV5 . . . . 28 A3
Stamford Ave CV3 . . . . . . 48 A2
Standard Ave CV4 . . . . . . 36 C1
Standish Cl CV2 . . . . 41 C2
Stanier Ave CV1 . . . . 38 C4
Stanley Rd
Coventry CV5 . . . . 47 A4
Rugby CV21, CV22 . . . . . . 91 B3
Stansfield Gr CV8 . . . . . . 75 C4
Stanton Bridge Prim Sch
CV6 . . . . 31 A2
Stanway Rd CV5 . . . . 47 B4
Staples Cl CV12 . . . . 8 C3
Starcross Cl CV2 . . . . 32 A3
Stare Gn CV4 . . . . 46 B1
STARETON 77 C3
Stareton Cl CV4 . . . . 47 A2
Star Ind Pk CV2 . . . . 33 A1
Starley Ct CV3 . . . . 51 B3
Starley Pk CV7 . . . . 14 B4
Starley Rd CV1 . . . . 97 A2
Startin Cl CV7 . . . . 13 C3
Station Ave CV4 . . . . 44 B4
Station Rd
Clifton u D CV23 . . . . 87 A3
Kenilworth CV8 . . . . 74 B4
Station St E CV6 . . . . 30 C3
Station St W CV6 . . . . 30 C3
Station Sq CV1 . . . . 97 B1
Station Street W Bsns Pk
CV6 . . . . 30 B3
Staveley Way CV21 . . . . . 86 C4
Staverton Cl CV5 . . . . . . 47 B4
Staverton Leys CV22 . . . 90 A1
Steele St CV22 . . . . 84 C1
Steeping Rd CV23 . . . . . . 83 C3
Steeplefield Rd CV6 . . . . 29 B1
Stennels Cl CV6 . . . . 29 A4
Stephenson Rd CV7 . . . . 14 C3
Stephen St CV21 . . . . 85 A1
Stepney Rd CV2 . . . . 40 B4
Stepping Stones Rd
CV5 . . . . 38 A4
Stevenage Wlk 2 CV2 . . 33 B3

Stevens Ho CV1 . . . . 96 C4
Stevenson Rd CV6 . . . . . . 29 B4
Stewart Cl CV4 . . . . 37 B2
Stirling Cl CV3. . . . . 51 A4
STIVICHALL 48 B1
Stivichall Croft CV3. . . . . 47 C2
Stivichall Prim Sch CV3 47 B2
Stockley Rd CV6. . . . . 14 C2
Stocks Ct CV2 . . . . 89 A2
Stocks La CV23 . . . . 93 A1
Stockton Rd CV1 . . . . 96 D4
STOKE 41 A2
STOKE ALDERMOOR . . . 49 C4
Stoke Gn CV3. . . . . 40 B2
Stoke Green Cres CV3 . . 40 C1
STOKE HEATH 31 B2
Stoke Heath Prim Sch
CV2 . . . . 31 B2
STOKE PARK 40 B2
Stoke Park Mews CV2 . . 40 B3
Stoke Park Sch & Com
Tech Coll CV2 . . . . 40 C4
Stoke Prim Sch CV2. . . . 40 B4
Stoke Row CV2 . . . . 40 B4
Stonebridge Highway
CV3 . . . . 60 C4
Stonebridge Trad Est
CV3 . . . . 61 C4
Stonebrook Way CV6 . . . 21 C3
Stonebury Ave CV5 . . . . 35 C4
Stonechat Rd CV23 . . . . 80 B3
Stonefield Cl CV2. . . . . . 33 B4
Stonehall Rd CV22. . . . . 88 A2
Stonehaven Dr CV3. . . . . 60 A3
Stonehills CV21 . . . . 80 A1
Stonehouse La CV2 . . . . 62 A4
STONELEIGH 69 C2
Stoneleigh Abbey★
CV8   76 B3
Stoneleigh Ave
Coventry CV5 . . . . 47 A3
Kenilworth CV8. . . . . 67 B2
Stoneleigh Cl CV4 . . . . . 59 A4
Stoneleigh Deer Park Bsns
Village CV8. . . . . 77 C4
Stoneleigh Park National
Ag Ctr★ CV8   76 C4
Stoneleigh Rd
Baginton CV8 . . . . 61 A1
Coventry CV4 . . . . 58 C2
Kenilworth CV8. . . . . 67 B2
Stoneleigh CV8 . . . . 77 A3
Stone Mdw CV7 . . . . 12 A2
Stoney Ct CV3 . . . . 51 B3
Stoney Rd CV1, CV3 . . . . . 97 B1
Stoney Stanton Rd CV1,
CV6 . . . . 30 C1
Stoneywood Rd CV2 . . . 33 A4
Stoop The CV3. . . . . 42 C1
Stowe Pl CV4. . . . . 35 A1
Stradey Cl CV3 . . . . 42 C1
Stratford St CV2 . . . . 40 B4
Strath Cl CV21. . . . . 92 A1
Strathmore Ave CV1 . . . 39 C1
Strawberry Wlk CV2 . . . 23 A2
Streamside Cl CV5. . . . . 27 B4
Stretton Ave CV3 . . . . . . 50 A2
Stretton Ct CV21. . . . . . . 80 B1
Stretton Rd CV8 . . . . 65 B2
Stuart Ct CV6. . . . . 31 B4
Stubbs Cl CV12 . . . . 6 A4
Stubbs Gr CV2. . . . . 31 C1
Studland Ave CV21 . . . . 91 C3
Studland Gn CV2 . . . . . . 42 B4
Sturley Cl CV8. . . . . 67 C2

Sturminster Cl CV2 . . . . . 42 B4
Styvechale Ave CV5. . . . . 47 B4
Sudeley Rd CV10 . . . . 3 B4
Suffolk Cl
Bedworth CV12. . . . . 6 A3
Coventry CV5 . . . . 36 C3
Sulgrave Cl CV2 . . . . 32 C3
Sullivan Ct CV6 . . . . 31 C3
Sullivan Rd CV6 . . . . 31 C3
Sunbeam Cl CV21. . . . . . 86 A1
Sunbridge Terr CV21. . . . 86 A1
Sunbury Rd CV3 . . . . 50 A1
Suncliffe Dr CV8. . . . . . . 74 C2
Sundew St CV2 . . . . 23 A2
Sundorne Cl CV5 . . . . . . 36 B4
Sunningdale Ave
Coventry CV6 . . . . 21 A2
Kenilworth CV8. . . . . 75 A4
Sunny Bank CV1. . . . . . . 96 A3
Sunnybank Ave CV3 . . . 49 C1
Sunnyside Cl CV5. . . . . . 38 A3
Sunshine Cl CV8. . . . . . . 74 C2
Sun St CV21. . . . . 86 A1
Sunway Gr CV3. . . . . 47 C2
Sussex Rd CV5 . . . . 38 A4
Sutherland Ave CV5 . . . 36 B4
Sutherland Dr CV12. . . . . 6 A4
Sutton Ave CV5 . . . . 35 B4
Sutton Ct CV6 . . . . 14 C2
Sutton Ho CV22. . . . . 88 C3
Sutton Stop CV6. . . . . . . 14 B1
Swaledale CV4 . . . . 46 B2
Swallow Cl CV12 . . . . 12 C4
Swallowdean Rd CV6 . . 28 C4
Swallowgate Bsns Pk
CV6. . . . . 21 A1
Swallow Rd CV6 . . . . 20 C1
Swanage Gn CV2 . . . . . . 42 B4
Swancroft Rd CV2 . . . . . 31 B1
Swan La CV2 . . . . 40 A4
Swanswell St CV1 . . . . . 96 C4
Swift Cl CV8. . . . . 74 C2
Swift Pk CV21 . . . . 79 B1
Swift Point CV21 . . . . . . 79 A3
Swift's Cnr CV3. . . . . 48 C4
Swift Valley Ind Est
CV21. . . . . 79 A2
Swillington Rd CV6. . . . . 29 C1
Swinburne Ave CV2. . . . 41 B2
Swindale Croft CV3. . . . . 51 A4
Sycamore Ct CV5. . . . . . 27 A3
Sycamore Gr CV21. . . . . 85 B2
Sycamore Rd CV2 . . . . . 22 B2
Sycamores The CV12. . . . . 5 B2
Sydnall Fields CV6. . . . . 21 C4
Sydnall Rd CV6 . . . . 21 C4
Sydney Ct ■ CV12 . . . . . . 5 C2
Sylvan Dr CV3 . . . . 47 A2
Synkere Cl CV7 . . . . 12 A2
Sywell Leys CV22 . . . . . . 95 A4

T

Tachbrook Cl CV2 . . . . . . 22 C2
Tackford Rd CV6. . . . . . . 31 B4
Tainters Hill CV8. . . . . . . 67 B2
Talisman Cl CV8 . . . . 74 B3
Talisman Sq CV8. . . . . . . 74 B4
Talland Ave CV6 . . . . 31 B2
Tallants Cl CV6 . . . . 31 B4
Tallants Rd CV6. . . . . 31 B4
Tamar Cl CV23 . . . . 83 C3
Tamar Rd CV12. . . . . 8 B2
Tamworth Rd CV6, CV7 . . 11 A1
Tanners Gr CV6. . . . . 21 A4
Tannery Ct CV8. . . . . 74 B4
Tanser Ct CV22 . . . . 94 A1
Tanyard Cl CV4 . . . . 35 B1

Tapcon Way CV2. . . . . . . 33 A1
Tappinger Gr CV8. . . . . . 68 A1
Tara Ct CV2 . . . . 40 C4
Tarlington Rd CV6 . . . . . 28 C2
Tarn Cl CV12 . . . . 6 A2
Tarquin Cl CV3 . . . . 50 B3
Tarragon Cl CV2 . . . . 23 A1
Tarrant Wlk CV2 . . . . 33 B1
Taunton Way CV6. . . . . . 20 A2
Tavistock Wlk CV2 . . . . . 32 A3
Taylor Cl CV8. . . . . 67 C2
Tay Rd CV6 . . . . 29 C2
Teachers Cl CV6 . . . . 29 B1
Tea Gdn The CV12 . . . . . 13 B4
Teasel Cl CV23. . . . . 80 B2
Ted Pitts La CV5 . . . . 18 B2
Telephone Rd CV3 . . . . . 41 A2
Telfer Rd CV6 . . . . 29 C3
Telford Rd CV7 . . . . 14 C4
Templar Ave CV4 . . . . . . 36 B1
Templars' Fields CV4 . . . 45 C3
Templars Prim Sch CV4 36 B1
Temple Ct CV22 . . . . 90 C4
Temple St CV21, CV22 . . 90 C4
Tenby Cl CV12 . . . . 4 C1
Teneriffe Rd CV6 . . . . . . 21 C1
Tennant Cl CV21. . . . . . . 91 B3
Tennyson Ave CV22 . . . . 89 B1
Tennyson Cl CV8. . . . . . . 75 B4
Tennyson Rd CV2 . . . . . . 41 A3
Ten Shilling Dr CV4 . . . . 44 C2
Terry Rd CV1 . . . . 40 A1
Tewkesbury Dr CV12. . . . . 6 C3
Thackeray Cl CV22. . . . . 89 C1
Thackhall St CV2 . . . . . . 40 A4
Thames Cl CV12 . . . . 8 A3
Thamley Rd CV6 . . . . 38 B4
Thatchings The CV22 . . . 94 B1
Theddingworth Cl CV3. . 50 C4
Thickthorn Cl CV8 . . . . . 75 A2
Thickthorn Mews CV8 . . 75 A2
Thickthorn Orchs CV8 . . 75 A2
Thimbler Rd CV4 . . . . . . 46 A3
Thirlestane Cl CV8. . . . . 68 A2
Thirlmere CV21. . . . . 80 A1
Thirlmere Cl CV4 . . . . . . 35 C3
Thirlmere Rd CV12 . . . . . . 6 A2
Thirsk Rd CV3 . . . . 48 A1
Thistle Way CV23 . . . . . . 80 B2
Thistley Field E CV6 . . . 29 B3
Thistley Field N CV6 . . . 29 B3
Thistley Field S CV6 . . . 29 A2
Thistley Field W CV6. . . 29 A3
Thomas King Ho ⑥
CV1 . . . . 39 C4
Thomas Landsdail St
CV3 . . . . 48 B4
Thomas Lane St CV6. . . 22 A1
Thomas Naul Croft CV4 . 36 A3
Thomas Sharp St CV4 . . 45 B3
Thomas St CV12 . . . . 6 A2
Thomas Way CV23 . . . . . 83 B3
Thompson's La CV7. . . . 11 B2
Thompson's Rd CV7 . . . 11 C2
Thomson Cl CV21. . . . . . 85 C4
Thornbury Ho CV8. . . . . 74 C3
Thornby Ave CV8 . . . . . . 75 A3
Thorn Cl CV21. . . . . 86 A4
Thorney Rd CV2 . . . . 31 C2
Thornhill Rd CV1. . . . . . . 30 B1
Thorns Com Inf Sch
CV8 . . . . 75 A4
Thornton Cl CV5. . . . . . . 35 A4
Threadneedle St CV1 . . 30 B2
Three Spires Ave CV6 . . 29 B2
Three Spires Ind Est
CV6 . . . . 14 A1
Three Spires Jct CV6 . . . 21 B1

Three Spires Sch CV6 . . 28 B2
Thruppence Cl CV4 . . . . 44 C2
Thurlaston Dr CV22. . . . . 93 C4
Thurlestone Rd CV6 . . . . 29 A4
Thurnmill Rd CV23. . . . . 84 A2
Tiber Cl CV5. . . . . 36 A4
Tiber Way CV21. . . . . 79 A1
Tideswell Cl CV3 . . . . . . 42 B1
TILE HILL 35 C1
Tile Hill La
Coventry, Allesley CV4,
CV5 . . . . 37 B2
Coventry, Tile Hill CV4. . 36 C1
Tile Hill Sta CV4 . . . . 44 A4
Tile Hill Wood Sch &
Language Coll CV4 . . . 35 B2
Tilehurst Dr CV4. . . . . . . 35 B1
Tilewood Ave CV5 . . . . . 36 A4
Timber Ct CV22. . . . . 90 C4
Timothy Gr CV4 . . . . 36 C1
Tintagel Cl CV3. . . . . 50 B1
Tintagel Gr CV8 . . . . 75 A4
Tintern Way CV12. . . . . . . 6 C3
Tisdale Rise CV8. . . . . . . 67 C2
Tiverton Gr CV2 . . . . 32 B1
Tiverton Rd CV2 . . . . 32 B1
Tiverton Sch CV6 . . . . . . 28 B1
Tiveycourt Rd CV6. . . . . 22 A3
Tocil Croft CV4 . . . . 58 B4
Toledo Cl CV5 . . . . 37 A1
Tollard Cl CV2 . . . . 33 A1
TOLLBAR END 62 A4
Tom Brown St CV21. . . . 86 A1
Tom Ellis Ct CV7. . . . . . . 14 A4
Tom Henderson Cl CV3 . 51 A3
Tomson Ave CV6. . . . . . . 38 C4
Tom Ward Cl CV3 . . . . . . 50 C3
Tonbridge Rd CV3 . . . . . 49 B2
Topp's Dr CV12 . . . . 5 B1
Topp's Heath CV12. . . . . . 5 B1
Top Rd CV7, CV12. . . . . . 16 B3
Torbay Rd CV5. . . . . 37 A4
Torcastle Cl CV6. . . . . . . 31 A3
Torcross Ave CV2 . . . . . . 32 A2
Torpoint Cl CV2 . . . . 32 A3
Torrance Rd CV21. . . . . . 85 A1
Torrington Ave CV4. . . . 44 C4
Torwood Cl CV4 . . . . 45 A2
Totnes Cl CV2 . . . . 32 A3
Tove Ct CV23 . . . . 83 C3
Tower Rd
Bedworth CV12. . . . . 6 A4
Rugby CV22. . . . . 90 C3
Towers Cl CV8. . . . . 74 B2
Tower St CV1. . . . . 96 B3
Town Feilds Cl CV3 . . . . 27 C3
Townsend Croft CV3 . . . 48 A3
Townsend La CV23. . . . . 83 C2
Townsend Rd
Coventry CV3 . . . . 48 A4
Rugby CV21. . . . . 86 B1
Towpath Cl CV6 . . . . 14 B2
Trafalgar Ho ❸ CV1 . . . . 38 C2
Tredington Rd CV5 . . . . 36 A4
Treedale Cl CV4 . . . . 44 B4
Treforest Rd CV3 . . . . . . 50 A4
Tregorrick Rd CV7 . . . . . 14 A4
Treherne Rd CV6 . . . . . . 29 C4
Trelawney Rd CV7 . . . . . 14 A3
Trenance Rd CV7 . . . . . . 14 A4
Treneere Rd CV7 . . . . . . 14 A4
Trensale Ave CV6 . . . . . . 38 A4
Trentham Gdns CV8 . . . 68 A1
Trentham Rd CV1. . . . . . 40 A4
Trent Rd CV12 . . . . 8 A2
Tresillian Rd CV7 . . . . . . 14 B4
Treviscoe Cl CV7. . . . . . . 14 A3

Trevor Cl CV4.......... 44 B4
Trevor White Dr CV22.. 90 B3
Trevose Ave CV7....... 14 B4
Trewint Cl CV7 .... 14 A4
Triangle The CV5 ...... 36 C4
Trimpley Dr CV6 ...... 30 A2
Trinity Churchyard CV1 . 96 B3
Trinity Cl CV21 .... 85 C1
Trinity La CV1 .... 96 B3
Trinity St CV1......... 96 B3
Triton Pk CV21 .... 79 A2
Triumph Cl CV2........ 41 C3
Triumph Ho CV1....... 97 B2
Trossachs Rd CV5...... 36 A3
Troubridge Wlk CV22 .. 88 C4
Troughton Cres CV6 ... 29 B1
Troutbeck Rd CV5 ..... 36 A4
Troyes Cl CV3 .... 48 C3
Trussell Way CV22 ..... 88 A2
Tudor Ave CV5......... 36 A4
Tudor Ct
  Bedworth CV7......... 13 B3
  Coventry CV3 .... 48 A4
Tulip Tree Ave CV8 .... 67 C1
Tulip Tree Ct CV8 ..... 75 A4
Tulliver Cl CV12 ....6 B3
Tulliver St CV6 .... 29 C1
Turchil Rd CV22 ...... 88 A2
Turchil Wlk CV22 ..... 88 A2
Turlands Cl CV2 ...... 33 B3
Turner Cl
  Bedworth CV12......... 6 A4
  Rugby CV21........... 92 B2
Turner Rd CV5......... 37 B3
Turnstone Cl CV23..... 80 A2
Turpin Ho CV21....... 80 A1
Turton Way CV8 ...... 75 B4
Tutbury Ave CV4...... 46 C2
Tuthill Furlong CV23.... 80 B3
Twickenham Way CV3 .. 42 C1
Tybalt Cl CV3......... 50 A1
Tylney Cl CV3......... 42 C2
Tynemouth Cl CV2..... 15 A1
Tynward Cl CV3....... 47 C1
Tysoe Croft CV3 ...... 51 A4

U

Ufton Croft CV5 ...... 36 B3
Ullswater Rd
  Bedworth CV12........ 6 A2
  Coventry CV3 .... 41 C1
Ulverscroft Rd CV3 .... 48 B3
Ulverston CV21........ 80 B1
Underhill Cl CV3....... 60 B3
Unicorn Ave CV5 ...... 35 C4
Unicorn La CV5........ 36 A4
Union Bldgs CV1 ...... 97 B2
Union Pl CV6.......... 21 C4
Union St CV22......... 90 A4
Unity Ho CV1......... 96 C4
University Hospl-
  Walsgrave CV2 .... 33 B1
University Rd CV4 ..... 46 A1
Univ of Warwick CV4 ... 58 A4
Univ of Warwick (Gibbet
  Hill) CV4 .... 58 B3
Univ of Warwick Science
  Pk CV4 .... 46 A1
Univ of Warwick
  (Westwood) CV4..... 45 C2
Uplands CV2 .... 31 B1
UPPER EASTERN GREEN
  .... 35 B4
Upper Eastern Green La
  CV5 .... 26 C1
Upperfield Way CV3 ... 42 B1

Upper Hill St CV1...... 96 A3
Upper Ladyes Hills CV8 . 67 B2
Upper Pk CV3 .... 50 B2
Upper Prec CV1 .... 96 B3
Upper Ride CV3 .... 50 B1
Upper Rosemary Hill
  CV8................. 67 A1
Upper Spon St CV1 .... 38 B3
Upper Spring La CV8 ... 67 A3
UPPER STOKE 40 C4
Upper Well St CV1..... 96 B3
Upper York St CV1 .... 38 C2
Upton Rd CV22 .... 84 B1
Utrillo Cl CV5......... 37 A3
Uxbridge Ave CV3 ..... 41 A2

V

Vale Cl CV21.......... 92 A2
Valencia Rd CV3....... 42 B2
Vale The CV3 .... 50 A4
Valley Dr CV21........ 79 B2
Valley Rd CV2 .... 31 B2
Van Dyke Cl CV5...... 37 A3
Vanguard Ave CV5..... 37 A1
Vanguard Ctr CV4 .... 46 A2
Vardon Dr CV3 .... 60 B4
Vauxhall Cl CV1 ...... 39 C3
Vauxhall St CV1 ...... 39 C3
Vecqueray St CV1 ..... 39 C2
Ventnor Cl CV2 .... 41 C3
Verbena Cl CV2....... 22 B1
Vere Rd CV1.......... 91 C3
Vernon Ave CV22 ..... 91 B2
Vernon Cl CV1 .... 39 C3
Vernon Ct CV1 .... 39 C4
Viaduct Cl CV21 ...... 86 B2
Vicarage Hill CV23..... 86 C3
Vicarage La
  Coventry CV7 .... 13 A3
  Dunchurch CV22...... 94 B1
Vicarage Rd
  Rugby CV22.......... 85 A1
  Stoneleigh CV8........ 69 C2
Victoria Ave CV21..... 85 A2
Victoria Cl CV5....... 37 B4
Victoria Mews CV3 .... 41 C2
Victoria St
  Coventry CV1 .... 96 D4
  Rugby CV21.......... 84 C1
Victory Rd CV1 .... 21 B1
Vienna Ho CV5 .... 37 C2
Villa Cl CV12 ....8 C2
Villa Cres CV12 ....8 C1
Village Mews CV22 .... 88 C1
Villa Rd CV6.......... 29 C2
Villiers Rd CV8 .... 67 C1
Villiers St CV2 .... 40 B3
Vincent St CV1 .... 38 C2
Vincent Wyles Ho CV2 . 41 C3
Vinecote Rd CV6...... 21 C4
Vine St CV1 .... 96 C3
Violet Cl
  Bedworth CV12........5 B2
  Coventry CV2 .... 22 C3
  Rugby CV23........... 80 C2
Virginia Rd CV1....... 39 C3
Vogue Cl CV1......... 96 D3

W

Wade Ave CV3........ 47 C1
Waggoners Cl CV8..... 72 A1
Wainbody Ave N CV3... 47 B2
Wainbody Ave S CV3... 47 A1
Wainbody Wood Sch
  CV4 .... 58 B2
Wakefield Cl CV3 ...... 51 A3

Walford Pl CV22 ...... 91 C2
Walkers Orch CV8 ..... 69 C2
Walkers Way
  Bedworth CV12........ 5 C1
  Kenilworth CV8....... 74 B2
Wallace Rd CV6....... 29 B4
WALL HILL 18 A4
Wall Hill Rd CV5, CV7 ... 18 B3
Walnut St CV2........ 22 B2
Walnut Tree Cl CV8 ... 74 C3
Walnut Way CV22..... 88 B3
Walsall St CV4........ 45 C3
Walsgrave CE Prim Sch
  CV2 .... 33 B2
Walsgrave Gdns CV2. 33 B3
WALSGRAVE ON SOWE
  .... 33 C3
Walsgrave Rd CV2 .... 40 C3
Walsgrave Ret Pk CV2. 33 C3
Walsingham Dr CV10 ...2 C3
Walter Scott Rd CV12 ...6 C1
Walton Cl CV3........ 50 C3
Wanley Rd CV3 .... 48 B2
Wansfell Cl CV4 ...... 45 B3
Wappenbury Cl CV2 ... 22 C2
Wappenbury Rd CV2... 23 A2
Warden Rd CV6....... 29 C2
Wardens Ave The CV5... 27 C2
Wardens The CV8...... 68 A1
Wareham Gn CV2...... 33 B1
Waring Way CV22..... 94 B2
Warmington Cl CV3.... 50 C4
Warmwell Cl CV2 ..... 42 A4
Warner Row CV6...... 31 A3
Warren Cl CV8........ 63 B1
Warren Field CV8...... 63 B1
Warren Gn CV4....... 45 A3
Warren Rd CV22 ...... 91 A3
Warton Cl CV8........ 75 B4
Warwick Ave CV5..... 47 B4
Warwick Ct CV3 ...... 97 B1
Warwick Gn CV12..... 8 C1
Warwick La CV1 ...... 97 B2
Warwick Rd
  Coventry CV3 .... 97 B1
  Kenilworth CV8....... 74 C1
  Wolston CV8......... 65 B3
Warwick Row CV1 .... 97 B2
Warwickshire Coll
  CV21 .... 91 A4
Warwick St
  Coventry CV5 .... 38 A1
  Rugby CV21.......... 90 A4
Washbrook La CV5 .... 18 A1
Wasperton Cl CV3 .... 51 A4
Waste La CV6........ 19 C1
Watch Cl CV1......... 96 A3
Watchmaker Ct CV1 ... 97 A2
Watcombe Rd CV2.... 32 C4
Watercall Ave CV3..... 48 A2
Waterford Way CV3... 41 A1
Water Lily Way CV10 ...2 C4
Waterloo St CV1 ...... 39 C4
Waterman Rd CV6..... 31 A2
Waterside CV6........ 14 C2
Waterside Dr CV21..... 86 A3
Watermeet Gr CV2.... 31 C2
Watermeet Rd CV2.... 31 C2
Water Tower La CV8 ... 67 A2
Watery La
  Coventry CV6 .... 20 A4
  Keresley CV7 .... 19 C4
Watling Rd CV8....... 67 C2
Watson Rd CV5....... 37 B2
Watts La CV21 .... 92 B2
Wavebeck Ct CV23..... 83 C3
Waveley Rd CV1....... 38 B3
Wavendon Cl CV2...... 23 C1

Wavere Ct CV21 ...... 80 B1
Waverley Rd
  Kenilworth CV8....... 74 C4
  Rugby CV21.......... 92 A3
Weaver Dr CV23 ..... 84 A2
Weavers Wlk CV6...... 31 C4
Webb Dr CV23........ 80 B2
Webb Ellis Bsns Pk
  CV21 .... 85 C2
Webb Ellis Rd CV22 ... 89 B4
Webster Ave CV8 ..... 67 C1
Webster St CV6....... 30 C3
Wedgewood Cl CV2.... 32 C4
Wedge-Woods CV5.... 47 A4
Wedon Cl CV4........ 44 C3
Welford Pl CV6....... 30 B3
Welford Rd CV21...... 86 A2
Welgarth Ave CV6..... 29 A2
Welland Cl CV23...... 84 A3
Welland Rd CV1 ...... 40 A1
Wellesbourne Rd CV5... 36 B3
Wellington Gdns ◨
  CV1................ 38 C2
Wellington St CV1 .... 96 D4
Wells Ct CV3 .... 49 A3
Wells St CV21 .... 85 C1
Well St CV1 .... 96 B3
Welsh Rd CV4 .... 40 C4
Welton Pl CV22 ...... 91 A2
Wendiburgh St CV4.... 45 C3
Wendover Rise CV5.... 37 A4
Wentworth Dr CV6.... 20 B4
Wentworth Rd CV22 .. 89 C3
Wesley Rd CV21 ...... 92 A3
Wessex Cl CV12.......6 A4
West Ave
  Bedworth CV12........ 7 A2
  Coventry CV6, CV7 ... 12 A1
  Coventry, Middle Stoke
  CV2 .... 40 B2
Westbourne Gr CV22... 89 C3
Westbrook Ct CV5 .... 36 B4
Westbury Ct CV2 ..... 40 B3
Westbury Rd CV5..... 28 B1
Westcliffe Dr CV3..... 47 C1
Westcotes CV4 .... 36 C1
Westfield Rd CV22..... 89 C4
Westgate Rd CV21 .... 91 B3
Westhill Rd CV6 ...... 29 A2
Westleigh Ave CV5.... 47 A3
West Leyes CV21...... 85 B1
Westmede Ctr CV5 ... 37 A4
Westminster Rd CV1... 97 A1
Westmorland Rd CV2... 42 A4
Westonbirt Cl CV8.... 68 A2
Weston Cl CV22 ...... 94 A2
Weston Ct CV21 ..... 86 A2
Weston Hall Stables
  CV12 ....8 A3
WESTON IN ARDEN ... 8 A3
Weston La CV12 ....8 B3
Weston St CV1 ...... 96 C4
West Orchards Sh Ctr
  CV1 .... 96 B3
West Ridge CV5 ...... 27 B1
West View Rd CV22 ... 89 B4
Westway CV21........ 85 B1
Westwood Bsns Pk CV4. 45 A2
WESTWOOD GARDENS
  .... 46 B4
WESTWOOD HEATH ... 44 C2

Westwood Heath Rd
CV4 . . . . 44 C2
Westwood Rd
Coventry CV5 . . . . 38 B1
Rugby CV22. . . . . 91 C1
Westwood Way CV4. . . . . 45 B2
Wetherell Way CV21 . . . . 80 A1
Wexford Rd CV2 . . . . 23 A1
Weymouth Cl CV3 . . . . . 50 B1
Whaley's Croft CV6 . . . . 29 C4
Wharf Rd CV6 . . . . 31 A1
Whateley's Dr CV8. . . . . . 67 B1
Wheate Croft CV4 . . . . . . 36 A2
Wheatfield Rd CV22 . . . . 89 A3
Wheelwright La CV6,
CV7 . . . . 20 C4
**Wheelwright Lane Prim
Sch** CV7 . . . . 13 A1
Wheler Rd CV3 . . . . 49 B3
Whernside CV21. . . . . 80 A1
Whetstone Dr CV21. . . . . 80 C1
Whiley Cl CV23 . . . . 87 A3
Whimbrel Cl CV23 . . . . . 80 A2
Whitaker Rd CV5 . . . . 37 A3
Whitburn Rd CV12. . . . . . .4 C1
Whitchurch Way CV4 . . . 45 A4
Whitebeam Cl CV4. . . . . . 35 B1
Whitefield Cl CV4. . . . . . 44 B2
Whitefriars Dr CV22 . . . . 88 A3
White Friars La CV1 . . . 97 C2
White Friars St CV1 . . . 97 C2
Whitehall Rd CV21. . . . . . 90 B4
Whitehead Dr CV8. . . . . . 68 A3
Whitehorse Cl CV6 . . . . . 14 B2
Whitelaw Cres CV5 . . . . . 28 A2
WHITEMOOR 67 C1
Whitemoor Rd CV8. . . . . . 67 C1
WHITEMORE PARK 20 C1
Whiteside Cl CV3 . . . . 51 A4
Whites Row CV8. . . . . 74 C3
White St CV1 . . . . 96 C3
Whitley Abbey Com Sch
CV3 . . . . 49 A2
Whitley Abbey Prim Sch
CV3 . . . . 49 B2
Whitley Ct CV3 . . . . 49 A3
Whitley Village CV3 . . . . . 49 A3
Whitmore Park Prim Sch
CV6 . . . . 20 A1
Whitmore Park Rd CV6 . 21 A3
Whitnash Gr CV2 . . . . 32 B1
Whittle Cl
Coventry CV3 . . . . 51 A4
Rugby CV21. . . . . 89 A1
Whitworth Ave CV3. . . . . 40 C1
WHOBERLEY 37 B2
Whoberley Ave CV5. . . . . 37 B2
Whoberley Hall Prim Sch
CV5 . . . . 37 A3
Wickham Cl CV6. . . . . . . 19 C2
Wickmans Dr CV4 . . . . . . 35 A2
Widdecombe Cl CV2. . . . 32 B3
Widdrington Rd CV1. . . . 30 A1
Wiggins Cl CV21. . . . . . . 92 B2
Wigston Rd
Coventry CV2 . . . . 23 C1
Rugby CV21. . . . . 92 A2
Wildcroft Rd CV5 . . . . 37 A3
Wildey Rd [1] CV12. . . . . .5 A2
Wildmoor Cl CV2 . . . . . . 22 B4
WILLENHALL 50 B2

Willenhall La CV3. . . . . . . 51 A3
Willenhall Wood Prim Sch
CV3 . . . . 50 B2
William Arnold Cl CV2 . . 40 B4
William Batchelor Ho
CV1 . . . . 96 B4
William Bree Rd CV5. . . . 26 A1
William Bristow Rd CV3. 48 C3
William Cree Cl CV8 . . . . 65 A3
William Groubb Cl CV3 . 50 B3
William Kirby Cl CV4. . . . 36 B1
William McCool Cl CV3 . 51 A3
William McKee Cl CV3 . . 50 C3
William Malcolm Ho
CV2 . . . . 41 C3
William Sheriden Ho
CV2 . . . . 41 C3
William St
Bedworth CV12. . . . . 7 A2
Rugby CV21. . . . . 85 C1
William Thomson Ho [2]
CV1 . . . . 96 D4
Willis Gr CV12 . . . . .6 C3
Willoughby Ave CV8 . . . . 74 A3
Willoughby Cl CV3. . . . . . 50 C4
Willoughby Pl CV22. . . . . 91 A1
Willow Brook Rd CV8 . . . 65 B4
Willow Cl CV12 . . . . .2 C1
Willow Ctyd CV2. . . . . 32 B3
Willow Gr CV4. . . . . 36 C2
Willowherb Cl [5] CV3. . . 51 A4
Willow La CV2. . . . . 90 C4
Willow Meer CV8 . . . . 67 C1
Willows The CV12. . . . . . . .5 B2
Willow Tree Gdns CV21. . 92 B2
Wilmcote Gn CV5. . . . . . . 36 B3
Wilson Cl CV22 . . . . 88 C4
Wilson Gn CV3 . . . . 42 A1
Wilson Gr CV8. . . . . 75 B4
Wilsons La CV7. . . . . 14 A2
Wilson's La CV6 . . . . 13 C2
Wiltshire Cl
Bedworth CV12. . . . . 6 A3
Coventry CV5 . . . . 36 C3
Wimborne Dr CV2 . . . . . . 42 B4
Winceby Pl CV4 . . . . 35 B1
Winchat Cl CV3. . . . . 42 A1
Winchester Ct CV22 . . . . . 94 A1
Winchester St CV1. . . . . . 39 C3
Windermere Ave
Coventry, Binley CV3. . . . . . 41 C1
Coventry, Upper Eastern Green
CV5 . . . . 35 C4
Windermere Cl CV21. . . . 80 A1
Winding House La CV6,
CV7 . . . . 20 C4
Windmill Cl CV8 . . . . 67 B2
Windmill Ct CV6. . . . . 22 A3
Windmill Hill The CV5. . . 27 B3
Windmill Ind Est CV5 . . . 27 A3
Windmill La CV22. . . . . . . 93 B2
Windmill Rd
Bedworth CV12. . . . . 14 A4
Coventry CV6 . . . . 22 A3
Windridge Cl CV3. . . . . . . 50 A2
Windrush Way CV23 . . . . 83 C3
Windsor Ct CV4 . . . . 36 C2
Windsor St
Coventry CV1 . . . . 38 C2
Rugby CV21. . . . . 86 A1
WINDY ARBOUR 75 A3
Windy Arbour CV8. . . . . . 75 A4
Winfield St CV21. . . . . 86 B1
Wingfield Way CV6 . . . . . 20 A2

Wingrave Cl CV5 . . . . 27 B2
Winifred Ave CV5. . . . . . . 38 B1
Winnallthorpe CV3 . . . . . 50 C2
Winsford Ave CV5. . . . . . . 36 C4
Winsford Ct CV5 . . . . 37 A4
Winsham Wlk CV3 . . . . . . 60 A3
Winslow Cl CV5 . . . . 36 C3
Winslow Ho [11] CV1 . . . . 38 C2
Winster Cl CV7 . . . . 12 A3
Winston Ave CV2 . . . . 32 B4
Winston Cl CV2. . . . . 32 B4
Winterton Rd CV12. . . . . . .8 C2
Winwick Pl CV22 . . . . 88 C2
Wise Gr CV21. . . . . 91 C4
Wisley Gr CV8 . . . . 68 A1
Wistaria Cl [2] CV2 . . . . . 22 B2
Withybrook Cl CV2 . . . . . 23 A2
Withybrook La CV7 . . . . . 17 C1
Withybrook Rd CV12. . . . . .9 A2
Witnell Rd CV6 . . . . 30 A2
Wolfe Rd CV4 . . . . 45 A4
Wolsey Rd CV22 . . . . 94 B4
WOLSTON 65 C4
Wolston La CV8 . . . . 64 C2
**Wolston St Margaret's CE
Prim Sch** CV8 . . . . 65 B4
Wolston Way CV3. . . . . . . 50 A2
Wolverton Rd CV5 . . . . . . 36 B3
Wolvey Rd CV12 . . . . .9 B2
Woodbridge Ct CV21. . . . 85 B1
Woodburn Cl CV5. . . . . . . 36 C4
Woodclose Ave CV6 . . . . . 29 A2
Woodcote Ave CV8 . . . . . . 66 B2
Woodcraft Cl CV4 . . . . . . 36 B2
Wood Ct CV2 . . . . 32 B3
WOOD END 22 C1
Woodend Croft CV4 . . . . 44 C4
Woodfield Rd CV5 . . . . . . 46 C4
Woodford Cl CV7 . . . . 13 A1
Woodhams Rd CV3 . . . . . 62 A3
Wood Hill Rise CV6 . . . . . 21 A2
Woodhouse Cl CV3 . . . . . 50 C4
Wood La CV7 . . . . 17 A1
Woodland Ave CV5 . . . . . . 47 A3
Woodland Rd CV8 . . . . . . 67 C3
Woodlands Ct
Binley Woods CV3. . . . . 52 B3
Coventry CV5 . . . . 47 B4
Woodlands La CV12. . . . . .5 B4
Woodlands Rd
Bedworth CV12. . . . . 5 C3
Binley Woods CV3. . . . . 52 B3
Woodlands Sch The
CV5 . . . . 35 B3
Woodleigh Rd CV4. . . . . . 45 A1
Woodmill Mdw CV8. . . . . 67 C2
Woodridge Ave CV5 . . . . . 27 B2
Woodroffe Wlk CV6. . . . . 22 A4
WOODSHIRES GREEN . 13 B1
Woodshires Rd CV6. . . . . 13 C1
Woodsia Cl CV23 . . . . 80 A2
Woodside Ave N CV3. . . . 47 A2
Woodside Ave S CV3. . . . 47 A1
Woodside Bsns Pk
CV21. . . . . 85 B2
Woodside Park Cvn Pk
CV8 . . . . 73 C2
Woodside Pk CV21. . . . . . 85 C3
Woods Piece CV7. . . . . . . 11 C2
Wood St
Bedworth CV12. . . . . 3 A1
Rugby CV21. . . . . 85 C2
Woodstock Rd CV3 . . . . . 48 B3
Woodway Cl CV2 . . . . 33 A4

Woodway La CV2 . . . . 23 C3
WOODWAY PARK 32 C4
**Woodway Park Sch & Com
Coll** CV2. . . . . 23 C3
Woodway Wlk CV2. . . . . . 32 C4
Woolgrove St CV6 . . . . . . 22 A3
Wooll St [9] CV21 . . . . 85 B1
Wootton Ct CV2 . . . . 32 B1
Wootton St CV12 . . . . .7 A1
Worcester Cl CV5. . . . . . . 27 C3
Worcester Ct CV6. . . . . . . 22 B4
Worcester Rd CV8 . . . . . . 75 A3
Worcester St CV21. . . . . . 85 B2
Wordsworth Dr CV8 . . . . 75 B4
Wordsworth Rd
Bedworth CV12. . . . . 7 A1
Coventry CV2 . . . . 41 A4
Rugby CV22. . . . . 94 C4
Worsdell Cl CV1 . . . . 38 C4
Worsfold Cl CV5. . . . . 27 B3
Wortley Cl
Cawston CV22. . . . . 88 A2
Cawston CV22. . . . . 88 A2
Wrenbury Dr CV6. . . . . . . 22 A4
Wren St CV2. . . . . 40 A3
Wright St CV1 . . . . 39 C4
Wrigsham St CV3. . . . . . . 48 B4
Wroxall Dr CV3 . . . . 50 B1
Wyatt Ho CV2 . . . . 32 B3
Wyatts Ct CV12 . . . . .6 B3
Wych-Elm Cl CV22. . . . . . 88 B3
Wychwood Ave CV3. . . . . 60 A3
Wycliffe Gr CV2 . . . . 31 C1
Wycliffe Rd W CV2. . . . . . 32 A1
Wye Cl CV21. . . . . .8 B2
Wykeham Ho CV21. . . . . . 80 A1
Wykeley Rd CV2 . . . . 41 A4
WYKEN 32 B1
Wyken Ave CV2. . . . . 32 B1
Wyken Croft CV2 . . . . 32 C1
Wyken Croft Nature Pk *
CV2 . . . . 32 B2
Wyken Croft Prim Sch
CV2 . . . . 32 C1
Wyken Grange Rd CV2 . . 32 C1
WYKEN GREEN 32 A2
Wyken Way CV2 . . . . 31 C1
Wyke Rd CV2 . . . . 41 A4
Wyld Ct CV5 . . . . 27 C1
Wyley Rd CV6 . . . . 29 C1
Wyncote Cl CV8 . . . . 74 C4
Wynter Rd CV22 . . . . 84 B1
Wythburn Way CV21 . . . . 80 B1
Wyver Cres CV2 . . . . 41 A3

Y

Yardley St CV1. . . . . 39 C4
Yarmouth Gn CV4. . . . . . . 44 C4
Yarningale Rd CV3. . . . . . 50 B1
Yarrow Cl CV23 . . . . 80 B2
Yates Ave CV21 . . . . 85 A4
Yelverton Rd CV6. . . . . . . 30 B4
Yew Cl CV3. . . . . 41 A1
Yewdale Cres CV2 . . . . . . 23 B1
Yewdale Ct CV2 . . . . 23 C1
Yews The CV12 . . . . .5 B2
York Ave CV12. . . . . .7 A2
York Cl CV3 . . . . 50 A1
York St
Coventry CV1 . . . . 38 C2
Rugby CV21. . . . . 85 A2
Yule Rd CV2 . . . . 32 B1

n some busy areas of the maps it is not always possible to show the name of every place.

Vhere not all names will fit, some smaller places are shown by a number. If you wish to find out the name associated with a number, use this listing.

The places in this list are also listed normally in the Index.

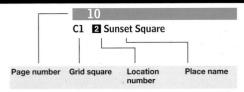

Page number	Grid square	Location number	Place name

5

A2 **1** Wildey Rd
2 Himley Rd
3 Campion Way
4 Daffodil Dr
5 Larkspur Gr
6 Speedwell Cl
C2 **1** Sydney Ct
2 Canberra Ct
3 Melbourne Ct
4 Queensland Gdns

6

A2 **1** Darwin Ct
2 Brisbane Ct
3 Adelaide Ct
4 Old Penn's Yd
5 Buckler's Yd
B3 **1** Old Meeting Yd
2 Bede Arc
3 Congreve Wlk

22

B1 **1** Alice Arnold Ho
2 Emily Smith Ho
3 Joseph Latham Ho
4 Dewis Ho
5 Samuel Hayward Ho
B2 **1** Camellia Rd
2 Wistaria Cl
3 Fuchsia Cl
4 Pear Tree Cl

5 Spruce Rd

29

B1 **1** Nethermill Rd
2 Chiltern Ct
3 Pake's Croft
4 Humberstone Rd

31

A3 **1** Adam Rd
2 Warner Row
3 St Nicholas Ct
4 Paradise Ho

32

B4 **1** Lyne Ho
2 Harry Edwards Ho
3 Friswell Ho

33

B3 **1** Bracknell Wlk
2 Stevenage Wlk
3 Basildon Wlk
4 Redditch Wlk
5 Walsgrave Gdns
6 Peterlee Wlk
7 Cumbernauld Wlk
8 Harlow Wlk
9 Dawley Wlk
10 Runcorn Wlk

38

B4 **1** Bateman's Acre S
2 Chiltern Leys
3 Priorsfield Rd N
4 Priorsfield Rd
5 Radford Circ
6 Lammas Ho
7 St Catherine's Lodge
8 Elizabeth Ct
9 Beaumont Ct
C2 **1** Wellington Gdns
2 Milestone Ho
3 Trafalgar Ho
4 Kerry's Ho
5 Grindley Ho
6 George Poole Ho
7 Drinkwater Ho
8 Gardner Ho
9 Givens Ho
10 Fennell Ho
11 Winslow Ho
12 St Thomas's Ho
13 St Thomas's Ct
C3 **1** Hawksworth Dr
2 Collett Wlk
3 River Ct
4 Compass Ct
5 Meadow Ho

39

C3 **1** Hillfields Ho
2 Jephcott Ho
3 Gilbert Cl
4 Vauxhall Cl

5 Vernon Cl
6 Spring Cl
7 Raglan Ct
C4 **1** Cawthorne Cl
2 Pensilva Way
3 Jacquard Ho
4 Leigh St
5 Clarence St
6 Thomas King Ho
7 Nelson St
8 Waterloo St
9 Vernon Ct

51

A4 **1** Cardale Croft
2 Kestrel Croft
3 Rutland Croft
4 Jim Forrest Cl
5 Willowherb Cl
6 Wasperton Cl
7 Joe Williams Cl
8 Deerdale Terr

85

B1 **1** Schoolfield Gr
2 Northway
3 Manning Wlk
4 Market Mall
5 Elborow St
6 Bloxam Pl
7 St Matthews St
8 Dukes Jetty
9 Wooll St
C1 **1** Bath Street Mews

2 Edward Ct
3 Pinders Ct
4 James Ct
5 Alexandra Ct
6 James Wlk
7 Alexandra Wlk
8 Central Bldgs
9 Arnold Villas
10 Clarendon Ct

88

A2 **1** Garard Pl
2 Garard Row
3 Garard Ct
4 Saxon Cl

91

C2 **2** Mercer Ct
3 Robbins Ct

92

A3 **3** Mews The

96

C4 **1** Little Church St
2 Russell St N
3 Joseph Halpin Ho
4 Pearl Hyde Ho
D4 **1** Sackville Ho
2 William Thomson Ho